With love -

7/6/24

WALKING WITH JESUS

WALKING WITH JESUS

A Collection of Talks and Reflections to Guide our Christian Journey

Anselm K. Jimoh

Nihil Obstat:
Very Rev. Fr. Dr. Anthony O. Ewherido
Rector,
SS. Peter and Paul Catholic Major Seminary,
Bodija, Ibadan.

Imprimatur:
His Grace,
Most Rev. Dr. Gabriel 'Leke Abegunrin
Archbishop of Ibadan

Published by
Ebony Books & Kreations
3, Gbolasere Street, Ologuneru
Ibadan, Oyo State
✆ 0802 208 2826, 0803 404 4405, 0905 710 6805
E-mail: ebonykreations1@gmail.com

ISBN 978–978–98009–5–7

First published February 2020

Dedication

To all who have supported me
in my priestly ministry
especially at the most challenging times

Acknowledgments

I give glory and thanks to God who has called me, unworthy as I am, to share in the sacred priesthood. I thank His Grace, Archbishop P. E. Ekpu; Archbishop (emeritus) of Benin-City, who ordained me a Catholic priest. I thank Very Rev. Msgr. Thomas Oleghe, who as my parish priest was a source of great inspiration to me. I thank Very Rev. Msgr. John Aniagwu, who as my Rector in the Seminary and till date remains an example of the priestly ministry to me. I am grateful to my Bishop, Most Rev. G. G. Dunia and priests of my diocese for their support and love.

In a very special way, I acknowledge the following priests who have had a special impact on my life and ministry; Very Rev. Msgr. Prof. Francis Ogunmodede, Very Rev. Fr. Dr. Anthony Ewherido, Rev. Fr. Yakubu-Gowon Salami, Rev. Fr. Ezekiel Owoeye, Rev. Fr. Steven Ogumah, Rev. Fr. Dr. John Odeyemi, Rev. Fr. Lawrence Adorolo, and Rev. Fr. Francis Ikhianosime. Sr. Elizabeth Agent has been a big sister to me and I will not forget to acknowledge her.

I thank and graciously acknowledge my parents and siblings, who, from the start till date, have given me a hundred percent family support. I cannot wish to belong to another family other than this wonderful and loving family God has generously given to me. You have all been a source of great strength and inspiration in the high and low moments of my life.

I thank and acknowledge all the laypersons who have been supportive in the course of my priestly ministry. Some of you have just been especially wonderful in your support of God's work in the places I have served as a priest. To you, I happily dedicate this work.

Finally, I acknowledge Rev. Frs. Anthony Ewherido, John Odeyemi, Lawrence Adorolo, and Godswill Ikiebeye, for their contributions to this work. I equally acknowledge the authors whose materials I used in the talks, papers, and homilies, in this collection. They are all duly acknowledged and cited within the text.

Rev. Fr. Anselm Jimoh, Ph.D.

Foreword

The collection that makes up *Walking with Jesus* is the product of the active priestly ministry of Very Rev. Fr. Anselm Jimoh, over a period of twenty-five years. The book is a testimony to Fr. Jimoh's ministerial efforts to walk with Jesus in his own life as a priest and as an individual disciple of Jesus. It is also a product of his missionary and evangelical zeal, which, in a very special way, underscores his understanding of the prophetic obligation that he has as a disciple of Jesus and as a priest of God. Called to serve God and God's people with the gift of his very life, he has put down, in a variety of ways, the character of his response to that vocation to minister to God's people.

The material contained herein is built up in response to a variety of contexts. First, there are homilies from his work on bringing the message of God to God's people in accordance with the demand of the liturgical arrangement of Sunday celebrations. Carefully documenting the fruits of his labour in that regard, he now shares with a wider audience what he zealously shared with his primary audience in parishes over the years to enrich the sowing of the word of God in countless hearts.

Second, there are the occasioned homilies, preached at different times when he was opportune or invited to be part of the celebration of events in the life of God's people. Such celebrations include the sacraments (marriage, baptism, Eucharist, Penance, etc.), funerals, birthdays and anniversaries, and at thanksgiving masses for various reasons.

The third group of material found in this book is the product of Fr. Jimoh's response to the call from God's people to share his faith and wisdom with them on different occasions. Such talks are either for the purpose of expanding Catholic Christian doctrine or moral issues. They are thoroughly catechetical and didactic at the same time, the product of painstaking research and reflection.

There are others that do not necessarily fall within the three groups mentioned but serve the same purpose. In terms of genre characterization, reading through these various works bring you through a hearing-again of homilies, lectures, reflections, catechesis, dogma, moral exhortations, and much more; all expressed in a way that one truly finds in them a spiritual journeying companion in the distilled words of this wonderful priest of God, who himself has journeyed with God's people through the different experiences of their lives for the past twenty-five years. In these journeys, he remained a companion to God's people, making Christ present to them in a variety of ways: in sadness and in joy, in times of need and in times of plenty, through penitential experiences and through joyful celebrations of God's grace and goodness, in the celebrations of time and in the hope of the future, in times of plenty and in times of dire need, and serving, leading, guiding, strengthening, consoling, exhorting and nurturing them every inch of the way.

With the mind of a philosopher, who is known for precision, candour and clarity, Fr. Jimoh has brought to bear on his ministry, his great philosophical learning. His passion as philosopher can be seen throughout the work, even though it is not a philosophical compendium.

Reading this book has nourished and enlightened me greatly. It is a book that meets the needs of both priests, religious and the people of God; throwing light in various places on the reasons we do what we do as Roman Catholics. I, therefore, recommend this book highly to everyone. It is not just a mere addition to the existing catholic volumes out there. It is peculiar and relevant in many ways to the experiences of our time and place.

I thank and congratulate Fr. Jimoh for sharing these outcomes of his priestly ministry with us and I wish him many more happy and fruitful years in the service of God and in the service of God's people.

Fr. Anthony Ovayero Ewherido
Rector
SS. Peter and Paul Catholic Major Seminary
Bodija, Ibadan

Contents

Introduction

On this 25th anniversary of my ordination to the priesthood, I humbly present this book as a souvenir to all who are genuinely interested in taking a walk with Jesus down the path of salvation. In the past 25 years as a priest, I have had the opportunity to share reflections with different groups and persons, write to clarify and explain some of the teachings of the Church that some Catholics find confusing.

Some years ago, a number of unrelated persons, at different places, and on different occasions, requested that I put in writing and possibly publish some of the reflections I shared with them, either as groups or as individuals. Precisely five years ago, I decided to take their request seriously. I collected from my files the scripted homilies I had delivered, the talks I gave to different groups at different times which I still had the manuscripts, and the articles I published in some newspapers and magazines at different times in the past. I was surprised to see that I had kept a good number of them. So I decided to dust them up and started to build up what today is the book in your hands.

You may find the arrangement a bit unconventional, even though that is not intentional. I also do not intend to arrange them in any particular order, especially the homilies. The homilies are presented as a guide for us to take a walk with Jesus, hence the title, *Walking with Jesus*. The idea is to provide a guide for us in our daily activities as disciples of our Lord Jesus Christ. Much more than presenting them as homilies, I present them as instructions and pieces of advice on how to follow the path that Jesus laid out for us. The talks and articles are meant to clarify some of the teachings of the Church on some issues that Catholics get confused about, especially in the face of contemporary misrepresentations and deliberately twisted teachings from all shades of self-proclaimed men and women of God whose aim is anything but evangelisation and the salvation of the souls of their audience.

I have provided themes for the various reflections as indicated in the chapters for the reader to choose whatever he/she wants to be guided on. The reader can select at random, based on his or her interest, at any given point in time. The reflections are deliberately brief and straight to the point. Each reflection is not more than three to five minutes read. The articles and talks are a bit longer. It is my sincere wish that the contents of this book would enlighten and guide the reader in his/her life as a Christian who is genuinely seeking the path of salvation, following the teachings of Jesus Christ, our Lord.

Rev. Fr. Anselm Jimoh

PART ONE

ARTICLES ON THE SACRAMENTS

1

The Sacraments of the Church

> The sacraments of the New Testament were instituted by Christ the Lord and entrusted to the Church. As actions of Christ and of the Church, they are signs and means by which faith is expressed and strengthened, worship is offered to God and our sanctification is brought about. Thus they contribute in the most effective manner to establishing, strengthening and manifesting ecclesiastical communion. Accordingly, in the celebration of the sacraments, both the sacred ministers and all the other members of Christ's faithful must show great reverence and due care.[1]

The word "sacrament" in the general sense describes the presence of the grace of God impacting on the life of his people. When applied to the seven sacraments of the Church, it means "some signs which can be perceived by the senses, instituted by Christ to signify and actually confer grace on those who receive it worthily."[2] Catholic catechism defines a sacrament as "an outward sign of inward grace ordained by Jesus Christ, by which grace is given to our soul."[3] This means that there are three things that are necessary to constitute a sacrament: (i) That it is instituted by Christ, (ii) that it is an outward sign, and (iii) that it has the power to give grace. The new Catechism of the Catholic Church

---

1 The *Code of Canon Law,* 1983 edition, English translation, (London: Collins Liturgical Pub.), Can. 840.

2 John F. McDonald, *The Sacraments in the Christian Life* (Slough: St. Paul Publications, 1983), p. 1.

3 *A Catechism of Christian Doctrine*, Revised Edition, (London: Catholic Truth Society, 1971), Q.249, pp. 42-43.

(CCC) corroborates this when it states categorically that, "Christ instituted the sacraments of the new law."[4] Only Christ instituted the sacraments since it is only God that can furnish signs with powers that give grace. Holy Scripture, the sacred tradition and teaching of the Church, makes it clear that Christ instituted the sacraments.

By 'outward sign' we mean something that the senses can perceive. This refers to what is called the *matter* and the *form* of a sacrament. While the *matter* refers to the external thing or action, the *form* refers to the formula or words. For instance, in the sacrament of baptism, we see water and hear the words pronounced as the water is poured over the forehead of the person baptized. The water and words constitute the outward signs as perceived by our human senses of sight and sound.

The sacraments signify the graces they bestow on the receiver. For instance, in baptism, the pouring of water over the head of the person being baptised signifies the cleansing of the soul from sin. This obtains if there are no obstacles being unprepared to receive the sacrament, on the part of the person to be baptised. Thus, the sacraments are channels by which the graces of God nourish and purify us. The Council of Trent in 1547 declared the sacraments as acting *ex opera operato*,[5] which means that the sacraments give grace to our souls by themselves (by virtue of the fact of the action performed). This is distinguished from *ex opera operantis*, which means by virtue of the one who performs the action – when the efficacy of what is done depends on the worthiness of the one who does it. The efficacy of the sacraments comes from Christ by whose merit we possess the sacraments. Therefore, they give grace to our souls by themselves irrespective of the worthiness of the person who administers them. The sacraments are efficacious in the life of the recipient, if the recipient is properly disposed to receive it. It is like saying that good medication is good regardless of the druggist or physician that administers it.

---

4 *The Catechism of the Catholic Church* (Nairobi: Paulines Publications – Africa, 1994), n. 1210.

5 *DS* 1608.

According to Richard McBrien, Catholicism has been described as a sacramental faith-tradition.[6] This means that very few things are more characteristic of the Catholic faith than its sacramental life. John McDonald describes the church as the universal sacrament of salvation.[7] The history of the development of Christian theology provides us a number of understandings of the function and role of the sacraments. These include the following: they convey grace, strengthen faith, enhance unity and commitment within the Church; and reassure us of the promises of God to humanity/his people.[8]

There are seven sacraments; baptism, confirmation, holy Eucharist, reconciliation, anointing of the sick, holy orders and matrimony. They can be broadly divided into three headings: (i) The sacraments of initiation, namely, baptism, confirmation and holy Eucharist; (ii) The sacraments of forgiveness and healing, namely, reconciliation or penance and anointing of the sick; (iii) The sacraments of vocation and commitment or the sacraments at the service of communion, namely, holy orders and matrimony or marriage. They, each, touch on all the stages and important moments of the Christian life, giving birth and increase, healing, and mission to the Christian faith.[9] "The sacraments are acts of Christ who personally sanctifies each individual through contact with him in them."[10] Though she is the guardian and interpreter of the will of Christ as far as the sacraments are concerned, the Church however cannot invent new sacraments nor delete from the existing sacraments. She cannot even change the existing elements of the sacraments insofar as Christ has determined them.

---

6 Richard McBrien, *Catholicism*, 3rd edition, (London: Geoffrey Chapman, 1994), p. 785.

7 John F. McDonald, p. 1

8 Alister E. McGrath, *Christian Theology: An Introduction*, 3rd edition, (Oxford: Blackwell Pub, 2001), pp. 516 – 522.

9 *The Catechism of the Catholic Church*, n. 1210.

10 John F. McDonald, p. 2.

2

The Sacrament of Baptism[11]

The "Christian initiation is accomplished by three sacraments together: Baptism, which is the beginning of the new life; Confirmation, which is its strengthening; and the Eucharist, which nourishes the disciple with Christ's body and blood for his transformation in Christ."[12] These sacraments lay the foundations of the Christian life and according to Pope Paul IV, Christians receive in an increasing measure the treasure of divine life and therefore, advance towards perfection of charity by means of these sacraments of initiation. Through these sacraments of initiation, the faithful are freed from the power of darkness, for they die with Christ, are buried with him and also rise with him to a new life. They become adopted children of God and celebrate the memorial of the Lord's death and resurrection.[13]

Baptism is the very first of the sacraments of initiation. As a sacrament, it serves as the gateway to the other sacraments; thus, it is the foundation on which the sacramental life of the Christian is built. It is the gateway to life in the Spirit. It gives to our soul a new life of sanctifying grace by making us children of God and heirs to his kingdom. It is a sacrament that cleanses us from the original sin, makes us members of Christ and incorporates us into his church. It is a sacrament of regeneration through water and the Holy Spirit.[14]

---

11 Originally published in *The Promise Newspaper*, a monthly publication of the Catholic Diocese of Auchi.

12 *The Catechism of the Catholic Church*, n.1275.

13 Richard McBrien, p. 806. See also Rom. 6:4.

14 *The Catechism of the Catholic Church*, n. 1213.

Christ instituted baptism as a sacrament and we recall that he was baptised at the Jordan (Mt. 3:13-16; Mk 1:9-11 & Lk. 3:21-22). He commanded his disciples to baptise at his ascension. “Go, therefore and make disciples of all nations, baptizing them in the name of the Father, and of the Son, and of the Holy Spirit.” (Mk 16:15-16). In his discussion with Nicodemus, Jesus made allusions to the necessity of baptism for salvation. “In truth I tell you, no one can see the kingdom of God without being born from above” (Jn. 3:3). To be born from above is translated by many versions of the bible as ‘born again.’ In explaining to Nicodemus what this meant, Jesus referred to being born through water and the Spirit. St. Paul took on this theme in his letter to the Romans, in Rom 6:1-11.

According to Paul, “By our baptism into his death we were buried with him, so that as Christ was raised from the dead by the Father’s glorious power, we too should begin living a new life” (Rom. 6:4). Commentaries on this verse show that Paul was not contrasting baptism with faith but making a categorical statement that baptism goes with faith. He expressed this same fact in Galatian 3:26 and Ephesian 4:5. The author of the Letter to the Hebrews equally expressed the same fact (Heb. 10:22). Therefore, as the sinner is immersed in the waters of baptism, he is buried with Christ (Col. 2:12), with the same Christ, the sinner as a Christian rises as in the resurrection (Rom. 8:11), to be a new creature (2 Cor. 5:17) or new person (Eph. 2:15).

According to the gospel of St. John, Jesus himself baptised people, “After this, Jesus went with his disciples into the Judean countryside and stayed with them there and baptized” (Jn. 3:22). He also approved of his disciples to baptise (Jn. 4:1-4). It was however, at the Pentecost gathering that the outpouring of the Holy Spirit became associated with baptism (Acts 2:1-39). As the bible tells us, over three thousand were baptised on this day. And ever since this very day, the Church has celebrated and administered the sacrament of baptism.[15]

---

15 *The Catechism of the Catholic Church*, n. 1226.

Baptism imprints an indelible spiritual sign or character on the recipient. This means that the recipient of the sacrament of baptism is configured into the person of Christ as he/she is sealed with the mark of God's ownership, which cannot be effaced. The term 'effaced' means the character so imprinted cannot be eliminated nor made indistinct. For this very reason, the sacrament of baptism once validly administered and received is not repeated.[16] For baptism to be validly administered, it must follow the essential rite, which consists in "immersing the candidate in water or pouring water on the head of the one to be baptized, while pronouncing the invocation of the Most Holy Trinity: the Father, the Son, and the Holy Spirit."[17] This is properly referred to as the Trinitarian formula for baptism.

The fruits of baptism are manifold. "It is a rich reality that includes forgiveness of original sin and all personal sins, birth into the new life by which man [and woman] becomes an adoptive son [and daughter] of the Father, a member of Christ and a temple of the Holy Spirit. By this very fact, the person baptised is incorporated into the Church, the Body of Christ, and made a sharer in the priesthood of Christ."[18] With this manifold fruit of the baptismal grace, it is only proper and wise that nobody is excluded from the reception of the sacrament. Therefore, the Church teaches that, "Every person not yet baptised and only such a person is able to be baptised."[19] In other words, the young and the old, the adult and the infant are eligible for baptism so long as they have not been baptised earlier.

There are however, some controversies concerning the baptism of infants. Some other Christian faiths or Churches differ from the Catholic Church on whether infants should be baptised or not. Catholic teaching subscribes to infant baptism while others do not. In the opinion of the latter, the practice of infant baptism by the Catholic Church is either mistaken or outrightly wrong. The Catholic Church teaches that,

---

16 *DS* 1609 and 1624.

17 *The Catechism of the Catholic Church*, n. 1278.

18 *The Catechism of the Catholic Church*, n. 1279.

19 Can. 864. See also *The Catechism of the Catholic Church*, n.1246.

> Born with a fallen human nature and tainted by original sin, children also have need of the new birth in baptism to be freed from the power of darkness and brought into the realm of the freedom of the children of God, to which all men are called. The sheer gratuitousness of the grace of salvation is particularly manifest in infant baptism. The Church and the parents would deny a child the priceless grace of becoming a child of God were they not to confer baptism shortly after birth.[20]

From time immemorial, infant baptism has been a practice of the Church with explicit testimony to its practice from the second century.[21] At the beginning of the apostolic preaching, there were records of whole households receiving baptism (Acts 16:15, 18:8; 1 Cor.1:16). It is highly probable that these households had children and infants among them.

The difficulty connected with the baptism of infants has to do with whether we can say infants have faith, since baptism is tied to faith. In response to this, St. Thomas Aquinas compared baptismal (spiritual) rebirth to physical birth. According to him, as the infant does not receive independent nourishment while in the mother's womb, but is sustained by the nourishment of the mother, so also children who are yet without the use of reason, as if in the womb of the Church, receive salvation through the activity of the Church. This submission of Aquinas takes into consideration the fact that baptism is a grace and a gift of God. This means that it does not presuppose any human merit. It is not a result of anyone's worthiness that he or she is baptised. Thus, children are rightly baptised into the faith of the Church.

We talk about conditional baptism, which is usually administered when there are doubts about the validity of an earlier baptism. Such doubts are about the formula of baptism, for instance, whether the recipient was baptised using the Triune name of God (the Trinitarian formula) and about the validity of the manner of baptism in the church from which the recipient of

---

20 *The Catechism of the Catholic Church*, n. 1250.
21 *The Catechism of the Catholic Church*, n. 1252.

conditional baptism is converting to the Catholic faith. It is called conditional baptism to indicate the fact that it is not a repetition of baptism but given in case the recipient was not validly and/or properly baptised. If the earlier baptism is valid, then the conditional baptism does not apply, if the earlier baptism is not valid, the conditional baptism applies.

One issue that sometimes generate controversy is the manner in which baptism is given, either by immersion or by infusion. Baptism by immersion is the total dunking of the person being baptised in water, while baptism by infusion or sprinkling involves pouring water over the head of the person. Fundamentalists insist that the only true way to baptise is by immersion because the Greek word *baptizo*, found in the New Testament means "to immerse" and that it is only through immersion that we symbolically reflect the significance of Christ's being buried and raised (Rom. 6:3-4). Although the Catholic church usually uses infusion, she teaches that immersion and sprinkling are also valid ways to baptise. The Catholic church disagrees with the inference that *baptizo* implies immersion only. Other uses of the same term in scripture indicate that it also means just "washing up", as in the case of washing hands before eating (Lk. 11:38 and Mk 7:3-4).

3

The Sacrament of Confirmation[22]

The sacrament of confirmation completes the sacraments of Christian initiation. "By the sacrament of confirmation, (the baptised) are more perfectly bound to the church and are enriched with a special strength of the Holy Spirit."[23] According to the CCC,

> The sacrament of confirmation brings about an increase and a deepening of our baptismal grace. It makes us more firmly united to Christ as it increases the gifts of the Holy Spirit in us. It also bounds us more perfectly to the church and gives us a special strength of the Holy Spirit to spread the faith and defend the same faith, both in words and deeds.[24]

The sacrament of confirmation is given only once like baptism and it also imprints an indelible character, which is a spiritual mark on the soul. This character is the sign that the Christian has been sealed by the Holy Spirit to witness to Christ. Every baptised person who has not received this sacrament is eligible and should receive the sacrament of confirmation.

As a sacrament that indicates the outpouring of thc Holy Spirit, it has its biblical roots. In the Old Testament, the prophet Isaiah proclaims that the Holy Spirit would rest on the expected Messiah. "On him will rest the spirit of Yahweh, the spirit of wisdom and insight, the spirit of counsel and power, the spirit of knowledge

---

22 Originally published in *The Promise Newspaper*, a monthly publication of the Catholic Diocese of Auchi in 2010.

23 Austin Flammery O.P. (ed.), *Vatican Council II: The Conciliar and Post Conciliar Documents*, 1988 Revised Edition (Iperu-Remo: The Ambassador Book Centre, 1990), *Lumen Gentium*, no. 11.

24 *The Catechism of the Catholic Church*, no. 1303.

and fear of Yahweh" (Is. 11:2). This prophecy was restated in Isaiah 61:1 as well as fulfilled in Lk. 4:18.

There are explicit references in the New Testament to the coming down of the Spirit upon Jesus Christ. In some of these references, the experience was presented as a confirmation of Jesus as the expected Messiah. The CCC tells us that "The descent of the Holy Spirit on Jesus at his baptism by John was the sign that this was he who was to come, the Messiah, the Son of God."[25] The coming of the Spirit upon Jesus at his baptism which is recorded in Mk 1:10 and Mt. 3:13-17 was not temporal, it was permanent. According to the gospel of John, "I saw the Spirit descend as a dove from heaven and remained on him" (Jn. 1:32).

Jesus was conceived of the Holy Spirit (Lk. 1:35, Mt. 1:20). His whole life and ministry was lived and carried out under the guidance of the Holy Spirit. That is to say, he lived completely in communion with the Holy Spirit. This Spirit, according to John 3:34 has been given to him by the Father in full measure. This fullness of the Spirit, which Jesus had, was not to remain exclusively with him, he was also to communicate it to God's people. "I shall pour clean water over you and you will be cleansed; I shall cleanse you of all your filth and of all your idols. I shall give you a new heart, and put a new spirit in you..." (Eze. 36:25. See also Joel 3:1-2).

At various times in the Scriptures, Jesus promised that he was going to send the Spirit to his followers. In the gospel of St. Luke, Jesus told his disciples not to be afraid that the Spirit will be with them in their mission so that they can bear fearless witness to their faith. "When they take you before synagogues and magistrates and authorities, do not worry about how to defend yourselves or what to say, because when the time comes, the Holy Spirit will teach you what you should say" (Lk. 12:11-12). In Jn. 7:37-38, Jesus promised his followers living water, and the evangelist went on to say, "He was speaking of the Spirit which those who believed in him were to receive; for there was no Spirit as yet because Jesus had not yet been glorified" (Jn. 7:39).

---

25 *The Catechism of the Catholic Church*, no. 1286.

The entire section of Jn. 16:5-15, discusses the sending of the Spirit by Jesus upon his disciples. Specifically, verse 7 says, "Still, I am telling you the truth: it is for your own good that I am going, because unless I go, the Paraclete will not come to you; but if I go, I will send him to you." In verses 12 and 13, Jesus says, "I still have many things to say to you but they would be too much for you to bear now. However, when the Spirit of truth comes he will lead you to the complete truth, since he will not be speaking of his own accord, but will say only what he has been told; and will reveal to you the things to come." There is also this reference to the coming of the Spirit, which Jesus was going to send from the Father to his disciples, "When the Paraclete comes, whom I shall send from the Father, the Spirit of truth who issues from the Father, he will be my witness. And you too will be witnesses, because you have been with me from the beginning" (Jn. 15:26-27). Even after his resurrection, Jesus Christ restated the fact that he will send his disciples the Spirit, "And now I am sending upon you what the Father has promised. Stay in the city, then, until you are clothed with the power from on high" (Lk. 24:49). The reference here to, "What the Father has promised," according to commentaries is a reference to the Holy Spirit.

Of utmost significance is the fulfilment of these promises, which took place, first on Easter Sunday and then on the day of Pentecost. On the day of his resurrection, when he appeared to the disciples, having greeted them, "Peace be with you," He continued; "As the Father has sent me, so am I sending you." He then breathed on them and said; "Receive the Holy Spirit. If you forgive anyone's sins, they are forgiven; if you retain anyone's sins, they are retained" (Jn. 20:22).

According to John McDonald, "We know that on the feast of Pentecost the Holy Spirit came down in an extraordinary way on the apostles together in the upper room and they were so 'filled with the Holy Spirit' that by divine inspiration they began to proclaim 'the mighty works of God."[26] McDonald is referring to Acts 2:1-41. The CCC, quoting Pope Paul VI, says:

---

26 John F. McDonald, p. 32.

> From that time on, the apostles, in fulfilment of Christ's will, imparted to the newly baptized, by laying on of hands, the gift of the Spirit that completes the grace of Baptism. For this reason, in the Letter to the Hebrews the doctrine concerning Baptism and the laying on of hands is listed among the first elements of Christian instruction. The imposition of hands is rightly recognized by the Catholic tradition as the origin of the sacrament of confirmation, which in a certain way, perpetuates the grace of Pentecost in the Church.[27]

The reference here by Pope Paul VI is to the Letter to the Hebrews. "Let us leave behind us then all the elementary teaching about Christ and go on to its completion, without going over the fundamental doctrines again: the turning away from dead actions, faith in God, the teaching about baptisms and the laying-on of hands, about the resurrection of the dead and eternal judgment" (Heb. 6:1-2).

The sacrament of confirmation enables us to attain spiritual maturity. This is what St. Thomas Aquinas referred to as the 'spiritual coming of age.' Spiritual maturity is reflected in our serious spiritual activities, which arise from our convictions and our deep knowledge of God, the church and the world. Thus, confirmation bestows on us great spiritual and moral responsibilities. According to McDonald,

i. A Christian who is spiritually mature is able to evaluate the things and affairs of this world at their proper worth in relation to the Christian life.
ii. Spiritual maturity enables us to discover our proper place in the life of the Church and the duties that go with it. We are made aware of our personal and social responsibilities as members of the Mystical Body of Christ.
iii. Hand-in-hand with spiritual maturity goes the freedom to make a responsible choice, the wisdom to make the

27 *The Catechism of the Catholic Church*, no. 1288.

> necessary adjustments that are called for in one's growth in the Christian life and a maturity of judgment.[28]

Confirmation is a sacrament given for the purpose of receiving the fullness of the Holy Spirit who works in many different ways. The essential rites of confirmation consist in the anointing of the forehead with the sacred oil of chrism and the laying on of hands. This is accompanied with the words, "Be sealed with the gift of the Holy Spirit." Thus, it gives us a further share in the priesthood of Christ, makes us more perfectly conformed to Christ, strengthens us in the Holy Spirit, and therefore, strengthens us to bear witness to Christ.

---

28 John F. MacDonald, p. 33.

4

The Sacrament of the Holy Eucharist (I)

According to the documents of the Second Vatican Council (VC II), the Holy Mass, which is also referred to as the Eucharist, or the Lord's Supper, is the centre and summit of Catholic worship, and in fact, the Christian life.[29] It is the greatest treasure of the Church. It is the source of the Church's power and the visible sign on which the Church's unity is built. It is both a sacrifice and a meal. In the Eucharist, the Church keeps alive the sacrifice of Christ that perfectly achieves our salvation at Calvary and enables her members to share in the sacred banquet of the body and blood of Christ to which Christ himself in Jn. 6:32-58 invites us to partake.[30] The Eucharist "contains Christ himself, who in it is present to the Church not merely by power of his grace but in the reality of his glorified humanity."[31] Contrary to the opinion of some that the Holy Mass detracts from the uniqueness of the sacrifice of Christ at Calvary; it rather enhances it, keeps it alive, and applies its power.[32]

Anyone, who has a full appreciation of what is involved and what takes place at Mass, cannot but be grateful to God for this great treasure. It seems that this treasure is hidden to many – Christians and non-Christians alike. It is poorly understood by many of those who seem to have found this treasure. Like the man who found a treasure in one of the parables of Jesus, replaced the

---

29 Austin Flammery O.P., *Sacrosanctum Concilium*, no. 11.

30 Jacques Dupuis, (ed.), *The Christian Faith in the Doctrinal Documents of the Catholic Church*, 7th Revised and Enlarged Edition, (Bangalore: Theological Publications in India, 2001), p. 605.

31 Jacques Dupuis, p. 605.

32 Jacques Dupuis, p. 605.

earth to cover up the treasure in view of his return, went home and sold off all he had so as to raise enough money to secure the land for himself and thereafter take possession of the treasure, (Mt. 13:44-46), we are supposed to value the Mass in like manner. Such an attitude as this is however, only possible when we know the value and worth of what we have.

Concerning the Mass, Pope Pius IV, said:

> I also profess that in the Mass there is offered to God a true sacrifice, properly speaking, which is propitiatory for the living and the dead, and that in the most Holy Sacrament of the Eucharist the body and blood together with the soul and the divinity of our Lord Jesus Christ are truly, really and substantially present, and that there takes place a change (*conversio*) of the whole substance of wine into the blood; and this change the Catholic Church calls transubstantiation. I also confess that under each species alone (*sub altera tantum specie*) the whole and entire Christ and the true sacrament is received.

Pope Pius IV's profession of faith in relation to the Mass is a beautiful summary of what the Holy Eucharist is. It brings to the fore several aspects of the Eucharist. Some of these aspects have been the subject of controversies in the history and growth of the Church's life, ditto, the Eucharist.

The Institution of the Holy Mass: Concerning the institution of the Eucharist, scripture says, "For the tradition I received from the Lord and also handed on to you is that on the night he was betrayed, the Lord Jesus took some bread, and after he had given thanks, he broke it, and said, 'This is my body, which is for you; do this in remembrance of me'. And in the same way, with the cup after supper, saying, 'This cup is the new covenant in my blood. Whenever you drink it, do this as a memorial of me'. When you eat this bread, then, and drink this cup, you are proclaiming the Lord's death until he comes. Therefore, anyone who eats the bread or drinks the cup of the Lord unworthily is answerable for the body and blood of the Lord" (1 Cor. 11:23-27).

Anyone who has heard about the man Jesus would equally have heard about the Lord's Supper. While it may be true that Jesus is not synonymous with the Lord's Supper, it is definitely the case that you cannot think of the Lord's Supper independently of Jesus Christ. In the passage of scripture above, St. Paul reports an account that is most closely connected with the Lord's Supper. He refers to it as a tradition he received from Christ. We know this was not part of the dialogue between Paul and Christ on his way to Damascus (Acts 9:1-9). Therefore, Paul is very likely referring to tradition that dates back to the Lord. As he did in 1 Cor. 15:3-7 where he talks about the death and resurrection of the Lord Jesus Christ, Paul is using the technical terminology of the rabbis for the passing on of tradition. From all indications, he was quoting the earliest Christian tradition about the Eucharist. And for those familiar with the writings of St. Paul, the language used here is not typical of him.

At the Last Supper, (Mt. 26:26-29; Mk 14:22-25 and Lk. 22:19-20), when everybody had settled down at table, according to John's account (Jn. 13:1-17); after washing the feet of his disciples, Jesus took bread, said the blessing and gave it to his disciples as his body. The same he did with the cup of wine and he said, "... whenever you drink it, do this as a memorial of me." Jesus Christ thus, invited his disciples with whom he shared his Lord's Supper to continue what they have seen him do. The invitation is not an ordinary one, it was an invitation backed with authority to do as he has done. And they did; for the description of the early Christian community highlighted it as one of the identifying marks of the early Church (Acts 2:42).

The Lord's Supper was a solemn and great occasion. It was as solemn as what obtains when a father gathers his children around his deathbed to give them a final instruction. He tells them the "yet unknown" secrets of the family and points to family possessions unknown to the children. In the same way Christ gathered his apostles around himself, just before he walked the long and painful way of the cross to his vicarious death. The apostles were his closest associates; he gathered them to give them the final lesson on the path to life, and most importantly, to bequeath to humankind through his apostles a memorial service.

Catholics do not doubt the fact that the Holy Mass is a true sacrifice instituted by Christ at the Lord's Supper, and that as a sacrifice, it is to perpetuate the memory of the sacrifice of the cross. The general council of Trent in its 22nd session upheld that the "Holy Mass is not a sacrifice independent of the cross." As a matter of fact, it is the sacrifice of the cross that is now offered by the Church following the command of Christ, whenever the Church celebrates the ritual of the Lord's Supper in which Christ offered himself.[33]

Accordingly, the council, in order to retain the Holy Catholic Church and preserve in its purity the ancient, absolute, and completely perfect faith and doctrine on the Eucharist and to prevent errors and avert heresies, vested with the rightful authority, declares and teaches that;

> As the Apostle testifies there was no perfection under the former Covenant because of the insufficiency of the Levitical priesthood. It was, therefore, necessary (according to the merciful ordination of God the Father) that another priest arise after the order of Melchizedek [cf. Gen. 14:18; Ps 110 (109):4; Heb. 7:11], our Lord Jesus Christ who could make perfect all who were to be sanctified [cf. Heb. 10:14] and bring them to fulfilment. He, then our Lord and God, was once and for all to offer himself to God the Father by his death on the altar of the cross, to accomplish for them an everlasting redemption. But, because his priesthood was not to end with his death [cf. Heb. 7:24, 27], at the Last Supper, "on the night when he was betrayed" [1 Cor. 11:23], in order to leave to his beloved Spouse the Church a visible sacrifice (as human nature demands) by which the bloody sacrifice which he was once for all to accomplish on the cross would be present, its memory perpetuated until the end of the world and its salutary power declaring himself constituted "a priest

33 Jacques Dupuis, p. 625.

> forever after the order of Melchizedek" [Ps 110 (109):4], he offered his body and blood under the species of bread and wine to God the Father, and, under the same signs (*sub earundem rerum symbolis*) gave them to partake of to the disciples (whom he then established as priests of the New covenant), and ordered them and their successors in the priesthood to offer, saying: "Do this as a memorial of me", etc. [Lk. 22:19; 1 Cor. 11:24], as the Catholic Church has always understood and taught.[34]

The *Catechism of Christian Doctrine* defines the holy Eucharist as, the sacrament of the body and blood of Christ, together with his soul and divinity, which is really present on the altar under the appearances of bread and wine.[35] The Holy Eucharist is a sacrament with many and varied aspects.

Man is both material and spiritual, therefore, man is made up of the physical and spiritual substances. For instance, the body and blood of man constitute the physical or material aspects of man, while the soul and intellect constitute his spiritual aspects. Theologians opine that man is like God in his soul and intellect because man enjoys immortality in his soul and rationality by virtue of his intellect. Based on this exposition of man, the Catholic Church describes the Eucharist as entirely Christ in his human and divine nature. That is, the Eucharist is Christ as entirely man and entirely God. The Holy Mother Church teaches that Christ is one person with two natures; the nature of man and the nature of God. This is explained in the teaching on the hypostatic union.

The Eucharist or Holy Mass is a memorial sacrifice that is tri-dimensional. It is the sacrifice of the new law, the sublime sacrifice of Christ himself, and the sacrifice of the people for the people. This is explained in the next chapter that deals with the Holy Mass as a sacrifice.

---

34 *DS* 1739 and 1740.

35 *A Catechism of Christian Doctrine*, Q. 266, p. 45.

The Holy Eucharist is truly the real and loving presence of God in our midst. The simple act of preserving the sacred species of the Body and Blood of Christ in the tabernacles all over the world is a testimony to this. The Blessed Sacrament or the Eucharist, is Jesus Christ in the real sense and Jesus Christ in the real sense is God in the real sense. God humbly dwells in our midst in the tabernacles of our Catholic Churches all over the world but we (the sons and daughters of men) arrogantly, sometimes insultively and contemptuously, continue to treat God with disrespect every day in our churches. We ignore His presence in the tabernacle and talk (make noise) away inside the church, neither praying nor allowing those praying to concentrate. We are on social media chatting and socially interacting with friends but ignoring Jesus who is there with us in the Blessed Sacrament. We steal in the Church and from the Church as we count collections of different designations, be it offertory, second collections, harvest offerings, launching collections, and feel great and happy thinking we have out-smarted the priest. But do we out-smart God? Some come purposely to Church to show off their new collections of clothing, some to sample the girls and the girls dress to attract the male folk in Church.

5

The Sacrament of the Holy Eucharist (II)

The Real Presence of Christ in the Eucharist[36]

Jesus Christ is truly and really present in the Sacrament of his Body and Blood, the Holy Eucharist. There is nowhere this is more obvious and attested to than the Lord's Supper itself. One of the very significant events of this supper was the reference of Jesus Christ to bread as his body and wine as his blood. The portrait we have of Jesus, both in religious and secular literature, is that of a serious minded man, a man with a singular sense of purpose and mission, one who goes about his set goals with integrity, and commitment not equivocating or trying to please any person. Even pagan historians, like Josephus Flavius, who at times spoke scornfully about a man called Christ who was the root cause of civil unrest in the Roman Empire, never referred to him as someone not to be taken seriously. On this account therefore, we cannot say that Jesus was not serious when he referred to bread as his body and wine as his blood during the Supper. So too we cannot say that he was out of his mind when he made these pronouncements. The occasion was solemn, the audience was his disciples, to whom he was to entrust his mission, and it was a moment of great significance and importance. A specific occasion Christ chose to institute a special form of prayer. Jesus did not say this bread looks like my body and the wine like my blood. Neither did he say that the bread represents his body and the wine his blood. These are possibilities of what he could have said so as to

---

36 First published in *The Promise Newspaper*, a monthly publication of the Catholic Diocese of Auchi, 2009.

avoid equivocation. He did not say any of these, rather he said; "This is my Body" and "This is my Blood."

The issue of Jesus giving his body as food and his blood as drink for our eternal salvation, goes back to his discourse in the theological gospel of St. John. This discourse opens with the miracle of the loaves (Jn. 6:1-15), a miracle whose setting recalls the anguish of Moses when the people cried out in tears to him in the desert for meat and Yahweh's subsequent response (Num. 11:13ff). It also recalls the multiplication of loaves by the prophet Elisha at Gilgal (2Kings 4:42-44). Out of compassion for the crowd, Jesus Christ asked Philip how to get some bread to feed the crowds surrounding him. In the opinion of Philip, this would not be easy, as it will cost some good money. Besides, the only boy selling food around has just five loaves and two fish. Little did Philip know that the five loaves and two fish were all that the master needed. Having given thanks, the five loaves and two fish fed all present and twelve whole baskets of leftover were collected.

Impressed by this great miracle, the crowds went in search of Jesus the following day. When they found him at Capernaum, they displayed their relief by telling him how much they have searched for him. Jesus however was not given to their material way of thinking. He puts it straight to them that they were seeking him because of bread and not because they really loved him and his teaching. He used the opportunity to advise them once again to seek and work for bread "that endures for eternal life which the son of man will give."

This was how he started the gradual exposition of the great mystery of the Eucharist. This is the mystery of the vicarious death of the Son of man, who has come to give new life to the human race, by inviting the human race to share in the life-giving meal of his Body and Blood. Jesus directed the attention of the crowd to the manna their ancestors had in the desert. He explained to the crowds that it was his Father, God, who gave them the manna and not Moses as they thought. This same God, he tells them, is going to give them the true bread "which comes down from heaven and gives life to the world." In response to the crowd's craving for this bread, he declared; "I am the bread of life. No one who comes to me will ever hunger; no one who believes in me will ever thirst" (Jn. 6:35). With this declaration, which is more of an invitation, Jesus presents himself as the wisdom of God, which invites all peoples to her table (Prov. 9:1ff).

The Jews had problems with this. They knew the father and mother of Jesus; how could he start claiming to have come from heaven as the bread of life? They started to complain. Aware of their rather quiet grudge, Jesus explained further and concluded the explanation by declaring again, "I am the living bread which has come down from heaven. Anyone who eats this bread will live for ever and the bread that I shall give is my flesh for the life of the world" (Jn. 6:50-51). Gradually, Jesus Christ is exposing the meaning and purpose of the incarnation and the mystery of his passion. The Jews, however, were not following. They were still thinking on the human realm and their disapproval of his claims was becoming louder; "How can this man give us his flesh to eat." They definitely do not understand what Jesus meant. Again, Jesus tried to lead them from the darkness of their human thoughts to the light God is offering them. His efforts seemed futile as the crowds started to leave him one after the other, afraid of being lured by him into cannibalism. They described Jesus' talk as "intolerable teaching," unacceptable to anyone. The listeners of Jesus are agreeable in their understanding that Jesus meant what he has said to be taken literally and not to be understood in any other way. In other words, they knew Jesus was not speaking in metaphors.

At the point they started leaving Jesus one after the other, we expect that Jesus, who does not want anyone entrusted to him to be lost (Jn. 17:2), would call back his followers and soften his teaching so as to make it agreeable to them. No! Jesus would not do that. He meant every word he spoke, exactly as he had said each word. For him the Jews were unteachable (Mt. 19:8) and he will not water down the truth or twist it so as to win their continuous followership. The truth, no matter how bitter, is the truth and only the truth shall set you free. He turned to his disciples instead and made it clear to them that they too can leave if they so desired (Jn. 6:67). To this, Simon Peter, who often played the role of the spokesman for the apostles, replied: "Lord to whom shall we go? You have the message of eternal life, and we believe; we have come to know that you are the Holy One of God" (Jn. 6:69).

The reference of Jesus at the Lord's Supper to bread and wine as his body and blood respectively is related to the above discourse. The bread and wine offered on the altar at Mass becomes the Body and Blood of Christ after the words of consecration ordained by Christ himself (Mt. 26:20-26, Lk. 22:19-20, Mk 14:22-25) are pronounced by a validly ordained Catholic priest. This whole process is called transubstantiation.

Transubstantiation

What happens on the altar during consecration at Mass is a great mystery, which the Church calls transubstantiation. The doctrine of transubstantiation was formally defined by the 4th Lateran Council of 1215 based on the Aristotelian distinction between 'substance' and 'accident.' For Aristotle, the substance is the essential nature of a thing while the accident is the outward appearance, for example, taste, colour, shape, smell, etc. Therefore, the doctrine of transubstantiation holds that the accidents (the outward appearance) of the bread and wine (smell, taste, colour, shape, etc.), remain unchanged at the moment of consecration but its substance changes from the bread and wine to the Body and Blood of Jesus Christ.

This doctrine was fiercely criticised by the Protestants during the reformation period. The 1551 Council of Trent however vigorously defended both the doctrine and the terminology of transubstantiation in its *Decree on the Most Holy Sacrament of the Eucharist*. The opening statement of the Decree strongly affirms that, "after the consecration of the bread and wine, our Lord Jesus Christ is *truly, really,* and *substantially* contained in the venerable sacrament of the Holy Eucharist under the appearance of those physical things." It proceeds with the affirmation that; "By the consecration of the bread and wine a change is brought about of the whole substance of the bread into the substance of the body of

Christ and of the whole substance of the wine into the blood of Christ. This change the holy Catholic Church properly and appropriately calls transubstantiation."

In other words, at consecration during the celebration of Holy Mass, there is a change in the ontological reality; in the significance and in the purpose of bread and wine. When we talk about a change in the significance, we are talking about a change in the meaning of the bread and wine, a change in what the bread and wine represent or signify. Hitherto, the bread and wine meant nothing other than earthly food, food for human (material) nourishment and satisfaction. With the spoken words of consecration, this meaning is changed. The bread and wine now means more than earthly food. It is now the body and blood of Christ, a heavenly food. It now signifies food and drink for human spiritual satisfaction. This mystery can, therefore, be expressed as "*transignification,*" that is, a transformation in the significance or meaning of the bread and wine. This concept however, does not fully express and explain what has happened. It leaves out the change in purpose of the bread and wine. It is therefore, not a correct expression but a one-sided expression of the mystery that has taken place. In addition to the change in significance, there is also a change in purpose. The purpose of the earthly bread and wine lies in ministering to the natural bodily life. After consecration, a new thrust and dynamism appears. The bread and wine, which are now the body and blood of Christ, minister and nourish the life of God in us and therefore, strengthen us for eternal life. Because of this change in finality, the mystery may be expressed as "*transfinalization.*" Again, like the former expression this expression is incomplete as it expresses the change in purpose alone and not the change in meaning.

A full and complete expression is obtained in the concept of *transubstantiation*. It expresses both the new significance and new purpose that the bread and wine now assume after consecration. The changes involved affect the whole being, the substance, of the bread and wine. So it is more complete to talk about a transformation in the substance; the substance being what makes a thing what it is.

There is a change from the substance of bread and wine to the substance of the Body and Blood of Jesus Christ. A transformation from the substance of bread to the substance of the Body and Blood of Jesus Christ. Though it still looks like bread and wine, it still tastes like bread and wine, it is in fact, the Body and Blood of Christ since the substance that makes it bread and wine is now the substance of the Body and Blood of Christ.

The official position of the Catholic Church is that as long as *transignification* and *transfinalization* are understood within the context of the traditional understanding of *transubstantiation*, they are acceptable.[37] According to Pope Paul VI, in his 1965 encyclical letter, *Mysterium Fidei*;

> As a result of transubstantiation, the species of bread and wine undoubtedly take on a new signification and a new finality, for they are no longer ordinary bread and wine but instead a sign of something sacred and a sign of spiritual food. Yet they take on this new significance, this new finality, precisely because they contain a new "reality." ... For what now lies beneath the aforementioned species [that is, what is now the new substance of the elements] is not what was there before, but something completely different ... namely, the body and blood of Christ.[38]

As long as the appearance of bread and wine remains, Jesus Christ remains sacramentally present in the consecrated species. This is why in the Catholic Church, the sacred species, that is, the Holy Communion, the Blessed Eucharist, the consecrated bread is preserved in the tabernacle and adored even outside the Holy Mass, like at benedictions.

This teaching on the Eucharist is very central to Catholic doctrine and it is not to be confused with the teaching on *consubstantiation* of some other Christian churches. The concept of consubstantiation, which is especially associated with Martin Luther, talks about the simultaneous presence of both the bread

37 Cf. Alister E. McGrath, p. 526.

38 Pope Paul VI, *Mysterium Fidei*. Cited in Alister E. McGrath, p. 527.

and the body of Christ at one and the same time. Meaning that, Christ comes to dwell with the substance of the bread and wine. In other words, the bread and wine do not become the body and blood of Christ, Christ only comes to dwell with the bread and wine. After the "Communion Service," as it is often called in these other Christian churches, Christ departs from the substance of the bread and wine and it once again becomes ordinary bread and ordinary wine. There has, however, been a shift in recent times in this understanding by these other Christian faiths as there is an increasing reverence given to the elements of bread and wine and a tendency to consume all that is left-over and not just dispose of them. There is however, a fundamental difference between consubstantiation and transubstantiation as Christian doctrines concerning the body and blood of Christ.

Finally, I want to mention that while in the other sacraments of Baptism, Confirmation, Penance, Anointing of the sick, Holy Orders, and Matrimony, we encounter Christ in person, in his action and power, in the Eucharist we meet Christ in person. That is why we talk about the real presence of Christ in the Eucharist. This does not mean or even suggest that Christ is not present in the other sacraments, but that his presence in the Eucharist, which is the sacrifice of the Holy Mass is "presence in its fullest sense."[39]

39 Pope Paul VI, *Mysterium Fidei.*

6

The Holy Mass as a Sacrifice (I)[40]

The Holy Eucharist which is the same as the Holy Mass is a sacrifice. "The Holy Mass is the sacrifice of the Body and Blood of Christ really present on the altar under the appearances of bread and wine and offered to God for the living and the dead."[41] As a sacrifice, it is viewed from different dimensions; it is first and foremost a memorial sacrifice, meaning that, it is in remembrance of the sacrifice of Jesus Christ on Golgotha. It is also the sacrifice of the new law. That is, the sacrifice that replaced the old law sacrifice of the Passover. It is also the sublime sacrifice of Christ himself – the sacrifice in which he offered himself as the victim, where of course, he was also the priest offering the sacrifice. Finally, it is the sacrifice of the people for the people; a sacrifice offered by the people and offered for the people.

The Mass as a Memorial Sacrifice

The Mass is a living memorial of Christ's saving death, a sacrifice of the people and a sacrifice for the people. It is a sacrifice because it re-enacts the death of Christ on the cross: A death, in which, Christ offered himself as a living oblation, a spotless lamb, to appease humankind's sin. Thus the Church teaches that the Holy Sacrifice of the Mass is one and the same sacrifice with that of Christ on the Cross.

A sacrifice is the offering of a victim in form of a visible gift. The Mass is a Christian sacrifice. It is the offering of a victim by a

40 Originally published in three parts in *The Promise Newspaper*, a monthly publication of the Catholic Diocese of Auchi.

41 *A Catechism of Christian Doctrine*, Q. 277, p. 47.

priest, to God alone. In this case, the victim is Jesus Christ himself, offered under the appearances of bread and wine, as Christ himself did at the Lord's Supper.

For us Africans, the concept of a sacrifice had for a long time been tied down to traditional worship of idols. As such, it carries a negative connotation in Christian circles. Any mention of sacrifice immediately suggests idolatry. Within this context, the use of the concept for the Holy Mass has created some difficulties for some people. Hence I deem it fit to make a little preliminary explanation about sacrifice in the scripture. The aim is to enable us have a better understanding of our discussion.

Religious sacrifice has been part of our human history, dating back to even primitive man who in popular thinking is seen as uncultured. As a matter of fact, primitive man was quite sensible, child-like, and intelligent, as opposed to the beastly, savage, and ferocious picture many history books tend to present of him. We also find religious sacrifice of some kind in great and ancient civilisations and their religions. With the exception of a certain form of Buddhism, religious sacrifice constitutes an essential part of different religions in ancient and contemporary times. The Hindu religion of Vedism and Brahmanism, the Persian, Chinese, Egyptian, Greek and Roman religions all bear witness to this fact. In a special way, the Hebrew religion of Judaism, which immediately precedes Christianity, does.

Among the Hebrews, sacrifice was a frequent practice. The Old Testament gives, in fair details, the rules by which the sacrificial rites are to be performed. The book of Leviticus, for instance, chronicles the rules for peace offerings (Lev. 3), sacrifices of ignorance (Lev. 4), sacrifices for expiation of various sins (Lev. 5), sacrifices for sins of injustice (Lev. 6), sacrifices for expiation of trespasses and in thanksgiving for some favour (Lev. 7). The Old Testament actually gives a narration of various and individual sacrificial offerings, from the offerings of Cain and Abel (Gen. 4:1-4, also referred to in Heb. 11:4) to the sacrifice of Melchizedek (Gen. 14:17-19), the eternal priest (Heb. 7:3).

The Eucharist as the living sacrifice of Jesus on the cross is foreshadowed in the demand of God to Abraham to offer his only son, Isaac (Gen. 22:1-14). This act pre-empts what God was to do in history by giving His only son, Jesus Christ for the salvation of humanity. While Isaac, Abraham's son, was spared and replaced with a ram, God did not spare His only begotten son the sacrifice and death on the cross.

With the coming of Moses, God's chosen instrument in liberating His people from the bondage land of Egypt, sacrificial offerings took a definite form as outlined in the five chapters of the book of Leviticus mentioned above. Afterwards, an official priesthood, consisting of those in the order of Levites and the house of Aaron, was to offer sacrifices on behalf of the people. This is the context that the offering of the religious sacrifice we read in scripture concerning the presentation of Jesus in the temple, the sacrifice of Joseph and Mary falls into (Lk. 2:22-27).

The idea of religious sacrifice was carried over to the New Testament but it took a new dimension. Jesus Christ in Mt. 5:17 says, "Do not imagine that I have come to abolish the Law or the Prophets. I have come not to abolish but to complete them." This means that he has neither come to destroy nor revise the Old Testament but to give it a new and definitive form by his teaching and way of acting, so that the goal of the law and prophets may be fully realised. In accordance with his claim in Mt. 5:17, Jesus Christ instituted a new and perfect form of Christian religious sacrifice. While he did not throw out the idea of a religious sacrifice, he replaced the rather imperfect sacrifices of the Old Testament referred to in Heb. 7:18; 10:1-10 with a new and perfect sacrifice, which is the sacrifice of the New Law. The Holy Mass as a sacrifice is tri-dimensional. It is first of all, the sacrifice of the New Law. Secondly, it is the sublime sacrifice of Christ himself. Thirdly, it is the sacrifice of the people and for the people.

The Mass as the Sacrifice of the New Law

The event of the Lord's Supper is a very unique and significant one. It took place at the time when the Jews celebrated the Passover, a celebration in memory of their liberation from Egypt. It was at this memorial celebration that Christ instituted the Mass; the new and perfect sacrifice of the New Law. The Lord's Supper marked the last of the Old Law and signifies the first of the New Law.

At the announcement of the Law to the Israelites on Mount Sinai, Moses sprinkled half of the blood of the slaughtered bullocks on the altar and on the people saying, "This is the blood of the covenant which Yahweh has made with you..." (Ex. 24:8). At the Lord's Supper, where and when the sacrifice of the New Law was instituted, Christ took bread, said the blessing broke it and gave it to his disciples saying, "Take it and eat, this is my body." Then he took the cup filled with wine, having given thanks he gave it to his disciples and said, "Drink from this, all of you, for this is my blood, the blood of the new covenant, poured out for the forgiveness of sin" (Lk. 22:19-20, Mt. 26:26-29, Mk 14:22-25). Following what he has done, Christ gave his disciples the authority to do the same as he said, "... do this in remembrance of me" (Lk. 22:19, 1 Cor. 11:23-26).

Jesus Christ referred to the cup of wine as his blood poured out for the forgiveness of sins. This reference is understood in the light of the bitter experience of Calvary, which he was soon after going to embrace and by which he won salvation for humankind. In the old Passover celebration, the paschal lamb was slain and eaten, but in the perfect sacrifice of the New Law, Christ changed bread and wine into his Body and Blood.

The Mass as the Sublime Sacrifice of Christ Himself

On Calvary, Christ offered himself as a great sacrifice to God for our salvation. The Mass is therefore, not just a sacrifice of the New Law; it is the sublime sacrifice of Christ who freely gave up himself on the cross (Phil. 2:8). That is to say, Christ was both the priest who offered the sacrifice and the victim offered as a sacrifice on the cross.

An object of offering is always involved in a sacrifice; this is called the sacrificial victim. In the case of the Mass, Christ himself is the sacrificial victim. At every Mass, Christ is there present on the altar as the acceptable and infinitely more perfect and sublime offering that can be made to the Father as compared to the sacrificial victims of the Old Testament. As the Letter to the

Hebrews says: "The blood of goats and bulls and the ashes of a heifer, sprinkled on those who have incurred defilement, may restore their bodily purity, how much more will the blood of Christ, who offered himself, blameless as he was, to God through the eternal spirit, purify our conscience from dead actions so that we can worship the living God" (Heb. 9:13-14). In fact, the whole of Hebrews 10:1-18 explains the efficacy of Christ's sacrifice as compared to the ineffective sacrifices of the Old Testament. In the same vein, St. Peter talks of the precious blood of the blameless and spotless lamb by which the price of humankind's ransom from futile way of life was paid (1 Peter 1:18-19).

In relation to the Lord's Supper where Christ talked about shedding his blood for humankind, the Mass is seen as most closely connected with the sacrifice of Christ at Calvary. In other words, any time the Mass is celebrated, the same offering as at Calvary is repeated, Jesus Christ being the divine victim. And it is done for the same purpose for which Christ died, the forgiveness of sins and the glory and honour of God. The only difference between Calvary and the altar on which Mass is celebrated is that the bloody sacrifice of Calvary is presented in an un-bloody manner at Mass. Christ having died once at Calvary does not die again at Mass. The coming together of the elements of bread, wine and water, which indicates the body, blood and water from the side of Jesus, as the living water of baptism, which unites every baptized person at the Eucharistic table symbolises his death.

Christ's death at Calvary is not the end of his love for humankind. His life is a continuous sacrificing of himself; both before and after his death. Calvary is the supreme realization of his offering. At Mass, Christ continues to renew innumerable times, the offering of himself, for our salvation and God's glorification. The continuous renewal of the offering of himself is not an indication that his offering has not been acceptable, for it is rather impossible that his offering is unacceptable, but an opportunity for us to be freely united with the death of Christ for our sins. This is necessary, for it recognizes the gift of free will, which God had given to us. Since sin is a misuse of free will, the salvation of individual members of the human race is also to result from free choice.

The Mass as the Sacrifice of the People and for the People

Though the priest really represents the people at the celebration of the Mass, the Mass is nonetheless, a collective act of worship. In it the faithful of God have the right and the duty to play an active role. Thus, Pope Pius X once said, "the people should not pray ***at*** the Mass but pray ***the*** Mass." So, the Mass is truly the sacrifice of the people.

When the Holy Father, Pope St. John Paul II declared October 2004 to October 2005 as **The Year of the Eucharist**, he issued an Apostolic Letter titled, *Mane Nobiscum Domine* in which he stressed the same point made here by one of his predecessors, "I urge all the faithful" he said, "to celebrate the Eucharistic sacrifice with due reverence, offering to Jesus present in the Eucharist, both within and outside Mass, the worship demanded by so great a Mystery."[42]

The text of the Mass makes the priest the spokesman of the people at Mass. Despite this, it provides what we may call a dialogue in which the people and the priest have their different parts to play. The words of the text of the Mass leave no doubt as to the fact that all present are expected to join their minds and hearts to the action of the priest. By so doing, all the faithful; the people and the priest, offer up the sacrifice together under the leadership of the priest. The priest sings or recites certain prayers of petition during the Mass. They are the Opening Prayer or *Collect*, the Prayer of *Offering* and the *Post-communion* prayers. These prayers are always in the collective pronoun "we" or "our". The priest in a manner that shows they are prayers of the people always introduces them. He invites the people to pray with him the Collect and the Post-communion prayers by the words "Let us pray" (*Oremus*) and as he says the *Collect* and *Post-communion* prayers, he extends his hands; a gesture that suggests the

42 *Mane Nobiscum Domine*, n. 10.

inclusion of all present. The priest introduces the prayer of offering by saying: "Pray brethren that **my** sacrifice and **yours** may be acceptable to God the almighty Father." To this the people respond, "May the Lord accept the sacrifice at **your** hands for the praise and glory of His name, for **our** good and the good of all His Church." This manner of introduction is an invitation to the people to unite their prayers with that of the priest. The corresponding response of the people indicates their acceptance of the priest as their representative and the willingness on the part of the people is as a result of the knowledge that the priest is offering the sacrifice for them. In all cases, after the prayers, the people respond "Amen," which means, "So be it." This signifies their assent to the prayers of the priest.

On Calvary Jesus Christ offered himself as the sacrificial victim for humankind's salvation. Prior to this, he gave humankind the celebration by which his supreme sacrifice is to be perpetuated for he said at the Lord's Supper that anytime they break bread and share the cup, which is his Body and Blood, they should do it as a memorial of him. Therefore, the Mass, which is one and the same with the offering of Christ on the cross, is not just a sacrifice, but also a memorial sacrifice of Christ.

7

The Holy Mass as a Sacrifice (II)

The Early History, Structure, and Rites of the Mass[43]

The setting of the Mass as we have it today is not exactly as it was at the Lord's Supper. At the Lord's Supper, Jesus Christ instituted the Mass in its core and essence. Over the course of time, it has been fashioned out as it is today with all the essential elements of the Lord's Supper still very much intact and present. The Lord's Supper itself has two principal component parts, the consecration and the communion. The consecration is the blessing of bread and the cup of wine (Mt. 26:26-28), and the communion is the sharing of the bread and wine. We find four accounts of the Lord's Supper in the Scriptures; the First Letter of St. Paul to the Corinthians, the gospels of Mark, Luke and Matthew. Although these accounts suggest two different traditions, they however, present the same structure:

i. Jesus "took" bread, then a cup of wine.
ii. He "gave thanks" (Gave the blessing).
iii. He "broke" the bread.
iv. He "gave" the bread and the cup to his disciples.

The same structure, determines today the course of the liturgy of the Eucharist:

i. The presentation of the gifts from which the offerings are taken and laid on the altar table.

---

43 Originally published in *The Promise Newspaper*, a monthly publication of the Catholic Diocese of Auchi, 2009.

ii. The Eucharistic prayer, which contains account of the Institution.
iii. The "blessing" and "breaking" of bread.
iv. The Communion rite.

We may not know precisely how the Mass was celebrated in the apostolic era, but we can be sure that it was celebrated with great reverence and devotion and that it corresponded to the action at the Lord's Supper. This insight is captured in the episode at Emmaus. The disciples never recognized Jesus until they sat at table where Christ assumed the role of the Chief Celebrant and scripture says; "he took the bread and said the blessing; then he broke it and handed it to them." (Lk. 24:30). So, the 'archetypal' formula for the celebration of the Mass shows that what the Apostles did was correspondent to the Lord's Supper (Acts 2:46, 20:11).

Apart from the Lord's Supper, the early Christians had another service, which included everybody unlike the sacrificial banquet of the Lord's Supper. It was adopted from their former Jewish religion and refashioned to suit their new Christian worship. It involved prayers, readings from the Law and the prophets, which constitute the Old Testament of the Bible as we have it today, and a sermon based on the readings. This service can be likened to the discussion on the way to Emmaus; where Jesus, starting with Moses, who symbolizes the law and going through the prophets, explained to the two disciples the passages concerning him, Jesus (Lk. 24:27). Later on, when the Eucharistic sacrifice, which is the Holy Mass, was separated from the Jewish charity banquet, fixed prayers and ceremonies were provided for it. The service of prayers and instruction was put in place with the whole liturgy, as a kind of introductory service. This is what we call the liturgy of the word today.

As early as the year 150 AD, just about a century after the apostles, the general outline of the Mass was already fixed. In his writing, about the year 155 AD to the pagan emperor, Antoninus Pius (138-161 AD), St. Justin explained what Christians do.

According to him,

> On the day of the sun, all who dwell in the city or country gather in the same place. The memories of the apostles and the writings of the prophets are read, as much as time permits. When the reader has finished, he who presides over those gathered admonishes and challenges them to imitate these beautiful things. Then we all rise together and offer prayers for ourselves... and for all others, wherever they may be, so that we may be found righteous by our life and actions, and faithful to the commandments, so as to obtain eternal salvation. When the prayers are concluded, we exchange the kiss. Then someone brings bread and a cup of water and wine mixed together to him who presides over the brethren. He takes them and offers praise and glory to the Father of the universe, through the name of the Son and of the Holy Spirit and for a considerable time he gives thanks that we have been judged worthy of these gifts. When he has concluded the prayers and thanksgiving, all present give voice to an acclamation by saying; 'Amen'! When he who presides has given thanks and the people have responded, those whom we call deacons give to those present the 'eucharisted' bread, wine and water and take them to those who are absent.[44]

This witness of St. Justin shows that the basic structure of the Mass had been as it is now for a very long time.

The development that has taken place in the Mass has to do with its manner of celebration. This was to meet with growing assembly and for better understanding of the signs and gestures of the Mass. From the time it was celebrated in homes with small gathering of the faithful (Acts 20:7-8, 11) and in catacombs during the persecution, the Mass had to be adapted to the far larger congregation and church buildings of today. Basically, like it was from time, the Mass today is made of two component parts; the liturgy of the word and the liturgy of the Eucharist. The liturgy of

---

44 *The Catechism of the Catholic Church*, no. 1345.

the word comprises the introductory rites, the readings, homily/sermon, and the prayers of the faithful. The liturgy of the Eucharist on the other hand is made up of the offering, that is, the *epiclesis*, Eucharistic prayer and the rite of communion.

The Mass being a sacrifice needs a priest for its celebration. A sacrifice, in the biblical perspective is, "the offering of a victim by a priest to God alone, in testimony of his being the sovereign Lord of all things."[45] The Catholic Priesthood fulfils this requirement. As a point of note, Jesus Christ is both the priest and the victim of sacrifice of Calvary. In other words, he was "The Priest" at Calvary and was also the victim of offering. He did not offer bulls or rams, he offered himself as the spotless lamb acceptable to God. Thus, Catholic teaching holds that he is both the priest and victim at Mass. The role of the priest then at Mass, as in the other sacraments of the Church, is that of a representative of Christ. So, in the celebration of the Mass, the officiating priest stands in the person of Christ as another Christ, *alter Christus*.

---

45 *A Catechism of Christian Doctrine*, Q. 275, p. 47.

8

The Sacrament of Penance or Reconciliation[46]

Although, the Christian receives a new life in Christ through the sacraments of Christian initiation, which comprise Baptism, Confirmation, and Holy Eucharist, our human weakness however, leads us to sin and corrupts the new life we have received in Christ. According to St. Paul, "However, we carry this treasure in vessels of clay, so that this all surpassing power may not be seen as ours but God's" (2 Cor.4:7). This shows that our new life in Christ is still subject to human weakness and therefore, can be weakened or even lost by sin.[47] But the Lord has willed that the Church continues through the power of the Holy Spirit and for this, he instituted the sacraments of healing.[48] The sacraments of healing are the sacraments of penance or reconciliation and the anointing of the sick.

The sacrament of penance or reconciliation provides us the opportunity to be reconciled to the Father through the confession of our sins for which we are truly sorry with the firm purpose not to sin again. Referring to Canon 959, John McDonald writes, "When in the sacrament of penance the faithful confess their sins to a lawful minister; are sorry for them and have a firm purpose of amendment, they receive from God pardon for the sins which they have committed after baptism through the absolution given them

46 First published in *The Promise Newspaper*, a monthly publication of the Catholic Diocese of Auchi, 2009.

47 *The Catechism of the Catholic Church*, n. 1420.

48 *The Catechism of the Catholic Church*, n. 1421.

by the minister."[49] Apart from the forgiveness of sins that we obtain through this sacrament, we are also reconciled to the Church which our sins have caused some harm.

The sacrament of reconciliation is a personal encounter with Christ. Like the leper in the gospel of St. Mark, we come to the Father asking him to cure us of our sins and sinfulness, if he wills (Mk 1:40). And Jesus' response is always that he wills, thus, through the hands of the priest, Jesus reaches out to us and says, as he did to the leper, "I do want to, be cured." By this, he touches us personally and individually, healing us of the wounds of our sins and carrying on himself our iniquity. Thereby making us fit again for a renewed relationship with God. Through this sacrament we receive a new grace and strength through the Holy Spirit, who works in the Church and through the Church, in the words and actions of the Church's ministers, to say no to sin in future and yes to holiness. Even if we fall again, he is there to help us again. No matter how grave our sins are, his love is always stronger than our sin. For as scripture says, "though your sins may be red as crimson, I shall make you white as snow." The Holy Rule (HR) of St. Benedict testifies to this when it says, "His blood has infinite power to cleanse. Nothing we ever do could justify despair of his mercy" (HR 4:74).

The lawful minister of the sacrament of reconciliation is an ordained priest who has the faculty to hear confessions. The faculty to hear confession is given usually to the priest by his Bishop after ordination. If for any reason, the Bishop does not authorize a priest to hear confessions, he is not a *lawful minister* of the sacrament of penance. "Only priests who have received the faculty of absolving from the authority of the Church can forgive sins in the name of Christ."[50]

Contrition is a very important part of the sacrament of reconciliation and the forgiveness of our sins is dependent on our contrition for our sins. Contrition includes our sincere resolve not to sin again. In other words, the efficacy of the words of

---

49 John F. McDonald, p. 69.
50 *The Catechism of the Catholic Church*, n. 1495.

absolution is to some extent dependent on the sincerity of our contrition. According to the Council of Trent in 1551 and as quoted in *The Catechism of the Catholic Church*, no. 1451, "Among the penitent's acts contrition occupies first place. Contrition is 'sorrow of the soul and detestation for the sin committed, together with the resolution not to sin again." If we were not truly sorry and sincerely willing to turn away from sin, our confession would be but a mere ritual. To gain forgiveness we have to first of all, be truly sorry and be willing to makc cfforts not to sin again.

The sins from which the sacrament of penance cleanses us are the sins we commit after baptism. The Church refers to the sins we commit after baptism as actual sins. It is not the priest *per se* who forgives our sins; God is the one who forgives, for only God forgives sins.[51] "How can he speak like this insulting God? Who can forgive sins except God?" (Mk 2:7). This verse of the gospel of Mark corroborates Isaiah 43:25, "I it is, I am He who blots out your offenses for my own sake, and remembers your sins no more" and Psalm 103:3, "He forgives all your sins and heals all your sickness." The priest is God's instrument in bringing about our forgiveness. The words of absolution clearly articulate this:

> God the Father of mercy has reconciled the world to Himself through the death and resurrection of His son and has sent the Holy Spirit among us for the forgiveness of sins. Through the ministry of the Church, may God grant you pardon and peace. I absolve you from your sins, in the name of the Father and of the Son and of the Holy Spirit.

We live in an extremely permissive society today and our Christian values have been greatly eroded. There are many mistaken opinions today about confession, some unfortunately propagated by priests either out of their laziness to sit in the confessional and therefore, want to rationalize its value or out of ignorance of the truth of the sacrament, for which in fact, they are also culpable. Many Catholics today find it difficult to go to confession because they have imbibed some of these erroneous

---

51 *The Catechism of the Catholic Church*, n. 1441.

popular opinions. For instance, some think and argue that we are only required to take grave sins like murder and adultery and perhaps any of the seven serious sins mentioned in scripture to confession. The others, they think, are not necessary since the penitential act at the beginning of the celebration of the Holy Mass can cleanse us of them. Among these erroneous opinions is the dangerous thinking that apart from the seven deadly sins; pride, covetousness, lust, anger, gluttony, envy and sloth, other minor offences, which we call venial sins are really no sins, they are just part of the gimmicks of life.

Imbibing such an erroneous idea puts us in the danger of falling into the shoes of the Pharisee who congratulated himself before God as his life bore a favourable comparison with that of his neighbours (Lk. 18:9-14). Sin, no matter the shape it takes and the depth it goes, is an offence against the infinite goodness of God. Therefore, no sin can be regarded as trivial and little. I am not trying to create fears in our minds, but asking that we wake up to the reality of the fact that at all times, we stand in need of the mercy of God. St. Paul writes in his letter to the Romans, "We have all sinned and fallen short of the glory of God" (Rom. 3:23). And in corroboration, St. John writes, "Anyone who says he is not a sinner is a liar and makes God a liar" (1 Jn. 1:10). How is one who denies his sinfulness a liar and makes God a liar? He is a liar because the incarnation, in the first place is a mission to redeem us from our sins. If we have not sinned, then what need would there be for such a mission of redemption? If only we learn to turn our gaze to God's love and all that his love entails, we would come to a greater understanding of how easily we offend him in our thoughts and actions with the wilful pleasures we derive from our thoughts and self-pride our so called trivial actions nurture in contrast to our Christian calling.

Some of us are overly aware of our sinfulness and have the great difficulty of always going to a priest for confession. We nurse the thoughts of what the priest might be thinking about us. My dear friend, the priest himself is a sinner who needs confession too. I can assure you that he is never shocked at anything you have to say. He would have heard them all several times and very too often from several others. He is the channel of God's grace and does not sit in the confessional as a judge to determine who goes to heaven or not, but as a minister of God's love and mercy. He is not interested in what your sins are but on how to put you in the presence of the Father of mercy, and by the authority vested on him, to ask for God's mercy for you in the name of the Church. Every confession is a moment of mercy where what matters is not how many sins, what sins, and how long you have last been to confession, even though these elements are required of the penitent, what matters most however, is that "Today salvation has come into this house, for this man (and woman) too is a son (and daughter) of Abraham" (Lk. 19:9-10). [The insertions are mine and not part of the scripture verse].

Again, many people are bothered by the fact that they have the same list of sins to confess every time they go to confession. The fact is this, we are the same person, and we live in the same circumstances and perhaps the same environment. We confront the same set of temptations and suffer the same weaknesses. So we commit the same sins over and over again. The best thing is to keep struggling by avoiding the occasion and circumstances of sin. And we must keep taking our sins to confession as often as we become victims of these sins. This is the only way we make progress, which is often a very gradual process. As long as each time we go to confession, we are genuinely sorry for our sins, we are on the right part but we have to be careful not to make it a ritual. This requires a sincere preparation in which we make a realistic firm purpose of amendment not to sin again and ready to follow our purpose through. We must strive to change from our ways of sin.

It is important to be truly sorry for all your sins. Some people say they do not know what to say, since they cannot recall any sin they may have committed. It is good to still go to confession and tell the priest just that. What matters here is the awareness that you are a sinner in need of the mercy of God, though you may not be able to articulate your sins. The publican said to God, "God, be merciful to me, a sinner." And scripture says, "This man, I tell you, went home again at rights with God ..." (Lk. 18:13).

That God can and indeed does forgive sins is clearly demonstrated in the ministry of Jesus as recorded in the New Testament. As the Son of God, Jesus said of himself that he had authority to forgive sins and did exercise that authority (Mk 2:5, 10). To the woman who washed his feet with her tears, wiped them with her hair and covered them with kisses, Jesus said, "Your sins are forgiven" (Lk. 7:48). Jesus not only exercised this authority, he gave the power to exercise this authority to the Church.

The Authority of the Church to Forgive Sins

Christ has willed that in her prayer and life and action his whole Church should be the sign and instrument of the forgiveness and reconciliation that he acquired for us at the price of his blood. But he entrusted the exercise of the power of absolution to the apostolic ministry, which he charged with the "ministry of reconciliation." The apostle is sent out "on behalf of Christ" with "God making his appeal" through him and pleading: "Be reconciled to God."[52]

Jesus conferred on the Church one of the powers he conferred on Peter and the other apostles, namely, the authority to bind and to loose. "In truth I tell you, whatever you bind on earth will be bound in heaven; whatever you loose on earth will be loosed in heaven" (Mt. 18:18). If you juxtapose this text with John 20:23, that says, "Receive the Holy Spirit. If you forgive anyone's sins they are forgiven; if you retain anyone's sins they are retained," you would immediately see that John's text is a clarification and explication of Matthew's "binding" and "loosing." This is to say that the "bind" and "loose" in Mt. 16:19; 18:18 involves the authority to forgive sins.

We know God alone can forgive sins, but it has pleased Him to make this means of grace available to the Church through the apostles (Jn. 20:23; Matt. 18:18), as Jesus did with Peter (Mt. 16:19). The Church in her wisdom, knowing that the Holy Father (the Pope), who occupies the chair of Peter and the Bishops; those who today occupy the position of the apostles, cannot reach out all alone to all the members of her community, entrusted the exercise

52 *The Catechism of the Catholic Church*, n. 1442.

of the authority to forgive sins, the power to bind and loose, to her ordained ministers; the priests. For Christ wills that all who have gone astray be reconciled to the Father (God) like the prodigal son was reconciled to the father (Lk. 15:11-24). For God does not wish the death of a sinner, but that the sinner should turn away from his sins and be saved.

The priest as a representative of Christ and his Church reconciles the contrite soul to God in the sacrament of penance. Through the beautiful words of absolution, he expresses the mystery of the sacrament, prays God's pardon and peace on the penitent and exercises the Church's authority to forgive and loose from the bondage of sin by absolving the penitent of his/her sins. He plays the role of a father who welcomes and celebrates the return of the prodigal child. He plays the role of a teacher who counsels and instructs the penitent to avoid sins and all occasions of sin. He is the merciful judge who absolves the penitent of his sins and teaches him to accept and reciprocate God's loving forgiveness.[53]

We cannot underestimate the value and importance of the sacrament of penance as it goes with numerous spiritual effects necessary for our Christian life. Amongst these are the following:

i. Reconciliation with God by which the penitent recovers grace
ii. Reconciliation with the Church
iii. Remission of the eternal punishment incurred by grave (mortal) sins
iv. Remission, at least in part, of temporal punishments resulting from sin
v. Peace and serenity of conscience, and spiritual consolation
vi. An increase of spiritual strength for the Christian battle.[54]

It is through individual and integral confession in which the penitent receives absolution that grave sins are forgiven and reconciliation with God and the Church is achieved.

---

53 Michael I. Mozia, *New Evangelization and Christian Moral Theology: An African Perspective*, (Ibadan: Newborne Publishers, 1994), p. 120.

54 *The Catechism of the Catholic Church*, n. 1496.

9

The Sacrament of the Anointing of the Sick[55]

The Code of Canon Law states that "the anointing of the sick can be administered to any member of the faithful who, having reached the use of reason begins to be in danger of death by reason of illness or old age."[56] The Church believes and confesses that among the seven sacraments, the sacrament of the anointing of the sick is one especially intended to strengthen those who are being tried by illness. This sacred anointing of the sick was instituted by Christ our Lord as a true and proper sacrament of the New Testament. The gospel of Mark alludes to this. (Mk 6:13). It is recommended to the faithful and promulgated by James (Jas. 5:14-15), the apostle and brother of the Lord.[57]

The CCC further tells us that the sacrament gives several graces and imparts strength through the Holy Spirit against anxiety, discouragement and temptation. It conveys peace and fortitude.[58] The source of these graces is of course the atoning death of Christ as the fulfilment of the prophet Isaiah that he took our infirmities upon himself and bore our diseases (Mt. 8:17). According to the Fathers of VC II, by the sacred anointing of the sick and the prayer of the priests, the whole Church commends those who are ill to the suffering and glorified Lord, that he may raise them up and save them. And indeed she exhorts them to

55 First published in *The Promise Newspaper*, a monthly publication of the Catholic Diocese of Auchi, 2010.
56 Can. 1004 no.1.
57 *The Catechism of the Catholic Church*, no. 1511.
58 *The Catechism of the Catholic Church*, no. 1520.

contribute to the good of the people of God by freely uniting themselves to the passion and death of Christ.[59]

The scripture is filled with references to God as the healer. His healing is both spiritual and material, that is, forgiveness of sins and restoration of physical health. While God led His people through the desert, he gave them statutes and laws to abide by. In one of such laws, he said, "If you listen carefully to the voice of Yahweh, your God, and if you obey his commands and statutes, I will not inflict on you any of the diseases I brought on the Egyptians, for I am Yahweh, the One who heals you" (Ex. 15:26). The Prophet Isaiah also referred to the time when God will usher in a time when he will forgive the offences of the people of Zion and heal their illnesses (Is. 33:24).

The New Testament is replete with stories of Christ as the healer. He has come to heal humanity in its entirety – both body and soul. He talks about himself as the physician who has come for the sick (Mk 2:17). The crowds, aware of the power that came out of him, struggled to touch him for by his power they were healed (Lk. 6:19). Jesus took pity on the sick and cured them. A leper came to Jesus and begged him, 'if you so will, you can make me clean.' Moved with pity, Jesus stretched out his hand and touched him, saying, 'I will; be clean.'

Based on the numerous healing actions of Jesus and specifically his instruction to his disciples to heal those who are sick as well as free the possessed (Mt. 10:1; Lk. 9:1) and the fact that the disciples actually carried out this instruction even during Jesus' lifetime (Mk 6:13), James declared, "If anyone is sick, let him call on the elders of the Church. They shall pray for him, anointing him with oil in the name of the Lord. The prayer said in faith will save the sick person; the Lord will raise him up and if he has committed any sins, he will be forgiven" (Jas. 5:14-15). Commentaries on this declaration of James agree that through the words of James, the Church continued and still continues Christ's ministry to the sick. Salvation includes both physical and spiritual health.

---

59 Austin Flammery O.P., *Lumen Gentium*, no. 11.

This sacrament unites the sick with the passion of Christ for his own good and the general good of the Church. It gives the sick the strength, peace and courage, to endure sickness in a manner that is Christian. It brings forgiveness of sin if the sick is not able to obtain it from the sacrament of penance and restores health if it is the will of God.[60]

The introduction of the will of God is deliberate as it directs our attention to the question whether God always heals physical infirmities? It is necessary to ask and answer the question because of two extreme positions that are rather common. Some people think that when one is sick, prayer is the answer and no need for medication. After so many prayer sessions and no improvement, they conclude that the sick person lacks the required faith. This is not correct; it is one extreme. The other extreme is that instant and automatic healing belongs to the apostolic age and not our present day. This is also extreme and not correct. But does God always heal physical illness? The answer is no, God does not always heal physical infirmities.

St. Paul made this clear in Gal. 4:13-14 when he addressed them concerning his bodily ailment. He does the same thing when he declared that he had to leave his companion Trophimus in Miletus because he was too sick to travel (II Tim. 4:20). And in his first letter to Timothy, he specifically instructed Timothy to take a little wine and not just water only, as this is good for the stomach and his frequent ailments (I Tim. 5:23). These passages are informative as they reveal Paul's counsel that illness should be managed through medical care as well as reveal that illnesses were not always healed in the apostolic age by prayer. Paul could have told Timothy to pray harder and strengthen his faith, rather, he advised him to use a little wine for medication.

Our healing is always subject to God's will. James pointed out that we do not know the future, so we cannot talk like we are sure, rather we should always depend on the will of God (Jas. 4:14-15). Our healing is conditional on the will of God. The sacrament of the anointing of the sick as we have it today in the

---

60 *The Catechism of the Catholic Church*, no. 1532.

practice of the Church is simply in compliance with Jesus' instruction. He laid his hands on the sick and when he sent out his disciples as missionaries, he asked them to lay their hands on the sick or anoint them with oil for the restoration of their health (Mk 6:13 & 16:18).

At this point, it is important to emphasize that the oil by which the sick is anointed sacramentally is not the popular olive oil that we find on the stalls around our churches and in the markets. It is a special oil, specially blessed by the Bishop at the Mass of Chrism on Holy Thursday. While I do not condemn the current trend of the lay faithful bringing all kinds of oil for blessing and using the same for private devotions, prayers and anointing, we should however, be educated as to the truth of the sacrament of anointing of the sick and be discouraged from the current near fetish practice of the use of olive oil at the slightest possible instance. The CCC, quoting from the Council of Trent and Canon 1003, n.1 declares that "Only priests (bishops and presbyters) are ministers of the Anointing of the sick."[61]

---

61 *The Catechism of the Catholic Church*, no. 1516.

10

The Sacrament of Christian Marriage[62]

Marriage is one of the two sacraments at the service of communion. The other sacrament at the service of communion is Holy Orders. These are sacraments directed to the body of Christ, that is, the Christian community. Thus, to what extent the recipients of these sacraments commit themselves to the service of the community to the extent that the sacrament sanctifies the recipient. They are sacraments meant to edify and build the body of Christ.

Marriage is an extensive subject both in the Church and civil society. Volumes of literature abound on the subject and yet new literature keeps emerging regularly on the subject. I do not intend to discuss it exhaustively as that cannot even be done in a short paper like this. However, I will outline its principal defining characteristics. The term marriage came from the Latin *matrimonium*, from *munus matris*, that is, the office of the mother. Married life is rightly described as a vocation; a human vocation that is blessed and ordered by God from the beginning of creation and one which will continue to the end of creation. Therefore, it requires a careful and adequate preparation before one goes into it.

Marriage is an enduring and exclusive covenant of love between a man and a woman.[63] It is a covenant not a contract. Although the term contract was used in the past to describe it, VC II avoided the use of the term. Contract deals with things where the services of people are engaged for a period of time. Against this notion, the Fathers of the council preferred the term

---

62 First published in *The Promise Newspaper*, a monthly publication of the Catholic Diocese of Auchi, 2010.

63 Thomas Pazhayampallil, *Pastoral Guide*, Vol. II, III Revised Edition, (Bangalore: Kristu Jyoti Publications, 1995), p. 665.

'covenant,' which signifies bond, mutual commitment, partnership and love. Covenant is a relationship of mutual trust and fidelity. According to the Fathers of VC II:

> The intimate partnership of married life and love has been established by the Creator and qualified by his laws. It is rooted in the conjugal covenant of irrevocable personal consent. Hence by that human act whereby spouses mutually bestow and accept each other, a relationship arises, which by divine will and in the eyes of society too is a lasting one. For the good of the spouses and their offspring as well as of society, the existence of this sacred bond no longer depends on human decisions alone. For God himself is the author of matrimony, endowed as it is with various benefits and purposes.[64]

Marriage is the covenant of love. Therefore, love is the basis of marriage. In love, one chooses to freely commit himself or herself to another. Marriage is not aimed at just "settling down," as it is secularly interpreted these days, nor is it aimed at obtaining social and economic status, or to legitimise the practice of sex in the society, as some pastors erroneously preach today. It is a covenant "by which a man and a woman establish between themselves a partnership of their whole life and which of its own very nature is ordered to the well-being of the spouses and to the procreation and education of offspring, has been raised by Christ the Lord to the dignity of a sacrament."[65]

Today, many look at marriage as a purely secular contract that can be made and unmade by the state. This is not true. Marriage is a sacred and religious phenomenon instituted by God from the very beginning of creation. "The rib which Yahweh God had taken from man, He formed into a woman and brought her to man. Then man said, 'Now this is bone of my bone and flesh of my flesh. She shall be called woman because she was taken from man.' That is why a man leaves his father and mother and is attached to his

---

64 Austin Flammery O.P., *Gaudium et Spes*, no. 48.
65 Can. 1055, no. 1.

wife and with her becomes one flesh" (Gen. 2:22-24). Thus, marriage is rightfully put as part of God's plan for humanity.

It is very important too to address the phenomenon of same sex union (marriage) which is beginning to spread all over the world. Pro-gay groups have lobbied for and succeeded in some western countries to legalise same-sex unions and in more recent editions of some literature, marriage is redefined without the gender implicate terms. For example, instead of considering marriage as a union between male and female it is seen as a union between two persons. This is an attempt to distort the authentic ontology of marriage. Marriage is a covenantal relationship of love between two persons, one male and one female. Therefore, two males or two females cannot validly and morally enter into the covenant of marriage; a man cannot marry a man or a woman marry another woman. The idea of lesbianism and homosexuality is an aberration, which has no basis in scripture. While we may admit that a relationship between two persons of the same sex can provide companionship, it is not true that such a relationship cannot lead to procreation. Companionship and procreation are the two primary aim to which the marriage covenant is ordered. The scriptural accounts of creation and the institution of marriage clearly state that it is a union between a man and a woman (Gen. 2:18). The attempts to redefine marriage along social and political lines is a disservice to the oldest institution in the world and an attempt to distort the creation of God. It is wrong and unacceptable.

Scripture begins with the creation of man and woman in the image and likeness of God (Gen. 1:26-27), affirms that man and woman were created for each other (Gen. 2:18) and concludes with the image of the wedding feast of the Lamb (Rev. 19:7, 9). And throughout, scripture speaks of the mystery of marriage, its meaning and origin, as well as its end. Jesus' discourse on marriage and divorce with the Pharisees in the gospel of Matthew give credence to this fact. "Jesus replied, 'Have you not read that in the beginning the Creator made them male and female, and he said: Man has now to leave father and mother, and be joined to his wife, and the two shall become one body? So they are no longer two but one body; let no one separate what God has joined" (Mt. 19:4-6).

Christian marriage is an efficacious sign of the presence of Christ among his people. The CCC explains this fact saying; "On the threshold of his public life, Jesus performs his first sign – at his mother's request – during a wedding feast. The Church attaches great importance to Jesus' presence at the wedding at Cana. She sees in it the confirmation of the goodness of marriage and the proclamation that thenceforth marriage will be an efficacious sign of Christ's presence."[66]

Marriage can only be brought about through the irrevocable consent, freely and lawfully, given by two partners; male and female who are capable of giving it. This consent is referred to as matrimonial consent. It is very important and cannot be supplied by any human power.[67] Those who can lawfully give matrimonial consent are: (i) Those who have sufficient use of reason. (ii) Those who are not impeded by any serious lack of judgment about the essential rights and duties of marriage. (iii) Those who are not impeded by their psychic nature as to become incapable of assuming marriage obligations.[68]

Marriage exists from the very moment spouses exchange consent. Where this freely given consent is lacking, there is no marriage. The consent must be an act of the will of both parties. It must be given without coercion, be it fear or physical threat. Where the freedom is lacking, the marriage is invalid. The Church holds the exchange of consent between the spouses as the indispensable element that establishes marriage.[69]

As a sacrament, marriage signifies the union between Christ and the Church. It confers grace upon the spouses to love each other with the love with which Christ loves his Church. This same grace of marriage as a sacrament strengthens the indissoluble unity that the spouses have entered and sanctifies them on the way to eternal life.[70]

---

66 *The Catechism of the Catholic Church*, no. 1613.
67 See Can. 1057, no. 1.
68 See Can. 1095.
69 *The Catechism of the Catholic Church*, no. 1626.
70 *The Catechism of the Catholic Church*, no. 1661.

11

The Sacrament of Holy Orders

Holy Orders is one of the sacraments at the service of communion, the other being the sacrament of Christian marriage. Both sacraments are directed towards the salvation of others. If they contribute to personal salvation, which they do, it is in their service to others that they do so.

> By divine institution some among Christ's faithful are, through the sacrament of order, marked with an indelible character and are thus constituted sacred ministers; thereby they are consecrated and deputed so that, each according to his own grade, they fulfil, in the person of Christ the Head, the offices of teaching, sanctifying and ruling, and so they nourish the people of God.[71]

By virtue of the sacrament of baptism, all the Christian faithful share in the kingly, prophetic and priestly function of Christ. Therefore, the Church talks about the priesthood of the faithful. This is however, different from the ministerial or hierarchical priesthood, which is the content of the sacrament of orders. The ministerial priesthood and the priesthood of the faithful differ essentially as well as in degree.

This sacrament consists of three levels; the diaconate, the presbyterate, and the episcopate, corresponding to the office of the deacon, the priest, and the bishop respectively. VC II teaches that "The divinely instituted ecclesiastical ministry is exercised in different degrees by those who from ancient times have been

71 Can. 1008.

called bishops, priests and deacons."[72] Explaining this further, the CCC acknowledges that the Magisterium, that is, the teaching authority of the Church, and the practice of the Church right from time, recognizes two degrees of ministerial participation in the priesthood of Christ, namely; the episcopacy, which is the bishopric and the presbyterate, which is, the priesthood. Thus, the term *sacerdos* is used to denote only priests and bishops and not deacons. This, notwithstanding the teachings of the Church in CCC, maintains that the degrees of priestly participation; episcopate and presbyterate, and the degree of service, diaconate, are conferred by the sacrament of Holy Orders.[73]

According to Pope St. John Paul II, the sacrament of Holy Orders is, "The fruit of the special grace of vocation and the basis of the priest's identity."[74] This sacrament is conferred by the imposition or laying on of hands and the prayer of consecration as prescribed for each grade by the liturgical books.[75] It is "The sacrament through which the mission entrusted by Christ to his apostles continues to be exercised in the Church until the end of time: thus it is the sacrament of apostolic ministry."[76]

Holy Orders take its name from *ordo,* which in Roman antiquity refers to a social group like the senatorial order and equestrian order. The Church adopted it for the clergy. The clergy, whose members are described as clerics, are a distinct group in the Church, which comprise the order of bishops, the order of priests and the order of deacons.[77] The term 'clergy' itself is from the Greek *kleros,* which means 'lot' or 'portion' or 'heritage.' It is used for those who have chosen the Lord as their special lot, portion or heritage.

---

72 Austin Flammery O.P., *Lumen Gentium,* no. 28.
73 *The Catechism of the Catholic Church,* no. 1554.
74 John F. McDonald, p. 129.
75 Can. 1009, no. 2.
76 *The Catechism of the Catholic Church,* no. 1536.
77 Thomas Pazhayampallil, p. 437.

Priesthood in Scripture

In the Old Testament, God constituted His chosen people into a kingdom of priest and a holy nation. "But you will be for me a kingdom of priests and a holy nation" (Ex. 19:6). 2 Mac. 2:17-18 refers to this when it talks about God saving his people and returning to them their heritage. This heritage among others includes the priesthood.

Though God has constituted the whole of Israel as a royal priesthood, He nevertheless, chose one of the twelve tribes of Israel, setting them apart for liturgical services. This was the tribe of Levi. "Yahweh spoke to Moses and said: 'Do not take any census of the Levites, or register them among the sons of Israel. You yourself must enlist the Levites to serve the Holy Tent of the Testimony and to look after its furnishings and its belongings. They are to carry the Holy Tent, and all its furnishings; they are to take care of it and set up their camp around it. Whenever the Holy Tent is to be moved, the Levites shall take it down; whenever the Holy Tent is to be set up again, they shall do this. Any layman coming near it shall be put to death. The sons of Israel are to set up their tents in formation, each man with his own group and under his own banner. But the Levites are to set up their tents around the Holy Tent of the Testimony, lest God's anger fall on the whole community of Israel. The Levites will take care of the Holy Tent of the Testimony" (Num.1:48-53). This instruction was authenticated by Joshua, "But to the tribe of Levi, Moses had given no land; Yahweh the God of Israel is their inheritance, as he has told them" (Josh. 13:33). There was therefore, a clear and definite distinction between the universal priesthood and the individual priesthood even in the Old Testament. The clarity of this distinction was further authenticated when Korah, Dathan and Abiram rebelled against Moses and Aaron, and denied the distinction between the individual and universal priesthood. For their punishment, the Lord opened up the earth and swallowed all of them (Num. 16:2-3, 32-33).

The place of Israel as God's chosen one is today a prerogative of all Christians; the sons and daughters of God. The promise of God to make Israel a kingdom of priests is therefore, applicable to

God's household today. In line with this, the Church teaches that all the faithful of God share the same dignity and equality by virtue of their baptism.[78] Baptism is the sacrament of an outward sign that gives us inward grace as God's children. In this wise, the Christian family can rightly be described as a "Kingdom of Priests." We all share in the priestly, kingly, and prophetic, mission of Christ. In the technical language of the Church, this is referred to as the priesthood of the faithful or the common priesthood of the faithful; all of us who are baptized in the Trinitarian formula share in this priesthood.

Those referred to as priests in the Old Testament are specially designated officials who are in-charge of performing rituals and conducting sacrificial services. The law of the Pentateuch, that is, the five books of Moses, while reserving the exclusive position of Aaron and his sons, who alone received the oil of anointing and have special priestly attire (Ex. 28-29), limited the priesthood to the Levites, the descendant of Levi (Deut. 10:8-9), who served at liturgical services in the temple. History shows that at a point there was no official priesthood among the Jews. Sacrificial services were performed by individual family heads in various holy places (Gen. 31:54). As the Israelites began to develop a structured society, a special class came to preside over their rather complex rituals. After the Canaan conquest, ordinary Israelites offered sacrifices at altars and high places (Judges 13:19-20, 1 Kings 3:3-4), but when it comes to sacrifice in the temple it was left to the priests of Levitical lineage.

The chief function of the priest in the Old Testament was to offer sacrifices, since only the priest is allowed to approach the altar. Even at that, the priest must be properly vested in specific vestments that portray his holiness. Other functions that the Old Testament Priest had include; judging (Deut. 17:9, Ezek. 15:1 & Num. 5:11-31) and teaching the law to the people (Deut. 33:10, Mal. 2:6-8).

Apart from the passion narrative in which the priests were prominent, much mention was not made of them in the New

---

78 Can. 208.

Testament. Jesus did not apply the title to himself, neither did he apply it to his disciples. In fact, the idea of the Christian priesthood in the New Testament was first applied to the whole Christian community in 1 Pet. 2:5 and Rev. 1:6, 20:5. These passages were references to Ex. 19:6.

The Letter to the Hebrews stands out in the New Testament in its treatment of Christ's priesthood (Heb. 3:3-8). The priesthood of Christ is likened to that of Melchizedek, the King of Salem, priest of the Most High God (Gen. 14:18). Melchizedek's priesthood is superior to Aaronic priesthood (Heb. 7:1-17; 8:1-13) and it is eternal like that of Christ (Ps 110:4, Heb. 5:6, 6:20). The priesthood of Christ is in itself perfect and does not need to offer his sacrifice over and over again (Heb. 3:1-4; 3:1-4; 7:27; 8:4-6; 9:12; 25; 10:5).

The Catholic priesthood stands parallel to the priesthood in the scripture. As God constituted Israel a kingdom of priests by virtue of their being his chosen people but chose from among them those to officiate at liturgical services so also his Church, the community of believers, are a kingdom of priests by virtue of their baptism, but from among them he has chosen some for ministerial services; the ordained priesthood.

The ministerial priesthood represents Christ the head of the Church. It acts in the name of the whole Church when presenting the prayer of the Church to God, especially during the celebration of the Eucharist. Only a baptized male Catholic can receive the sacrament of Holy Orders. No one has a right to the sacrament of Holy Orders. Anyone who feels he has a calling to the sacred priesthood must first submit himself humbly to the Church. Only the Church, through the bishop, has the right and responsibility to call anyone forward to receive the sacrament of Holy Orders.

The emphasis on baptized male as the only persons who can receive the sacrament of Holy Orders is necessary because in recent times some persons have clamoured for the ordination of women to the Catholic priesthood. The long history of the Church shows that women have never been candidates for the priesthood. This is in line with the Church's teachings that, "only a baptized man can validly receive sacred ordination."[79] In the Scriptures, Christ did not call or appoint a woman among the twelve (Mk 3:13-19; Mt. 10:1-4; Lk. 6:12-16) to whom the ordained ministry was entrusted at the Last Supper (Lk. 22:14-20).

Celibacy in the Catholic Priesthood

The CCC states that "in the Latin Church the sacrament of Holy Orders for the presbyterate is normally conferred only on candidates who are ready to embrace celibacy freely and who publicly manifest their intention of staying celibate for the love of God's kingdom and the service of men."[80] Celibacy in the Catholic priesthood has been a source of controversy even among Catholic priests. Some desire that it be abolished while others maintain that it should be retained as a necessary part of the priestly ministry. The sex scandal crisis that is recently splotching the image of the Church from North America, through Europe and now gathering momentum in Africa has again brought the question of the appropriateness of celibacy in the priesthood to the fore. I must note here that the issue of paedophilia, which properly speaking refers to the sexual abuse of children, which was specifically the problem in the American and European churches, is more an issue of sexual disorientation than an issue of celibacy. In fact, sexual misconduct has no intrinsic link to celibacy, as even chastity is demanded in the married state.

Celibacy, which consists in not marrying, is a vocation. It is a gift of the Holy Spirit. It is a call to be chaste in a special way. The vocation to celibacy is different from the vocation to the priesthood. The Church however, acting in her experience and wisdom, guided by the Holy Spirit and finding a backing in scripture, made celibacy a prerequisite vocation for vocation to the priesthood. In other words, vocation to the Catholic priesthood becomes complete only when an aspirant has the vocation to the celibate life. One appreciates the wisdom of the church in reaching this decision, when celibacy is properly conceived as a way of

---

79 Can. 1024.

80 *The Catechism of the Catholic Church*, no. 1599.

being completely and totally available and dedicated to the Lord so as to be "sent out" by him.

In the light of Old Testament tradition that requires continence both on the part of the Israelites and their priests before some specific engagements with the Lord (see Ex. 15:15, 1 Sam. 21:2-7), it is right to argue that the biblical tradition backing celibacy in the Catholic priesthood pre-dates the New Testament in a sense. In the New Testament, the example of Jesus as a celibate and the demands Christ made on his apostles, "... Truly, there is no one who has left house or brothers or sisters, or father or mother, or children, or lands for my sake and for the Gospel, who will not receive his reward" (Mk 10:29-30), show a certain preference on the part of Jesus, for celibacy over marriage. For instance, after responding to the Pharisees' question on marriage and divorce, the disciples thought that it might just be better not to marry. Jesus responds to this, saying, "Not everybody can accept what you have just said, but only those who have received this gift. There are eunuchs born so from their mother's womb. Some have been made that way by others. But there are some who have given up the possibility of marriage for the sake of the kingdom of heaven. Let the one who can accept it, accept it" (Mt. 19:11-12). Apart from these, the New Testament states no regulation on celibacy. Passages like 1 Tim. 3: 2; 1 Cor. 9:5 and Mk 1:29-31 make it clear that there is no hard and fast rule about celibacy in the New Testament. On the other hand, such passages like 1 Cor. 7:8; 32-35 and Mt. 19:11-12 portray a strong preference for celibacy by Christ and the apostle Paul.

Encouraged by such preferences in the scripture and the popularity priestly celibacy enjoyed, in the opinions of Pope Innocent 1 (AD 404), Pope Leo (AD 446) and Pope Gregory VII, the Council of Trent in AD 1563 moved for priestly celibacy. The Second Vatican Council of 1962-1965 later affirmed this. Here the fathers of the Church acknowledged that celibacy is not demanded by the very nature of the priesthood, nevertheless, they see it as a sign of the complete consecration of the priest, as well as a "transcendental and eschatological sign." This simply means that it is a pointer to the end and what is beyond this material world.

If viewed ecclesiologically, that is, from the point of the community of God's faithful, the Church, celibacy is a sign of the priest's total consecration and dedication to the Church. It is a renunciation of earthly and material fatherhood to embrace the higher and spiritual fatherhood. In relation to Christ, celibacy helps the priest to be configured, completely identified, and fitted with and into Christ. Being that the priest shares in the mediatory role of Christ as "another Christ" he is called to imitate Christ who exercised his mediation in a celibate state. Finally, by celibacy, the priest bears witness to the end of time and transitory nature of our world. His celibacy is a proclamation of the eschatological fact that in heaven there is no giving in marriage.

PART TWO

ARTICLES ON THE BLESSED VIRGIN MARY

12

The Blessed Virgin Mary in Scripture

The role of the Blessed Virgin Mary (BVM) in the history of salvation is often contested by non-Catholics who accuse Catholics of giving her undue respect that cannot be grounded on scriptural teaching. My aim therefore, is to shed some light on how the scripture referred to Mary. Hopefully, this will enable us establish how relevant Mary was in the economy of salvation as recorded in the sacred books of the scripture. There are two possible ways of reading the Old Testament. One of them is to read it as a purely Jewish literature without connection to the salvation mystery revealed in the New Testament and the other is to read as a Christian literature that foreshadows the activities of Jesus recorded in the New Testament. In this latter sense, we would have to read it with the knowledge of the practices of the Jews. If we read the Old Testament as a purely Jewish literature, we would see Mary as just any Jewish woman born of the religious race and cultural environment of Israel. In this case, Mary can only be seen as intervening in the past and thus, the Old Testament cannot be affirmed to be moving decisively towards Mary. Alternatively, when we read the Old Testament as a Christian literature, we would have a completely new meaning of the expressions, symbols and realities of the Old Testament. The new interpretations produced from this context overwhelm the ones from the first perspective of the Old Testament as a mere Jewish literature. If we read the Old Testament as a Christian literature, it enables us to see the Bible as a single literature in which the Old Testament is directed towards the New Testament with Christ as the end and goal. Since Mary is intimately related to

Jesus Christ in the New Testament, we would see her in that role in some parts of the Old Testament.

The Fathers of VC II express this fact beautifully by saying that:

> The books of the Old Testament recount the period of salvation history during which the coming of Christ into the world was slowly prepared for. These earliest documents, as they are read in the Church are understood in the light of a further and full revelation, bring the figure of the Woman, Mother of the redeemer, into a gradually sharper focus.[1]

The first pointer to our salvation, which is the sharpest image of Mary in the Old Testament, came immediately after the fall of humankind. "I shall put enmity between you and the woman, and between your offspring and hers; it will bruise your head and you will strike its heel" (Gen. 3:15). Biblical scholars refer to this as the *proto-evangelium*, which means, the first gospel. It opposes the human race, which is personified in the image of the woman's offspring to the devil, which is personified in the image of the snake. Significantly, the *proto-evangelium* is rendered in the singular, thus, it gives room for it to be interpreted as Jesus Christ. This passage hints on the ultimate victory of the woman's offspring. The Greek version of the Old Testament uses the masculine pronoun "he will bruise…" instead of the impersonal "it will bruise…" of the English version. This symbolically ascribes the final victory to one of the woman's descendant. Throwing more light on the issue, the Septuagint (LXX), which is the Latin translation of the Greek/Hebrew scripture and was popular among the first generation of Christians, uses the feminine pronoun, "she will bruise…" This allows an interpretation that specifically suggests a reference to Mary, since the Messianic interpretation of this text, in whatever version of the Old Testament, puts the Messiah and the Mother together.[2]

---

1 Austin Flammery O.P., *Lumen Gentium*, no. 55.
2 See Commentaries on Gen. 3:15 in the New Jerusalem Bible.

The prophet Isaiah tells Israel, the House of David, that though Ahaz, the king has refused to ask for a sign about what is to come, the Lord will, nonetheless, give a sign which is that of a young woman, who will give birth to a son called Immanuel. "The Lord will give you a sign in any case: It is this: the young woman is with child and will give birth to a son whom she will call Immanuel" (Is. 7:14). Later on, Isaiah talks about Immanuel as the future saviour of his people (Is. 8:8-9). Isaiah's 'young woman' could either be a virgin as the Greek translation renders it or a recently married young woman as the LXX renders it. This brief analysis of Isaiah's text suggests the idea that the prophet was referring to Mary, the virgin mother of Jesus Christ, who is the saviour of the human race. This is the opinion found in Christian tradition based on the claim that Mt. 1:23 identifies Mary as the 'young woman' of Isaiah, which, Matthew substitutes with 'virgin.'[3]

The prophet Micah, in reference to the distress plaguing the Davidic dynasty, chips in a word of hope as he mentions the glory that was to come, that though Bethlehem is considered least of the Kingdom of Judah, it will only be till, "she who is in labour gives birth" (Micah 5:2). Commentaries on this passage assume that Micah is perhaps thinking of the famous prophecy of Is. 7:14, which historically precedes Micah's prophecy with about thirty years.

Apart from these outstanding Old Testament Marian passages, other passages, which at least implicitly highlight Mary, can be found in the Old Testament. For instance, at the definition of the dogma of the Immaculate Conception, Pope Pius IX in 1854 described Mary as the prototype of the Ark of Noah, which was built at the instance of God's command to escape the effects of sin (Gen. 6). The early Fathers of the Church saw Mary as a personification of the burning bush since she held the presence of God but without corruption as the bush burns without being consumed (Ex. 3:1).

---

3 John K. Aniagwu, *The Role of Mary in the Work of Salvation* (Iperu-Remo: The Ambassador Publications, 1991), p. 3.

The temple of God talked about in 1 Kings 8, provides a picture of a sanctified dwelling place of God and therefore, foreshadows Mary as the future tabernacle of Jesus Christ. Among these models, the "Ark of the Covenant" stands out as a strong model of Mary, who is specially chosen to hold the presence of God (Gen. 6:14, Ex. 37:1). The richness of the Old Testament in foretelling the intercessory, virginal and pure nature of Mary through the use of models and archetypes cannot be overemphasized. VC II, in *Lumen Gentium* no. 55 cited above already, testifies to this fact.

The gospels, which form the main thrust of the New Testament, have significant references to the dignity of Mary. According to scripture scholars, we can identify three stages that the gospels passed through to its present and final end. The first stage is that of historical place. It forms the base of the gospels. The second stage has to do with the traditions that surround the events recorded in the gospels as they are interpreted from the point of view of faith. The final stage, which is the third stage, is the compilation of the gospels. This afforded the evangelists the opportunity to express their own theological vision.

In the light of this, we can claim that the New Testament is more than anything else, an encyclopaedia of documents of faith. Therefore, we should be careful in interpreting its material. When it applies to Mary, we should be extra careful that we do not read them as exact accounts of history. It does not seem to be the intention of any of the evangelists to give an exact historical account of events. They were more interested in presenting the mystery of Christ with the aim of building up faith in their readers. The evangelists cannot be accused of falsifying or inaccurately reporting the events in the light of the passion, death, resurrection and glorification of Jesus Christ. In other words, the gospels present concrete historical events as seen in the light of the Paschal event by men of faith.

The vision of Mary in the New Testament is that of a humble and obedient servant of God, one whose meekness enables her to put her total trust and confidence in God; a pious young woman.

Her prominent appearances in the New Testament are found in the infancy narratives of Matthew and Luke.

The Lucan account of the annunciation describes how the angel Gabriel was sent to a woman, named Mary, in Galilee. The dialogue that ensued between the angel and Mary is of special interest. The greeting of the angel, "Rejoice, you who enjoys God's favour! The Lord is with you" (Lk. 1:28) echoes the greeting to the daughter of Zion. A greeting that is motivated by the idea that God has come to His people. The prophet Isaiah puts it like this: "Cry and shout for joy, you who live in Zion, for the Holy One of Israel is among you in His greatness" (Is. 12:6).

The greeting of the angel is therefore, an invitation to be happy and joyful. No wonder Mary was disturbed. As scripture puts it, "she was deeply disturbed by these words and asked herself what this greeting could mean" (Lk. 1:29). The full import of the greeting in question is appreciated when it is correctly noted that the name of Mary was not included in the angelic greeting and that the '... you who enjoy God's favour' is rendered as 'full of grace' in other translations. The fact here is that no one with a fallen nature as all humankind have, can possess a fullness of grace. So, for Mary to be addressed as "Full of Grace" and by an angel of God is not a passing comment. It is an indication of her exemption from the stain of original sin. As the Catholic catechism puts it, "all mankind have contracted the guilt and stain of original sin except the Blessed Virgin who through the merit of her divine Son, was conceived without the least guilt and stain of original sin."[4] This teaching is the basis of the dogmatic pronouncement on Mary's Immaculate Conception.

Other than the angelic greetings, the New Testament gives other instances, although in seed form, of the revealed truths about Mary. Like the mustard seed, some of these have grown to be subjects of dogmatic definitions. Such instances include; the encounter between Mary and Elizabeth (Lk. 2:4-20), the presentation in the temple, which featured the prophetic words of Simeon, in which Mary's sorrow on account of her son Jesus was

---

4 *A Catechism of Christian Doctrine*, ques.117, p. 20.

foretold (Lk. 2:34-35), and the finding of the missing Jesus in the temple (Lk. 2:41-52). In his narrative, Matthew added the betrothal of Mary to Joseph (Mt. 1:18), the reluctance of Joseph to take Mary a "pregnant virgin" home as wife and the consequent interference of an angel of God (Mt. 1:20), the visit of the wise men from the East at the birth of Jesus (Mt. 2:1-12), the flight into Egypt, and the return of the Holy family to Israel (Mt. 2:13-23). The striking fact about these infancy narratives is the unity between Jesus and Mary as the references repeatedly pointed out. According to Mark Miravalle, this is "a sign of the profound union of Jesus and Mary that would continue for all time."[5]

The gospel according to St. John, whose main thrust is showing the divinity of Jesus, did not miss out on Mary. Interestingly, the two times the evangelist mentioned Mary were so strategic that one cannot just wave them aside as coincidental. John featured Mary at the beginning of the public ministry of Jesus, which is the wedding feast at Cana (Jn 2:1-11). Here, through Mary's intercessory role, Jesus performed his first miracle where he turned water into wine. According to Miravalle, the Marian words, "do whatever he tells you" (Jn. 2:5) were spoken and till today they continue to echo.[6]

It is perfectly in place to think that Mary's intercession on behalf of the celebrants at the Cana wedding was effective because Jesus had always listened to his mother. I infer this from Lk. 2:51, which tells us that after the incident in the temple (Lk. 2:41f), when Jesus was found among the teachers and scribes after three days of their search for him, he went to Nazareth with Mary and Joseph and lived under their authority.

John featured Mary again at the close of Jesus' public ministry, at the foot of the cross (Jn. 19:25-27). Here Jesus entrusted his mother to the care of his beloved disciple and also entrusted his beloved disciple to his mother as son. Mariologists opine that the act of Jesus by which he entrusted his beloved disciple to his

---

5 Mark Miravalle, *Introduction to Mary: The Heart of Marian Doctrine and Devotion* (Santa Barbara, CA: Queenship Publishing Company, 1993), p. 22.

6 Mark Miravalle, p. 22.

mother equally signifies that he is entrusting all who are his beloved (Jn. 15:10-15) to the care of his mother.

This opinion finds a basis in the exegesis of the scriptural passage which says, "... Woman, this is your son. ... This is your mother." According to this exegesis, the gesture of Jesus here is more than of one who is just a dutiful son, but implies "a declaration that Mary, the new Eve, is the spiritual mother of all the faithful, of whom the beloved disciple is the type and representative."[7] If the African proverb that says, "the biggest masquerade comes out last" is anything to go by, then the fact that John chose to mention Mary at the end of Jesus' public ministry and even the gesture of Jesus to give his mother as mother of all his beloved, at the end of his life as man, cannot be overemphasized.

Some persons make reference to the gospel according to Mark as a test case to show that Jesus had no regards for Mary. The question that follows is usually, why then do Catholics make such big deal out of Mary? In truth, the gospel of Mark has not always been easy for Mariologists to explain. But before we make an appraisal of Mk 3:31-34, which is often the passage quoted, it would be pertinent to observe that although Mark is historically the first gospel writing of the New Testament, it is not the complete New Testament revelation. Therefore, even if Mark is said to be anti-Mary literarily, which is not the case, it does not prove that Mary is irrelevant in the salvation history of humankind.

As a matter of fact, the text of Mk 3:34 in which Jesus asks, "who are my mother and my brothers?" reveals the exemplary lifestyle of Mary as a member of God's kingdom on earth. So much so that all who do the will of God are his brothers and sisters and mother. (Mk 3:35). Jesus not only signified the perfect manner in which his mother, Mary has cooperated with the will of God for our salvation (Lk. 1:38) by doing the will of God, but he has also pointed to Mary as a model of Christian obedience to God's will. Most importantly, he has given an insight into the relationship

---

7 See Commentary on Jn. 19:27 in the *New Jerusalem Bible*.

between himself and those who strive after doing God's will, that is, those who strive after righteousness.

The Acts of the Apostles also did not forget to mention the place of Mary in the beginning of the church. Mary was portrayed as being at the heart of the infant church. Her presence in what could be called the first congregation of the Church, at the upper room (Acts 1:13-24) was well noted. And lastly, but not the least in any way, the apocalyptic description of a woman clothed with the sun, with the moon under her feet and twelve stars for a crown (Rev. 12:1) paints a picture of Mary as typifying the Church.

13

The Person of the Blessed Virgin Mary

Issues about Mary have been a source of contention between Catholics and other Christian denominations for ages. The contentions are either about the veneration of the Blessed Virgin Mary by Catholics or the doctrinal teachings about the person of Mary. These doctrinal teachings include:

i. The proclamation of Mary as the mother of God.
ii. The proclamation that Mary was conceived without sin.
iii. The proclamation that Mary was a virgin before, and remained a virgin after the birth of Jesus Christ. This implies that Mary had no other children aside Jesus Christ.

We should not mix up the idea of adoration and veneration as they apply to Jesus and Mary respectively. There is a theological distinction between adoration and veneration. In classical theology, adoration is referred to as *latria*. It is the worship and homage that is rightly offered to God alone. On the other hand, veneration is called *dulia* in classical theology. It is the honour due to the excellence of a created person.[1] Adoration "is the acknowledgement of excellence and perfection of an uncreated divine person."[2] This is the worship that God alone deserves as the creator. Veneration refers to the recognition, honour and respect that are due to a created being on account of the excellence exhibited by that created being. This is not and does not compete with the adoration due to the creator. Adoration of Mary "has never been and will never be part of authentic Catholic doctrine

1 Mark Miravalle, p. 9.
2 Mark Miravalle, p. 9.

and devotional life."[3] Devotion to Mary in form of veneration is also not arbitrary nor extraordinary for God Himself has willed that she plays an important role in the work of the incarnation, that is, God becoming man, and the salvation of the humankind. Pope St. Pius X states this clearly in his *Ad Diem Illum*, thus:

> God could have given us the Redeemer of the human race and the Founder of the faith in another way than through the Virgin, but since Divine Providence has been pleased that we should have the God-man through Mary, who conceived Him by the Holy Spirit and bore Him in her womb, it remains for us to receive Christ only through the hands of Mary.[4]

Keeping this clarification in mind, we are better informed and positioned to look at the person of Mary and thus, try to understand the basis of the theological positions of the Catholic Church about Mary, Marian dogmas and devotions. Scripture says:

> And Mary said: My soul proclaims the greatness of the Lord and my spirit rejoices in God my saviour, because he has looked upon the lowliness of his servant. Yes, from now onwards, all generations will call me blessed, for the Almighty has done great things for me. Holy is his name, and his faithful love extends age after age to those who fear him. He has used the power of his arm; he has routed the arrogant of heart. He has pulled down princes from their thrones and raised high the lowly. He has filled the starving with good things, sent the rich away empty. He has come to the help of Israel his servant, mindful of his faithful love, according to the promise he made to our ancestors, of his mercy to Abraham and his descendants forever (Lk. 1:46-55).

The above is Mary's response to the greetings of Elizabeth, otherwise referred to the Magnificat. It recalls the song of Hannah, the barren wife of Elkanah;

---

3 Mark Miravalle, p. 10.

4 Pope Pius X, Papal Encyclical on the "Immaculate Conception," *Ad Diem Illum*, Laetissimum, 2nd February, 1904.

> My heart exults in Yahweh, in my God is my strength lifted up, my mouth derides my foes, for I rejoice in your deliverance. There is no Holy one like Yahweh, (indeed, there is none but you) no rock like our God. Do not keep talking as proudly, let no arrogance come from your mouth, for Yahweh is a wise God, his to weigh up deeds. The bow of the mighty has been broken but those who were tottering are now braced with strength. The full fed are living themselves out for bread but the hungry need labour no more; the barren woman bears sevenfold but the mother of many is left desolate. Yahweh gives death and life, brings down to Sheol and draws up; Yahweh makes poor and rich, he humbles and also exults. He raises the poor from the dust, he lifts the needy from the dunghill to give them a place with princes, to assign them a seat of honour; for to Yahweh belongs the pillars of the earth; on these he has poised the world. He safeguards the steps of his faithful but the wicked vanish in darkness (for human strength can win no victories). Yahweh, his enemies are shattered, the Most High thunders in the heavens, Yahweh judges the ends of the earth, He endows His king with power; He raises up the strength of his Anointed (1 Sam. 2:1-10).

This outstanding poem, which the compiler of the book of Samuel has put in the voice of Hannah, has its strong hold in its reference to the childless woman, an image depicted by Hannah. Hannah had known grief as one of the two wives of Elkanah, son of Jeroham (1 Sam. 1:1). Anytime Elkanah goes up to Shiloh, which was then the home of the Ark of the Covenant, to offer sacrifices he usually gives a portion to Hannah and a portion each to the other wife, Peninnah and all her sons and daughters. Peninnah on her part would taunt and provoke Hannah whom it has pleased the Lord to make barren (1 Sam. 1:16). Completely weighed down by such taunts and provocations from Peninnah, Hannah poured out her whole being to Yahweh in prayer asking for a child, a boy (1 Sam. 1:10-11). And Yahweh Sabaoth heard the prayer of His servant, taking note of her humiliation on account of her barrenness. Hannah was blessed with a son, Samuel. In thankful praise to God she prayed the poem above.

This beautiful prayer of thanks glorifies God who triumphantly vindicates His faithful followers. In a special way, it expresses the theology of the "poor of Yahweh," which is epitomized in the book of Zep. 2:3, "seek Yahweh, all you humble of the earth..." and the prophecy of Is. 57:15, "...but I am with the contrite and humble..." In the New Testament, this theology of the "poor of Yahweh" comes out conspicuously in the Beatitudes, "How blessed are the poor in spirit; the kingdom of Heaven is theirs" (Mt. 5:3). Jesus also makes this clear in the declaration of his mission in Lk 4:21, "this text is being fulfilled today even while you are listening." The text in question being that of Is. 61:1-2 and Lk. 4:18. "The spirit of the Lord is on me, for he has anointed me to bring the good news to the afflicted, to proclaim liberty to captives, sight to the blind, to let the oppressed go free, to proclaim a year of favour from the Lord." The "poor of Yahweh," namely, the oppressed and those whom society have humbled, hold a place of pride in the ministry of Jesus.

The account of the annunciation follows the pattern of the Old Testament angelic promise of a child to Samson's mother (Judges 13:2-7). It sets forth Mary's identity as one of God's lowly, the "poor of Yahweh." Ancient tradition has it that Mary was the belated offspring of the materially poor couple, Joachim and Anne. She was born when both parents ordinarily had passed the age of child bearing. Mary assents her lowliness in her loving submissive answer to the archangel Gabriel, "You see before you the Lord's servant, let it happen to me as you have said" (Lk. 1:38). As God has raised her from her lowly state, she affirms that "from now onwards all generation will call me blessed" (Lk. 1:48). The Lord the almighty has done great things for her. Mary is therefore, the humble servant of God, who is ready to do the will of God in her life. Her acknowledgement of her lowly state and perfect submission to the will of God brought her to the exalted position of the mother of the Son of God, who is our Lord Jesus Christ.

14

The Immaculate Conception of the Blessed Virgin Mary[92]

The doctrine that Mary was conceived without any stain of original sin was the second Marian doctrine (dogmatic teaching on Mary). It is otherwise referred to as the Immaculate Conception and was proclaimed by Pope Pius IX in 1854 and celebrated on the 8 of December according to the Roman Rite. Prior to its proclamation, it was a subject of prolonged debate. By the close of the 7th century, the Eastern Church established a feast called "the feast of the conception of the virgin." It was celebrated after the feasts of the Annunciation and the conception of John the Baptist. This new feast entails the celebration of Mary as the "all-holy woman in whom there was no trace of sin" (The *panhagia*).

The story in the Western Roman Catholic Church was however different as there were some difficulties with the understanding of the doctrine. From the time of St. Augustine, there was a stress on the sinful condition of all human beings, that is, the universality of original sin. This was occasioned by the need to emphasize the need for salvation through the grace of God given in Jesus Christ. To say that Mary did not share in original sin would be denying that she was saved by Christ as she should, in the first place, not needing salvation since she is already free from the sinful nature of humankind. It would also be undermining the universal character of Jesus' redemptive act.

The opinion of great theologians of authority like St. Thomas Aquinas and St. Bonaventure was that, Mary was not immaculate in the first instant of her conception. But thanks to Jesus Christ,

92 First published in *The Promise Newspaper*, a monthly publication of the Catholic Diocese of Auchi.

the perfect redeemer, Mary was perfectly redeemed from original sin in the second instance of her existence. John Duns Scotus, a renowned theologian of the Franciscan Order, held that precisely because Mary was most perfectly redeemed by the most perfect redeemer, she enjoyed the fullness of grace from the very first instance of her existence. The debate about when precisely Mary became immaculate went on till the end of the 15th century when Rome officially adopted the feast of the conception of Mary. The teaching that Mary was immaculate from the first instance of her existence was neither condemned nor affirmed by any Pope.

Pope Alexander VII, however, resolved the issue when he declared on the 8th of December 1661 in favour of the Immaculate Conception of Mary from the first instance of her existence. On the 8th of December 1854, almost two centuries after the papal declaration of Alexander VII, Pope Pius IX took a more definitive stand. He pronounced as an article of faith, the Immaculate Conception of Mary thus:

> For the honour of the holy and undivided Trinity, for the honour and renown of the virgin Mother of God, for the exaltation of Catholic faith and the increase of Christian religion, by the authority of our Lord Jesus Christ, by the authority of the blessed Apostles Peter and Paul, and by our own authority, We declare, pronounce and define: the doctrine that maintains that the most Blessed Virgin Mary in the first instance of her conception, by a unique grace and privilege of Almighty God and in consideration of the merits of Christ Jesus the saviour of the human race, was preserved free from all stain of original sin, is a doctrine revealed by God and therefore must be firmly and constantly held by all the faithful.[93]

The scripture provides two passages, which at least give an implicit idea of this revealed truth. Genesis 3:15, where God tells Satan that He will put enmity between Satan and the woman whose offspring shall crush Satan's head. This enmity extends also to the offspring of both parties; the woman and Satan. This

---

93 Pius IX, *Ineffabilis Deus*. Cf. *DS* 2803-2904.

passage points to the complete and absolute opposition between Jesus who is the offspring of the woman and sin which is the offspring of Satan. Mary, the woman so referred to in this passage, is given similar opposition to the serpent which is Satan in the passage. It is on this note that it will be inconceivable that at any point in Mary's existence, she took part in the fallen nature of humankind, which is the result of original sin.

The doctrine of the Immaculate Conception is revealed also in the angelic greetings of the annunciation. "Hail, full of grace, the Lord is with you" (Lk. 1:28). Mary's name was substituted for in this greeting with "full of grace." That this title served as a substitute for Mary's name in the sight of God who is all knowing, is to indicate that her very being is full of grace. It is true that no one with a fallen nature as all others of the human race have can be appropriately described as full of grace. Mary has been compared by the early Church Fathers to Eve in her original state. Thus, Mary is frequently referred to as the New Eve. Eve was conceived in grace without a fallen nature. So, to compare Mary to her is to talk of another like Eve who was conceived without the fallen nature.

Our understanding and explanation of the dogma of the Immaculate Conception ultimately depends largely on how we understand and explain the doctrine of original sin. One such way of understanding and explaining the doctrine of original sin is that we are conceived and born with a stain of sin on the soul or conceived and born without grace. Within this context, it would mean that only Mary was born in the state of grace. If alternatively, our understanding and explanation of original sin is that of a sinful condition in which every human being is born; a corporate alienation of the human race from God, then we may have to propose a different explanation for the Immaculate Conception. This explanation would be that in view of her role in the redemptive plan of God, she was exempted from this collective condition of alienation and God was fully present to her in grace from the beginning.

Whichever way we choose to explain the dogma of the Immaculate Conception, the fact remains that it teaches, "that

Mary was exempt in a unique and exceptional way from the normal and the usual impact of sin, and/or more positively, that she was given a greater degree of grace (God was more intensely present to her than to others) in view of her role as the 'God-bearer."[94] The dogma of the Immaculate Conception therefore, shows that God can be, and in fact, is utterly gracious to us not by our merits but by reason of divine love and mercy.

94 Richard McBrien, p. 1101.

15

The Perpetual Virginity of the Blessed Virgin Mary[95]

Pope St. Martin 1 at the Lateran Synod of 649 A.D defined the doctrine of Mary's perpetual virginity, which is the third central doctrine regarding the blessed virgin. This dogma enjoyed a unanimous acceptance among the Fathers of the Early Church. The dogma proclaims that Mary was a virgin before the birth of Jesus, during the birth of Jesus and she remained a virgin after the birth of Jesus. Thus, it has a threefold aspect. That Mary was a virgin before the birth of Jesus is a clear and straightforward scriptural fact. The prophecy of Is. 7:14 refers to "...the young woman" who is with child. The Greek version of this translates "young woman" as virgin. Mt. 1:22-23 makes reference to this Old Testament verse, in fact, it quotes it verbatim. Matthew points out that Mary's conception is a fulfilment of scripture therefore, authenticating Isaiah's prophecy. According to Deut. 18:20, the mark of an authentic prophet is the fulfilment of his prophecies, in this wise, Isaiah's prophecy in the light of Matthew's confirmation is authentic.

The evangelist Luke also records Mary's virginity before the birth of Jesus. He introduced the annunciation account thus: "In the sixth month, the angel Gabriel was sent by God to a town in Galilee called Nazareth, to a virgin betrothed to a man named Joseph ... And the virgin's name was Mary" (Lk. 1:26-27). Mary's response to the angelic message also confirmed her virginity. "But how can this come about, since I have no knowledge of man?" (Lk.

95 Originally published as an article in *The Promise Newspaper*, a monthly publication of the Catholic Diocese of Auchi.

1:34). Knowledge of man in the scriptural sense would mean to have had conjugal relationship with a man. Mary, in her response confirms that she has never done this.

Apart from being a virgin before the birth of Jesus, Mary is also considered to have retained her virginity during the birth of Jesus. This means that Jesus left the womb of Mary without her losing her virginity. The firm belief of the Church in the perpetual virginity of Mary after the birth of the Lord is based on her spiritual conception, which was possible by virtue of God's special divine action for God is all-powerful[96] and with God, nothing is impossible.

In his *Summa Theologica*, III, St. Thomas Aquinas explains that, "painlessly, and without change in Mary's virgin body, her son emerged from the tabernacle of the spotless womb as he was later to emerge from the tomb, without moving the stone or breaking the seal of Pilate."[97] The use of the term 'painlessly' by Thomas Aquinas is significant as it reminds us of the pain that goes with childbirth, from which Mary is exempted by virtue of her Immaculate Conception.

The virginity of Mary before and during the birth of Christ was confirmed at VC II. The Dogmatic Constitution on the Church *Lumen Gentium* records it in the following words, "This union of the mother with the son in the work of salvation is made manifest from the time of Christ's virginal conception ... then also at the birth of our Lord, who did not diminish his mother's virginal integrity but sanctified it..."[98]

The third aspect of Mary's perpetual virginity is that she remained a virgin after the birth of Jesus, till the end of her earthly life. According to St. Thomas Aquinas, it would have been disrespectful to the Holy Spirit on the part of Mary to allow a human conception to follow the miraculous conception by the Holy Spirit in her virginal womb.

---

96 Mark Miravalle, p. 46.

97 Thomas Aquinas, *Summa Theologica* III, Q28, a. 2.

98 Austin Flammery O.P., *Lumen Gentium*, no. 57.

Objections to Mary's perpetual virginity have been centred on the reference to the "brethren" or "brothers and sisters" of Jesus in Mt. 12:46, 13:55 and Mk 3:31. Those who make these objections often do not consider the fact that the Greek word "*adelphos*" that translates as brothers in English is often used in scripture to mean cousins and close relatives. For instance, Gen. 13:8 and 29:15, used the same word to denote the relationship between Lot and Abraham and between Jacob and Leban, who were in fact not brothers.

16

The Assumption of the Blessed Virgin Mary[99]

On the 1st of November, 1950, Pope Pius XII declared, "By the authority of our Lord Jesus Christ, of the Blessed Apostles Peter and Paul, and by our own authority, we pronounce, declare, and define it to be a divinely revealed dogma: that the Immaculate Mother of God, the ever Virgin Mary, having completed the course of her earthly life, was assumed body and soul into heavenly glory."[100] With these words, the age-long belief that Mary, after her death, was taken up to heaven, body and soul was declared as the fourth Marian dogma. This is the belief refer to as the Assumption of the Blessed Virgin Mary. According to McBrien:

> The dogma of the Assumption complements the dogma of the Immaculate Conception in the same way that the resurrection of Christ complements his crucifixion and life of sacrificial service to others. Just as the Immaculate Conception was not merely a personal privilege conferred upon Mary but a reality bestowed in view of her role in the economy of salvation, so the Assumption is not merely a personal privilege unrelated to the wider mission of her life. Her union with God in Christ was unique from the beginning. Her call to final union with God in Christ, in the totality of her human existence (body and soul), was also unique in the end. The dogma of the Assumption asserts

99 First published in *The Promise Newspaper*, a monthly publication of the Catholic Diocese of Auchi.

100 Pope Pius XII, "*Munificentissimus Deus* – Defining the Dogma of the Assumption," n. 44, (Vactican, November 1, 1950).

> something about human existence in asserting something about Mary: that human existence is bodily existence, and that we are destined for glory not only in the realm of the spiritual but in the realm of the material as well.[101]

In 1946, Pope Pius XII asked the bishops of the world whether to define Mary's assumption as dogma. Out of the 1232 bishops, 1210 answered in the affirmative. Thus, in 1950, on the first day of November, Pope Pius XII defined the assumption as a dogma. According to him, "the doctrine has deep roots in the scriptural teaching on the holiness, and dignity of Mary, and on the meaning of man, sin, death, and the resurrection of the body."[102]

The doctrine of assumption proclaims that after Mary's earthly life, she was taken up to heaven body and soul. This teaching is rooted in the firm belief of the Church that from the very first moment of the conception of Mary, she was free of all sin, including original sin. This is possible by the special favour that God granted her, that is, the Immaculate Conception, which was discussed above.

The feast of the Assumption of Mary is celebrated every year on the 15th of August. It brings to the mind of Catholics, the height to which the Church has elevated Mary as a special woman. It is a feast with a long history and it serves two purposes:

i. To celebrate the happy departure of Mary from this physical life on earth.
ii. To mark the assumption of her body into heavenly glory.[103]

The exact circumstances that surround the death of the Blessed Virgin Mary is not known, since the Bible did not provide any insight into that. One tradition has it that she died in Jerusalem, while another says, she died in Ephesus where the apostle John was living. The stories about her death were shaped in the first

---

101 Richard McBrien, p. 1101.

102 Pope Pius XII, *Munificentissimus Deus*.

103 See "Assumption of the Blessed Virgin Mary" in www.marypages.com, (Assessed 07 Aug. 2015).

centuries after her death and they were focussed on her deathbed and her body being carried up to heaven.

Historically, Assumption is a very old feast that was already celebrated universally by the 6th century. Its celebration started in the East as the feast of the Dormition. The word "dormition" means "the falling asleep." The first reference to the belief about the Assumption is traced to a 4th century document titled; "The Falling Asleep of the Holy Mother of God." This document recounts the death, laying in the tomb and assumption of the Blessed Virgin Mary.[104] It is written in the voice of John, the Apostle. Although the Eastern Orthodox accepts and celebrates the feast of Dormition, they think the Papal dogmatic definition of the feast of Assumption is not necessary.

About 200 years of Jerusalem being a pagan city, having being levelled by Emperor Hadrian in 135 A.D. and rebuilt as *Aelia Capitolina* in honour of Jupiter, with every memory of Jesus obliterated from the city, Emperor Constantine restored Jerusalem as a sacred city. With the Church of the Holy Sepulchre built in 336 A.D., other sacred sites were restored and the memories of the life of Jesus were celebrated by the people of Jerusalem. One of the memories celebrated was, "Memory of Mary" and it was centred on the "Tomb of Mary," which is where she was buried, close to Mount Zion, where the early Christian community is said to have lived.[105] The "Place of Dormition," which is the spot Mary died or fell asleep is right on the hill of Mount Zion. The celebration of the "Memory of Mary" is what has evolved to become the feast of the Assumption.

Initially, this celebration of the "Memory of Mary" was restricted to Palestine until the Emperor Constantine extended it to all the churches of the East. The celebration started in Rome in the 7th century as the "Falling Asleep" of the Mother of God. Later on, the title of the celebration was changed to the "Assumption of Mary" because the celebration involved much more than her

---

104 See "The Assumption of the Blessed Virgin Mary" in www.catholicism.about.com (Accessed 7/8/2015).

105 See "The Assumption of the Blessed Virgin Mary" in www.ewtn.com (Accessed 7/8/2015).

dying, but also included the belief that she was taken up to heaven, body and soul. This belief dates back to the apostles themselves. Two facts that seem to inform this belief are; (i) There were no relics of the Blessed Virgin Mary to be venerated, and (ii) There was an empty tomb located near the site of her death.

According to EWTN sources, when the Bishops from the Mediterranean world assembled in Constantinople, at the Council of Chalcedon in 451 A.D., Emperor Marcian requested for the relics of Mary to be brought to Constantinople, so that they can be enshrined in the capitol. The Patriarch of Jerusalem explained to the Emperor that the relics are not available. According to him, although Mary had died in the presence of the Apostle, when they later opened the tomb where she was buried, they found it empty, thus, they concluded that the body was taken up into heaven.[106]

In defining the dogmatic teaching on Assumption, Pope Pius XII made reference to Gen. 3:15 as the scripture that supports the belief that Mary was victorious over sin and death as 1 Cor. 15:54 states, "then shall come to pass the saying that is written, Death is swallowed up in victory." This implies that Mary shared in the same absolute victory of her son over Satan.[107] The Holy Father, Pope Pius XII also referred to Ps. 132, which commemorates the return of the Ark of God to Jerusalem as well as laments the subsequent loss. According to the second half of this Psalm, the loss will be recompensed in the New Covenant. Thus, it prays, "Arise, O Lord, into thy resting place: thou and the ark, which thou hast sanctified" (Ps. 132:8). The Church sees Mary as the New Covenant ark and therefore, understands that she was taken into Heaven, body and soul, in the same manner like the Lord Jesus Christ.[108] The Holy Father also alluded to Rev. 12:1-2, where John referred to the woman clothed with the sun. According to him, Mary is that woman as she is to be; body and soul in heaven.

We cannot say that scripture provides any explicit teaching on which we can base the Assumption of Mary, nevertheless, there

---

106 Ibid.

107 Mark Miravalle, pp. 75-78.

108 Pope Pius XII, *Munificenssimus Deus*, no. 26.

are seeds of the definition in scriptural passages like Lk. 1:28, where the Angel Gabriel referred to Mary as "full of Grace." The Assumption is seen as a natural effect of her being 'full of grace.' Paul equally teaches in his letter to the Romans that sin and death are the two-fold effects of evil (Rom. 5-8). Corruption we know, is the effect of original sin. Mary, by virtue of her sharing in her son's victory over Satan and evil would not know eternal death or bodily corruption. According to Lawler, *et al*, "since she had never been subject to sin, she, like her divine son, was not to remain in the grave, subject to the empire of death that sin had brought into the world."[109] Rev. 12:1 is also seen as confirming Mary's assumption, for Mary's coronation implies her preceding bodily assumption. One would have to admit however, that this verse of scripture is not primarily about Mary.

Some persons argue that Mary's assumption is out of place. This is not true if we consider the rising from the tomb recorded in Mt. 27:52 and 1 Cor. 15:23, which talks of the dead coming to life beginning with Christ and then those who belong to him. Among those who belong to Christ, Mary definitely comes first.

---

109 Ronald Lawler, Donald Wuerl, and Thomas Lawler, (eds.), *The Teaching of Christ: A Catholic Catechism with Study Guide*, (Bombay: St. Paul Publications, 1976), p. 244.

PART THREE

TALKS AND ARTICLES ON SELECTED THEMES

17

A Call to Repentance (I)[110]
(Let us go back to the Father)

> I will leave this place and go back to my Father (Lk. 15:18).
>
> Come back to me with all your heart ... Who knows if he will not come back, relent and leave a blessing behind him (Joel 2:12, 14).
>
> Wash, make yourselves clean, take your wrong-doing out of my sight. Cease to do evil. Learn to do good, search for justice, help the oppressed, be just to the orphan, plead for the widow. Come now, let us talk this over, says the Lord: though your sins are like scarlet, they shall be white as snow; though they are red as crimson, they shall be like wool (Is.1:16-18).

God invites us every Lenten season to come back to him. It is a call to repentance, a call to look into ourselves and renounce our deeds that are not pleasant in the presence of God. It is a time to seek reconciliation with God for walking away from his presence, seeking our own independence and wanting to live as we like. The parable of the Prodigal Son presents us a perfect point of reflection on repentance. It is the story of the son who left the father in search of his own independence and wanting to do things

110 One-day Lenten Recollection Talk delivered to the friends and associates of the Our Lady of Apostles (OLA) sisters at Maryhill Convent, Archdiocese of Ibadan, on the 15th March, 2014 with the title: "Let us Go back to the Father: A Call to Repentance".

his own way. He ran into difficulties and problems, but he had the courage to retrace his steps. According to him, "I will leave this place and go back to my Father..." (Lk. 15:18). Lent is an occasion to consider the same thing, to leave our present condition of sin and go back to a life of grace in the presence of the heavenly Father.

Contemporary society is overrun by sin and vices of various degrees, shades and kinds. We are constantly drifting away from virtue and from God. The need to be recognized and respected in the society has brought the craze for power, which is achieved by wealth, to the forefront, and therefore, money has become 'almighty.' Everyone craves for money with naked and unbridled appetite. As if this is not enough medium of bewitching humanity, the devil has introduced lust and unholy sexual desires, and the drive for sex into our world. We are no longer even satisfied with normal sexual relations between male and female, homosexuality and lesbianism (sexual relation between same-sex partners) is now something fashionable and adventurous, especially for our youths and people of middle age. The drives for money and sex are two very powerful weapons at the disposal of the devil today against humanity. Many people today are too ready and willing to do almost anything for money and sex. As Christians, we are called to live beyond this, even as we remain in the midst of the rat race that engulfs our communities. It is therefore, a call to become saints in the midst of sinners.

To give in to temptation is to sin and to sin is to revolt against God. It is to seek to be independent and therefore, disconnect from God. This is often accompanied with a sense of shame. The fall of humanity is premised on this. "The woman saw that the tree was good to eat and pleasing to the eye and that it was enticing for the wisdom that it could give" (Gen. 3:6). The reality of sin is such that after the initial enticement that leads us into sin, we suddenly feel the emptiness of the promise of temptation. This is followed by the sense of shame like the one felt by Adam after eating from the tree in the middle of the garden. After gaining his independence from God, so to say, he realized that he was just there, exposed to the elements, naked.

Adam had always been naked but it never mattered to him because he trusted himself to the care of God to cover him up. Now that he has drifted away from the presence of God, he could not be sure of God's protection anymore. God did not withdraw his protection or even walk away from Adam. Adam forfeited his dependence on God and walked away from God's presence. This is always the case when we succumb to temptation and sin. The joy however, is that in the story of our relationship with God is that God comes looking for us. God came looking for Adam with the aim of restoring the ruptured relationship resulting from Adam's disobedience. God found him and was willing to reconstruct the relationship Adam has broken.

The nature of man and the reality of human history with God is that despite our sinful nature, ingratitude and incapacity to rise above our sinful and weak nature, God is always the first to initiate the move of restoration of our lost dignity. This is typified in Jer. 3:12 where God cries out, "Come back, unfaithful Israel; it is Yahweh who speaks, I will not let my anger fall on you for I am merciful, I will not be angry forever." The same initiative of God is what Joel 2:12-14 and Is. 1:16-18, which we started this reflection with, refers to. God is calling us, taking the initiative to amend our relationship with him that we have destroyed with our sin. The Lenten season is the annual opportunity we have to take advantage of this initiative of God by playing our own part in the reconstruction work.

Sin is an offence against God and it injures humanity. The implications of sin are so great that it destroys our relationship with the community of Christians on the horizontal level and ultimately strains our relationship with God on the vertical level. In the case of very grave sins, until repentance, it closes the gate of salvation against us.

In the Old Testament, the children of Israel committed sins upon sins. God was always ready to forget His anger and forgive them, but they were always consistent in their acts of rebellion. Over and over again they offered sacrifices for sin until the blood of bulls and goats were no longer capable of taking away their sins (Heb. 10:4). When the appointed time came, God still sent His son to redeem the subjects of the law, so they could become His adopted children (Heb. 4:4-5). This shows the love of God for us, despite our sins. This love is so much that, according to St. Paul, it was while we were still in sin that He sent His only son to be the perfect sacrifice for our redemption (Rom. 5:8). By the death of this same Son of God, we are saved from the retribution of God (Rom. 5:9) and through him, we receive our reconciliation (Rom. 5:11).

In our journey back to God, we are besieged by temptation and sin. We find ourselves constantly falling prey to the devil. This is because of our human frailty since we are only earthen vessels. Thus, we need to constantly renew ourselves. Perfection is not achieved on a straight path; it involves ascending mountains and descending into valleys. As long as we remain human we will always need to renew our Christian commitments, wash our stained white garments and struggle with ever renewed vigour in our search for God. This is how we become saints in a world full of sin. The saint is one who sees his/her vulnerability and the constant tendency to disobedience and therefore, the need to struggle always to keep afloat in the tidal waves of a sinful world.

Jesus Christ is surely aware of our situation to fall prey to sin that is why he instituted the sacrament of reconciliation as indicated in the gospel of Jn. 20:19, 22-23. This sacrament avails us the opportunity to constantly be renewed. The sinner finds every reason not to take advantage of this, but the saint will always have a reason to go to confession at every available opportunity. Though the perfect sacrifice of Christ was once and for all, he understands our propensity to commit sin, for as scripture says, "The high priest we have is not incapable of feeling our weakness with us, but has been put to the test in exactly the same way as ourselves apart from sin" (Heb. 4:15).

As sincere as the true Christian may be in observing the covenant of love, s/he is between two forces, evil and good. Everyone carries an impediment with him/her no matter how light it may be. Besides the devil is always roaming around like a roaring lion looking for someone to devour. The 'saint' stands up to him strong in faith (1 Pet. 5:8-9).

What separates the saint from the sinner in our world is not that the saint does not sin but that despite his/her sins and weaknesses, s/he realizes that he/she is not a stranger to God and therefore, opens him/herself in his/her filth and dirt to God to be washed clean. The saint does not act like Adam, trying to hide from God. Unlike the saint, the sinner runs away from God, s/he does not want to confront his/her shame and vulnerability. So s/he travels farther away from God; farther into the darkness of the sinful world, walking away from the protective presence of God, like the prodigal son, leaving his home and inheritance to a foreign land (Lk. 15:11-32). But, then, he came to his senses and said himself, "I will leave this place and go back to my Father..." (Lk. 15:18). We too should summon the courage to say the same thing to ourselves and generate the will power to do the same as the prodigal son did (Lk. 15:19).[111]

The parable of the prodigal son, which is a model of repentance is full of meaning and virtually touches on every aspect of the Christian life. This is a parable that can be viewed from the perspectives of; (i) the younger son who was prodigal, (ii) the elder son who could not forgive, (iii) the father whose love and forgiveness could not be overstretched, (iv) the tax collectors and sinners who sought the company of Jesus, (v) the scribes and Pharisees who complained about the company of Jesus, and (vi) the open-ended nature of the parable, which leaves us to conclude whether the elder son joined the celebration or not.[112] Let us consider each of these briefly, not necessarily in the order I just outlined, to see what model of repentance we find in the prodigal son.

i. **Open-endedness of the parable:** Jesus leaves this parable open-ended without saying whether the elder son agreed to join in the celebration or not. It

111 Anselm K. Jimoh, *Pathways of Truth: Selected Talks of Rev. Fr. Anselm K. Jimoh to mark the 15th Anniversary of Ordination to the Priesthood. (December 3rd 1994 – December 3rd 2009)* (Benin-City: Amfitop Books, 2010), p. 4.

112 Anselm K. Jimoh, pp. 4-5.

simply passes across the message to us that it is our decision to join in the heavenly banquet or not. Salvation is an individual choice; no one is forced into the kingdom of God.

ii. **The complaining scribes and Pharisees:** This is better understood within the context of "the Company of Jesus." The company of Jesus refers to those notorious for what they do and who they are in the community. They are tax collectors, thieves, cheats, liars, and prostitutes, what business do such people have with Jesus? These set of persons found in Jesus, one who cares, who is ready to listen, and accept them as they are. The self-righteous ones, like the Pharisees and scribes would usually complain because they lack truth and sincerity. They want people to see them as righteous and law abiding as they strictly observe the letters of the law. Most importantly they do not understand, neither were they willing to be enlightened on who Jesus is and what his mission was. Their self-righteousness blinds them to the offer of salvation Jesus is making to all.

iii. **The younger son who was prodigal:** To be prodigal as the gospel of Luke presents it, is to be wasteful and thoughtless; to live recklessly and carelessly as if we hold the key to life. (i) The prodigal son was younger. Therefore, in his youthful exuberance he wants to be free. He does not want to be under the control of anybody; he wants to do things in his own way, he wants to be independent. He sought to be alone. (ii) The prodigal son was lazy and wants to live on the sweat of his father. (iii) The prodigal son was disrespectful and rude to his father because he asked for an inheritance he did not have a right to and which should come to him only after the passing of his father, the rightful owner of his wealth and benefactor of his heirs. (iv) The prodigal son rejected the father for material pleasure and satisfaction. (v) The prodigal son left his rightful home and place; he was not pushed out, he freely walked away on his own.

iv. **The elder son who could not forgive:** Like the Scribes and Pharisees who complained about the company of Jesus, so was the elder son. He could not forgive his younger brother. In fact, he was not ready to accept him as a brother anymore. (i) The elder son was full of resentment for the younger one. (ii) The elder son was comparing himself with the younger son. The question on his mind was 'why not me?'

v. **The father whose love and forgiveness cannot be over stretched:** Here is the father who is full of love and is able to forgive. (i) Forgiveness comes only from love. He offered his love equally to both sons. (ii) He reached out and responded to them in their own uniqueness, he never allowed their rivalry to affect him. In a world that is full of comparison, the father shows love that does not compare and contrast. (iii) The father calls for celebration for that is what life is about; the celebration of the love of God. It is unhealthy to compete and grade ourselves in the presence of God.[113]

The parable of the prodigal son is the great call to conversion by Jesus Christ. It is a call to move from belonging to the world to belonging to God. It is a call to be the younger son without being rebellious, to be the elder son without being resentful, and to be the father full of love and forgiveness. It calls on us to grow, for no father or mother ever becomes father or mother without having been a son or daughter, but every son and daughter has to consciously choose to step beyond their childhood and become

113 Anselm K. Jimoh, pp. 5-6.

father and mother for others. This is precisely what all true Christians are called to be; a father and a mother to others.[114]

God offers us reconciliation and calls us back to Himself. The response depends on us. We see the same offer and different responses to the offer in scripture. For instance, the offer to the woman caught in the act of sin (Jn. 8:3-11); the offer to the rich young man (Mt. 19:16-22; Mk 10:17-22; Lk. 18:18-23); the offer to Zacchaeus (Lk. 19:1-10) and the call of the disciples (Mt. 4:18-22, 9:9; Mk 2:14; Lk. 5:27-28). These are various offers and calls to repentance and we see two types of responses; (i) the positive response of the woman caught in the act of sin, Zacchaeus, and the disciples, and (ii) the negative response of the rich young man. Our response is our private business and God does not force it upon us.

---

114 Anselm K. Jimoh, pp. 6-7.

18

A Call to Repentance (II)

> Yet even now, says the Lord, return to me with your whole heart, with fasting and weeping, and mourning; rend your hearts, not your garments, and return to the Lord, your God. For gracious and merciful is he, slow to anger, rich in kindness, and relenting in punishment (Joel 2:12-13).

The passage from Joel on which this reflection is anchored contains three themes that go hand-in-hand. These themes are repentance, sincerity and discipleship. The passage calls us to *turn away from sin* (repent) not by verbal denial of sin but *sincerely* from our hearts and become a disciple of Christ (return to the Lord).

Joel's call to repentance is a call to conversion. It is a call to turn away from sin, a turn away from what offends God, a turn away from evil. It is equally an invitation to participate in the grace and mercy of God. This call is not novel to Joel as a prophet; it is a call that runs through the whole of scripture. Therefore, let us take an excursion through scripture and understand the call to repentance as the various prophets had put it and more importantly, as Jesus Christ himself had made the call.

In the book of 1 Sam. 12-13, the prophet Nathan went up to king David and asked him to be the judge over a case in which a certain rich man, who owns a lot of property and herds of flocks was in the same city with a certain poor man whose only property was a little ewe lamb that he had bought. This poor man liked the ewe so much that it was like a daughter to him. The rich man had a visitor, instead of taking from his own flocks and herds, he took the poor man's ewe lamb and prepared it as a meal for his visitor. David was filled with indignation and very furious. He pronounced the rich man guilty and asked that he makes restitution of the ewe lamb fourfold because he has been without pity for the poor man. Nathan told David, he (David) was the rich man. In that way the prophet Nathan confronted David with his sins. The prophet Nathan in this parable of the ewe lamb called David to repentance, a call that David immediately responded to. "I have sinned against the Lord," David said. Similarly, the prophet Jeremiah called the people of Judah to repentance by asking them to "Turn back, each of you, from your evil ways and from your evil deeds; then you shall remain in the land which the Lord gave you and your fathers, from of old forever" (Jer. 25:5).

The prophet Nathan proclaimed repentance as a prophetic doctrine in a rather thought-provoking manner to the adulterous King David (1Sam. 12-13). In a parable in which David was made to judge between right and wrong and prescribe punishment, Nathan called David to repentance. It was a call that he should turn from his evil deeds. David frankly confessed his sins and did penance. Nathan then, after declaring calamities that will befall the house of David ends his prophecy by announcing hope. Thus, the last word of God is hope for the repentant sinner. Jesus Christ echoes this same message in the Gospels. The call to repentance constitutes an essential part of Jeremiah's prophetic preaching (Jer. 25:3-6, especially v. 5). In simple terms, Jeremiah makes it clear that sin destroys and blocks favours from God, while avoidance and turning away from sin puts us in a vantage position to benefit from the favours of God.

The prophets Amos, Hosea and Isaiah, also denounced sin and called the Israelites to conversion. Amos who is fondly referred to as the prophet of justice was not content with calling his contemporaries to denounce sin, he insisted that they must seek God (Amos 5:4-6). This brings out what repentance entails. Repentance does not only require that we turn away from sin, but also that we turn to the Lord. When Amos called on his contemporaries to seek God, he implied that they should hate evil and love good (Amos 5:14f). In the same vein, Hosea called for a complete detachment from iniquity, which must come from within and which must be inspired by the love and knowledge of God (Hos. 6:1-6). Isaiah 1:16f says, "Wash yourselves! Purify yourselves! Take your wickedness away from my sight! Stop doing evil, learn to do good! Seek again the right way, help the oppressed, do justice toward the orphan!" And Eze. 18:31f says, "Cast far from you the transgressions that you have committed and make yourself a new heart and a new spirit. Why do you prefer to die, house of Israel? I do not desire the death of anyone! Be converted and you shall live."

The last of the prophets, John the Baptist, specifically and strongly too, called the house of Israel to repentance. "Repent, for the kingdom of heaven is at hand" (Mt. 3:2). Jesus Christ took up this same message of John the Baptist at the beginning of his public ministry. He made it clear that if he has come, he has come to call sinners to repentance (Lk. 5:32). And in the same words of John he preached, "Repent for the kingdom of heaven is at hand" (Mt. 4:17, Mk 1:15). The repentance that Christ calls us to is one that proceeds from humility, "Lord have mercy on me, I am a sinner" (Lk. 18:13). In calling for repentance, Jesus distrusted signs that were too showy (Mt. 6:16) and called for a change of heart that makes us become as little children. (Mt. 18:3). This means that we should regulate our lives according to the new law, which is to love God above all and to love one's neighbour as self (Jn. 13:34-35).

Repentance is an invitation to turn away from sin and enter into the kingdom. The evangelist Mark sums up the preaching of Jesus thus: "The time is fulfilled, and the kingdom of God has come near; repent, and believe in the good news" (Mk 1:15). This is an announcement of a divine act and a demand for a response from men and women.

What is repentance? In general terms, repentance means sorrow for sins and turning to God. It entails a conversion, which requires a change in intention or attitude. One can regret an action or evil deed; this does not necessarily translate as repentance because repentance means much more than regret. Judas' betrayal of Jesus makes my last point clear. Judas regretted his action but did not repent of it. Apart from turning away from sin, repentance involves also, turning to God and a new life.

Repentance is an invitation to change route, an invitation to retrace our steps. It is a call to turn away from what is bad and to turn towards God. It implies a change of conduct, a new orientation of the whole being. It essentially defines the idea of conversion. This is typically expressed in the Greek word, *metanoia*, which means a return to God through change in our practical conduct.

In the encounter between Jesus Christ and the paralytic at the pool of Bethzatha recorded in John 5:1-9, Jesus asked the sick man if he wants to be well again. It is rather surprising to ask a man who has been sick for thirty-eight years whether he wants to be well again. It is even more surprising when we consider the fact that this same sick man is by the side of the pool waiting for the water to be stirred so that he can go in. What is he going in to do? To get healing of course! And he is confronted with the question "do you want to be well again?"

It is however, possible that the sick man is now comfortable making money from alms that he gets from sympathisers that he may not wish to be well again. Becoming well again would mean that he loses that source of income. So he just sits there without putting genuine efforts into getting into the water before anyone else's when the water is stirred. Viewed from this angle, the question of Jesus begins to make sense and the element of surprise that one initially feels at the sound of the question begins to disappear.

In application to the call to repentance, we could ask this question again as; do you want to rise above your sin or you are already comfortable with it and want to remain there? We can become comfortable in our sinful ways and do not want to turn away from them. Such an attitude of being comfortable in sin can easily be noticed in the way we rationalise away some sinful actions. We rationalise what is sinful and what is not sinful. We become so accustomed to a sin that we now enjoy it and would not want to live above it. Very often, these are sexual sins and false acquisition of wealth. Some have claimed that because almost everyone is involved in fornication and adultery, it will no longer count as sinful in the sight of God, otherwise, almost everyone will be condemned.

The story of the barren fig tree in Lk. 13:6-9 shows God's patience with sinners. That God is seemingly not acting to destroy a sinful world today does not mean God has accepted our sinful ways of life. It is simply the graciousness of God that allows a sinner enough time and opportunity to change from his sinful ways. As the fig tree was given another opportunity to produce good fruit, so God continues to give us the chance to repent and be saved. If we do not take advantage of God's patience, we position ourselves to be damned.

19

Fraternal Love: The New Commandment[115]

Love is the central theme of the New Testament. Its importance is underlined when Jesus in his pre-passion discourse with his disciples specifically said, "Now I give you a new commandment: love one another ... by this everyone will know that you are my disciples, if you have love for one another" (Jn. 13:34-35). The act of love was practically displayed by Jesus prior to the issuance of this new commandment. He the Lord and Master, without clinging to his position as Lord and Master, did what only the lowest slaves do for their Jewish masters, for his disciples; he washed their feet. Why did he do it? According to him, "You call me Master and Lord, and you are right, for so I am. If I, then, your Lord and Master have washed your feet, you also must wash one another's feet. I have just given you an example that as I have done, you also may do" (Jn. 13:13-15). Thus, Jesus did not only give them a new commandment, he went the extra mile to teach his disciples how best to observe the commandment and very instructively, he made it clear to them that it is a command that is practicable; a commandment that our human and earthly positions and status do not exempt us from, but, in fact, our earthly status makes it imperative upon us to carry out.

Let us be a little more critical and detailed about the entire scenario so as to draw from its fullness the richness of this teaching. Jesus began by (i) getting up, (ii) removing his garment, (iii) taking a towel and wrapping it around his waist, (iv) pouring

115 Originally presented as a talk to the Knights and Ladies of St. John International, Benin Grand Commandery, on the occasion of their Grand Board of Trustees Meeting, at St. Paul's Minor Seminary, Airport Road, Benin-City in June, 2011.

water into a basin, washing, and (v) wiping the feet of his disciples.

'Getting up' was a conscious and deliberate effort that is best understood in the context of the story of the prodigal son (Lk. 15:11-32). The prodigal son said, "I will get up and go to my father..." (Lk. 15:18). He did not just wish to go to his father, neither did he just think about it, he decided and did it. The outcome was the reconciliation between him and his father. The reconciliation did not happen by chance, it was a deliberate and conscious action engineered by the prodigal son. In the same vein, the washing of the feet of his disciples was not a chance event, it was a deliberate and conscious action of Jesus. An action he used as an example for his disciples to follow. The meaning of this for us is that our love for one another should not be a product of chance, but some deliberate, conscious act of friendship towards one another.

Apart from getting up, Jesus properly and positively disposed himself with his next action – 'removing his garment.' By removing his garment, he shed himself of what could constitute an obstacle to what he wanted to do. The Jewish outer garment, which is what Jesus would most probably be wearing, is a long flowing garment which is often tied to the body at the waist with a girdle to enable the Jewish man walk freely. Such a garment will definitely not allow Jesus to bend down to wash the feet of his disciples. So, to effectively wash their feet, he needed to do away with the garment first, thus, he removed the garment. Jesus undid what will undo what he wanted to do. We can also view it as Jesus putting aside his Lordship and mastership so as to assume the position of the servant. Let us simplify this with the analogy of the father and husband of the house who wants to do the dishes. He will not go into the kitchen with his suit or *agbada*, he would most likely pull off these and put on a T-shirt and short. The point is, we need to put aside from our lives everything that will constitute obstacles to our practice of brotherly love. These may include our social and political position, our economic/financial status, our academic qualifications, etc. They can also include our personal pride, principles and policies, especially those that make us feel better and superior to others. If we do not put these aside, we cannot truly love one another in the sense Jesus has commanded us to. It is significant to note that the same verb used to describe Jesus removing his outer garment, is the same used in Jn. 10:12 to describe Jesus laying down his life for our salvation. As the Bible says, no greater love than this has anyone than to lay down his life for his friends (Jn. 15:13). This is the same kind of sacrificial love that Jesus asks us to show to one another as his followers.

Going back to the analogy of the father and husband who want to do the dishes, when he gets into the kitchen, he most likely will put on the apron and wear the plastic gloves for doing the dishes, as the case may be. This was precisely what Jesus did. After removing his garment, 'taking a towel and wrapping it around his waist and pouring water into a basin,' he armed himself with the basic necessities required to do what he wanted to do. It is insightful to note that it is not enough to do away with obstacles that would obstruct our carrying out the command to love one another, we must equip ourselves with the requisite attitude and disposition to love one another.

Why has Jesus referred to the command to love as a new commandment? Is it really a new commandment as in something that has never been mentioned before? Just in case, the answer to the latter question is affirmative, why a new commandment? Are the Ten Commandments outdated or needed to be revised or perhaps a new one needed to be added to make them eleven? What is really new in the new commandment? In the light of Mt. 22:37, where Jesus stated that the greatest commandment is love and went on to say in the next verse (38) that the entire law and prophets rest on this commandment, we understand that the command to love is not a new commandment as such, perhaps a new approach to the Ten Commandments.

Most of the Ten Commandments were expressed in terms of what we should not do but Jesus re-expressed them positively in terms of what we should do. This brings out the emphasis that it is not enough to avoid doing what is wrong; we should in fact do what is right. So it is not what we did not do that matters, but what we have done. Common sense in fact shows that what we did not do does not necessarily translate as what we have done, but what we have done necessarily eliminates what we did not do.

The foregoing analysis allows us to consider what Jesus did by wrapping the towel around his waist as what he has done to practice love. He did not only remove the obstacle of the garment, he now armed/equipped himself with the tools for what he wanted to do. Therefore, when we cast off the obstacles to love in our lives, we need to equip ourselves with the necessary tools to practice love. What are the tools for love? There is in fact, a single tool for love, which is the Christian heart that sees all others as our brothers and sisters; creatures of the same one God almighty who has made us in his image and likeness (Gen. 1:26-27), irrespective of our various physical looks and social, economic and political status and differences in this world.

Lastly, Jesus ensued that he completed what he started even when some obstructions in the form of the objection of Simon Peter came up. Peter's complain would not deter Jesus to follow through and complete what he had started. As the Bible says, "No one who lays his hands on the plough and looks back is worthy of the kingdom of God" (Lk. 9:62). Jesus had to do what he had to do; no distractions like that of Simon Peter would stop him. After washing the feet of his disciples, and wiping them with the towel, he explained to them what he has done. It is significant to note that from start to finish, Jesus did not ask for the assistance of any of his disciples. He could easily have asked one of them to bring the water and another to wipe the feet after the washing, but the burden of loving your neighbour can never be too much for any one person to bear. He did it all by himself and at the end the message was simple, direct, and very clear; "I have given you an example to follow."

When does love become fraternal or what is fraternal? Fraternal simply means comradeship; something relating to brothers. Fraternal is doing that which is suitable to a brother or that which is brotherly. The term comes from fraternity which is a company of people who regard each other as equals with the same interest.

The call for fraternal love is not new; we find it also in the Old Testament especially the books of the Law. The Christian human history opens with the jealousy and hatred between two brothers; Cain and Abel that eventually led to murder (Gen. 4:1-8). The relationship between Jacob and Esau was one of deep love despite the issues between them (Gen. 33:3-4). We can also talk about the relationships between Ephraim and Manasseh, between Moses and Aaron, Joseph and his brothers, but by far the most compelling lesson in the Old Testament on fraternal love is the relationship between David and Jonathan, which is lucidly described in First book of Samuel, chapters 1-15.[116] It is a moving story of two men each in-line for the kingship succession in Israel. They could have hated each other, they could have murdered each other, as is common practice among many Nigerians today, but they both rose above politics, family succession, reality, motives and aspirations that we experience everyday around us. They overcame their self-interest, hatred, jealousy and ego. Jonathan subjugated himself to help establish the Davidic line of kingship from which the Saviour of the world was to be born. While Cain chose to kill Abel so that he will be, Jonathan chose to give way so that David will be (I Sam.18:4ff). From Cain and Abel to David and Jonathan, we see two patterns of brotherly relationships; we see the absence of fraternity in one and the presence of fraternity in the other.

Fraternal love is an imperative not just to foster the bond between brothers and sisters but also a requirement that helps us fulfil our responsibility as light of the world. We have our differences on various issues, society, politics, personal wealth, social affiliations, tribe, etc. which have stratified and divided us, yet it has pleased God to bring us together as brothers and sisters. We owe each other and we owe God to ensure that this design of His does not break down because of our personal and selfish interest. Fraternal love among us is a collective responsibility.

---

116 You can also find a simple but wonderful analysis of the relationship between David and Jonathan in John Segun Odeyemi, *Friendship: Dating, Courtship, and Engagement, A Hand Book for Young Catholics* (Iperu Remo: The Ambassador Publications, 2010), pp. 21-22.

20

The Vocation to the Catholic Priesthood[117]

What is a vocation? I do not intend to define vocation but to generally reflect on what we call a vocation in relation to our desire to become catholic priests and religious. Every vocation is about serving others in a particular way or form. Serving others is the secret of happiness. It is holiness.

To discern and accept one's vocation is like building a pyramid. It has to be constructed from the bottom, which I refer to here as the primary vocation. One cannot accept a secondary vocation, which is a particular vocation or call to do or serve in a particular form of state of being, without first accepting the primary vocation, which constitute the foundation and the framework within which the secondary vocation is built. Our primary vocation is to be Christians; followers of Christ. We are a people who are dedicated and committed to serving God by the moral and spiritual injunctions we find in the scriptures as interpreted by the Catholic Church. Therefore, to become priests and religious is a secondary vocation that has its root in our primary Christian vocation.

We can easily identify certain characteristics that constitute the first indication that we indeed have a vocation to the priesthood or religious life. These characteristics include:

i. The vocation must be pre-determined or pre-destined by God.
ii. It must involve a permanent commitment on our part.

117 A Sharing with the Aspirants to the Catholic Priesthood and Religious Life at the Auchi Diocesan Vocations Rally for 2008.

iii. It must involve willingness to sacrifice oneself for God and others.
iv. It must be recognised by the Church as a vocation.
v. It must have the singular purpose of helping others and oneself towards God and heaven.

The absence of these characteristics would cast a shadow of doubt on our claim to a vocation to the priesthood or religious life. If we seek to be priests or religious because it provides us an easy means of employment in a situation where the rate of unemployment is very high, we cannot say we have an authentic vocation to the priesthood or religious life. Likewise, when we want to be priests or religious because of the desire to be placed on a higher pedestal in the society, get easy recognition in the circle of power, accorded respect by the low and mighty in the society and accumulate wealth easily. These negate the idea of self-sacrifice and the purpose of getting closer to God and moving towards heaven. The Church does not recognise such motives or characteristics as indicative of a vocation to the priesthood or religious life. And with such motives, we cannot truly talk about a permanent commitment.

Generally, there are four options of vocation for every true Catholic; namely, (i) Marriage, (ii) Holy Orders, (iii) Religious Life, and (iv) Generous Single Life in Christ. Every Catholic has a choice about which of these ways of life to live out his/her faith. In making our choice, it is important to seek the will of God for the absolutely best vocation for any person is the will of God for the person. We, therefore, have to discern our vocation properly. When we do this, we have to be conscious of the advice of St. Ignatius of Loyola that we pray with a "holy indifference." By this he means that we should not pray to be this or that, but to ask God to reveal to us what he wants us to do and be. St. Augustine puts it lucidly when he asked us not to pray to inform God but to pray to conform to the will of God.

Vocation to the priesthood and religious life, which is our concern here, is not primarily about self-fulfilment. It is about being the instrument of God in saving the lives of others for the kingdom of heaven. The story of Jonah in the scripture buttresses this point. The four chapters of the book of Jonah talk about the call of Jonah to go and preach repentance to the people of Nineveh. His initial reaction was to turn away because he does not like pagans and does not see why God should be concerned about them, let alone be interested in saving them. Eventually he went and Nineveh, with a population of over one hundred and twenty thousand people, was saved. Jonah was not pleased with this, but God made him realize that he had no right to be angry at his graciousness and mercy towards the Ninevites.

The primary morale for bringing out this story is to help us appreciate the fact that the ministry of the priesthood and religious life is towards the salvation of souls. God saves a lot of people through the ministry of the average diocesan priest. The purpose of the priest is to bring people to Jesus and bring Jesus to people. It is therefore, a powerful vocation, which influences many souls towards God.

Above, we talked about the characteristics of an authentic vocation to the priesthood and religious life. It would be helpful to outline here the signs of a vocation. But just before then, it is important to quickly mention that God does not always call the best to be priest, but God expects the best from those He has called and chosen. The story of the call of Gideon and the victory God gave him over the Midianites as narrated in the book of Judges 6-7 exemplifies this. If God calls you He has the power to qualify you to be what He has called you to be, even if you think you are not qualified. But you have to make yourself available for God to use you as He wants. In other words, allow yourself to be directed by the spirit of God and not by your own self thought-out ways or relying on your intelligence alone. In this wise, we can begin to identify certain signs that must be associated with a vocation to the priesthood and religious life.

i. A candidate for the priesthood must show undivided love for Christ and genuinely thirst to bring the teaching of Christ to the world. He must strive to have a real and personal relationship with Jesus. No one can be a priest if he does not love Jesus.

ii. The candidate for the priesthood must be a believing and practicing Catholic. One who regularly attends Masses on Sundays and weekdays. He must believe in regular use of the sacrament of reconciliation, that is, go to confession regularly. He must believe in the Eucharist and develop a deep and loving relationship with the Blessed Virgin Mary. He must study the teachings of the Church. He must respect and pray for the Holy Father. He must be attracted to things that are Catholic. These are what constitute being a believing and practicing Catholic.

iii. A candidate for the Catholic priesthood must strive to live a life of prayer. A priest, above all else, is a man of prayer. He should like to spend time with God in prayer and be comfortable even when the prayer is getting long.

iv. A candidate for the priesthood must live and desire to live a life of service. The life of service is expressed in the corporal and spiritual works of mercy. Service is seen in concrete works of charity that naturally springs from prayer. Service makes us become more like Christ. Therefore, a candidate who spends his day watching television and playing video games is not ready to begin his seminary training. A priest is called to serve others and not to be served by others.

v. A candidate for the priesthood must truly desire to be a priest and not one who is living out the desire of his parents to have a priest in the family. One who will eventually be a priest must be attracted to doing what a priest does and become who a priest is. This desire comes and goes in many people, but it never goes away from a good candidate for the priesthood. Note that this is not an intellectual appreciation of the priesthood, it is not admiration for the priesthood; a genuine desire that makes him fantasize celebrating Mass, hearing confession, and preaching homilies. This genuine desire separates those called by God from those who call themselves or are called by others.

vi. The candidate for the priesthood must have his call validated by others and scripture. By this, I mean people should be able to say of him that this young man will make a good priest just by seeing the way and manner he conducts himself. The things the scripture says about the priesthood should also be observable in his way of life.

vii. A candidate for the priesthood should be seen to make efforts towards living a life of virtues. He must be conscious of sins and be bothered by them. He must exhibit complete honesty, truthfulness, self-control and make committed efforts to be chaste. He must be courteous, responsible, and dependable.

viii. A candidate for the priesthood should have good human relations skills. According to *Pastores Dabo Vobis*, no. 43, "... a priest should become a bridge and not an obstacle for others in their meeting with Christ." Good human formation is a necessary criterion for today's priests. He must be able to converse well with others, make friends easily, and be hospitable and approachable. These are characters shaped by one's personality, family, and social relationships while growing up.

ix. A candidate for the priesthood must be intellectually mature. If a priest is not able to speak intelligently about many subjects, he will not be respected when he speaks from the pulpit about Christ and how to live the gospel in the modern world. No priest however, should assume that he is the smartest or most educated person in the Church, nor assume that people will or should accept everything he says as law.

x. A candidate for the priesthood must be physically, emotionally, and psychologically stable. The work involved in living the life of a priest is very hard and as such the priest needs the physical strength and psychological balance to do this every day.

xi. A candidate for the priesthood should be joyful, with a good sense of humour. It is definitely difficult and frustrating dealing with fallen human nature and as such priests must have a sense of humour. This enables the priest to laugh both at himself and with others when he deals with the sad realities of sin and death. According to Mother Theresa, "Joy is a net of love by which we can catch souls for God." The gospel is the good news and should be proclaimed with joy and happiness. As Pope Benedict XVI puts it, "The greatest poverty in the world is the inability to live our lives with joy."

xii. A candidate for the priesthood must have the heart of a priest. The heart of a priest is modelled after the Sacred Heart of Jesus. The Sacred Heart of Jesus is full of kindness and compassion for others like the Good Shepherd (Mk. 6:34). It means then that the heart of a candidate for the priesthood, like that of a priest, should always be ready and willing to sacrifice. You detect the kind of heart someone has by the way he reacts to others or speaks to others. The heart of a priest or a priestly heart is one of the best indicators for a vocation for the right reasons.

xiii. A candidate for the priesthood must have self-mastery. People expect a lot from the priest and they do have a right to expect as much as they do. In meeting up with the expectations of the people the self-mastery of the priest makes a lot of difference. The story is told of St. Clement Marie Hofbauer, the Patron Saint of Vienna. He started orphanages to take care of children on the street. He sustained these orphanages by begging for money to buy food for the children. On this particular day, he went into a place where some hooligans were drinking and playing cards. He begged for some money for the orphans and one of the hooligans abused him and spat right into his face.

St. Clement took out his handkerchief calmly, wiped his face and said, "That was for me. Now may I please have something for my orphans?" This attitude made them nervous not knowing how to respond to this self-mastery, never before had they seen such self-control. One of the hooligans laughed out loudly, grabbed the heap of money for gambling on the table and gave it to the priest, St. Clement. St. Clement won the day and the money for the orphans with his self-mastery and self-control.[118] Self-mastery entails that the priest maintains good impulse control of anger and emotions. He must be in control of what he says and how he says it. He must be conscious of the sensitivity of the people. He must be able to wake up on time, keep scheduled appointments, and do the things expected of him at the appropriate times.

xiv. A candidate for the priesthood must have a stable lifestyle. Priesthood is a lifetime commitment, a commitment that makes the priest do whatever the authority of the Church as it resides in his Bishop and superior requires of him. The Church needs priests who will go where they are assigned and remain there, taking care of God's people entrusted to their care. The people of God need pastors, shepherds, Fathers, who will be dependable, loving, strong, and present. Priests should do what they need to do according to the mind of the Church as they had promised on the day of their priestly ordination, not just what they want to do.

xv. A candidate for the priesthood must be a Christian gentleman. He must have a certain degree of social polish, excellent table manners, and neat appearance. He must be appropriately dressed at all times; he does not have to be lavish as to attract undue attention to himself. He must exercise courtesy and patience in dealing with others,

---

118 Lawrence G. Lovasik, *Treasury of Catechism Stories,* (Pittsburgh, PA: Marian Action Publications, 1966), s. 118.

speak correct grammar and must respect appropriate boundaries with men and women.

xvi. A candidate for the priesthood must be able to accept both success and failure peacefully and humbly. Failures and successes are part of our endeavours in life. We cannot always win and failure is not a permanent state, it applies to individual situations and cases, which come and go. Calmness and humble acceptance of the result of our activities be it failure or success, is an advantage for the candidate for the priesthood.[119]

These indicators of authentic vocation to the Catholic priesthood, which are drawn from what is expected of a committed priest are issues for thought in the process of discerning your vocation. It is always easy to want to fit ourselves into what we wish to be and pretend to be that most times. However, deep within ourselves, we know what we are and who we are. Discerning our authentic vocation would require that we are true to ourselves. These indicators are virtues we can also develop if we work honestly towards them.[120]

---

119 Brentt A. Brannen, *To Save a Thousand Souls: A Guide for Discerning a Vocation to Diocesan Priesthood*, (Valdosta, Georgia: Vianney Vocations LLC, 2010), pp. 77-104.

120 This entire discussion is largely drawn from Brentt A. Brannen, Chapters 1-5.

21

The Petrine Primacy: The Papacy[121]

Peter exercised primacy within the community or the Church, which has become noted for her unity, holiness and apostolicity. The Petrine primacy has central importance in the Catholic tradition. It is the belief that the Pope, who occupies the 'chair of Peter,' is the visible head of the whole Church on earth and he is infallible when he speaks solemnly in matters of faith and morals. This role was directly entrusted to Peter and his successors by Jesus when he (Jesus) promised, "I will give you the keys of the kingdom of heaven; whatever you bind on earth will be bound in heaven; whatever you loose on earth will be loosed in heaven" (Mt. 16:19).

Some other classic texts that affirm the Petrine primacy are Lk. 22:31-32, "Simon, Simon! Look, Satan has got his wish to sift you like wheat; but I have prayed for you, Simon, that your faith may not fail, and once you have recovered, you in your turn must strengthen your brothers" and Jn. 21:15-19, where Jesus asked Peter if he loved him thrice and upon Peter's affirmation that he does, handed him the responsibility to feed and care for his lambs and sheep. These passages suggest that Christ expected a more faithful love from Peter than the other disciples and on this basis, Christ appointed Peter and Peter alone to shepherd his (Christ's) flock. Whichever way we choose to interpret this passage, the fact would always remain that we cannot escape the impression that the whole body of the early Christians knew that Simon Peter bore a special relation to the stability of the Church. This unique

121 Originally published in *The Promise Newspaper*, a monthly publication of the Catholic Diocese of Auchi.

position of Simon Peter was derived from the express declaration of our Lord.

We recall that at creation God shared with humankind His immortality by endowing us with an immortal soul. God also shared with us His dominion over created things by mandating us to "subdue" the earth. (Gen. 1 and 2). In the same vein, Jesus mandates Peter to take charge of his faithful, members of his community or Church, as he hands Peter "the keys of the kingdom of heaven." It is significant to note here that the symbolic use of the "keys" dates back to ancient times. Keys in ancient times and in fact, till date, symbolize authority and power. The person who holds the keys reserves the right of entrance into the house. Such a person determines who enters and who does not enter. It is this right and prerogative that Jesus conferred on Peter. This is a prerogative that *ipso facto* makes him the head of the apostolic group and therefore, the head of the Church. This role is exercised today by the Holy Father, the Pope, who is the successor of Peter.

As a matter of correct expression, the reference to Peter as the successor of Jesus Christ by some writers and persons is wrong. Peter was the Vicar of Christ, the visible head of the visible Church on earth. The position of Jesus Christ is not an office and his death; the sacrifice on the cross, is perfect, once and for all. He does not need a successor. He appointed Peter not as a successor but as a visible head of a community for which he is in fact, the head. Therefore, while it is correct to call one Holy Father the successor of another, neither Peter, the first Pope and Holy Father nor any occupant of his chair can be correctly referred to as the successor of Christ.

In what seems like an emphasis on the exercise of the authority of 'the key' Jesus told Peter, "whatever you bind on earth will be bound in heaven; whatever you loose on earth will be loosed in heaven." The use of the terms "bind" and "loose" is very significant as both terms belong to the technical vocabulary of the rabbinic tradition – the technical language of the teachers of the law. Primarily, "bind" and "loose" in the rabbinic tradition have disciplinary connotation. To bind is to be found guilty and consequently condemned. To loose is to be acquitted or absolved of an offence. Secondarily, the use of both terms is linked to doctrinal decisions. When an opinion is forbidden, it is bound and when it is allowed, it is loosed. Certainly, Jesus who amazed the doctors of the law and all who heard him answer questions from the doctors of the law at the tender age of twelve years (Lk. 2:46-47) is aware of the implication and technical meaning of his choice of terms. Thus, we may comfortably submit that Jesus meant that Peter, whom he has made controller of God's household, as the keys symbolize in Is. 22:22, exercises the disciplinary power of admitting or excluding, as the case may be, those he thinks fit and unfit respectively. As Peter administers the Church, he is also to make doctrinal decisions as necessity calls for it. God in Heaven will ratify his pronouncements.

The profile of Peter after Christ's ascension clearly shows how he exercised the powers of "the keys" and affirmed his primacy among the apostles and his leadership of God's household, the Church of Christ. Scripture presents a new and confident post-ascension Peter, a Peter who is aware of his enormous responsibility of feeding the entire flock of the Son of God. A Peter, who sets out to discharge his responsibilities with courage and wisdom. He started by proposing the election of another to take the place of Judas Iscariot (Acts 1:21-26). With the advent of the Holy Spirit at Pentecost, he preached the first sermon that saw over three thousand people convert from Judaism to christianity and he admitted them into the fold (Acts 2: 14-41). He did the same with pagan converts in Acts 10:48. Apart from working the first miracle by the apostles, of making the man lame from birth to walk (Acts 3: 6-8), he meted out the first punishment of which Ananias and his wife Sapphira were victims (Acts 5:1-6). Peter was also the one who cast out the heretic Simon Magus who wanted to buy the powers of the Apostles (Acts 8:19-20). As an elder, he addressed other elders (1 Pet. 5:1) and he corrected others for doctrinal misunderstanding (2 Pet. 3:15-16).

Most important of all was Peter's role in the first council of the Church, the council of Jerusalem. After a long debate as regards upholding circumcision as God demanded in his covenant with Abraham (Gen. 17:10-11) with regards to Gentile converts or not,

Peter spoke and recognizing the efficacy of his powers to bind and loose, freely chose to exercise his powers as he declared that salvation is by the grace of the Lord Jesus and not by circumcision (Acts 15:7-11). We may argue that it was a collective decision, yes, indeed it was, but the onus was on Peter to voice it. Was Peter being contemptuous of God's covenant with Abraham, our father in faith? No, he was not. He only exercised his moral and legal authority to make doctrinal and juridical decisions as it will benefit and lead the community of Christ to her ultimate goal, which is the salvation of the human person.[122]

The Evangelists recognized and acknowledged the primacy and authority of Peter as they always put his name first any time they make a list of the apostles. Yet the fact remains that Peter was not the first apostle to be called by Jesus. This fact they also know.

Perhaps, we may want to ask whether the powers conferred on Peter are personal to him and as such end with him and his office as chief shepherd? Or are they also applicable to his successors? The simple answer is to be found in the fact that Christ did not intend his Church to die with Peter neither did he intend his Church to be a fold of sheep without a shepherd at any point in history. Therefore, the rank, dignity, and powers of Peter are to be handed on to his successors. And so, the Pope, who is the successor of Peter remains the Head of the Holy Roman Catholic and Apostolic Church. After Peter, we had St. Linus who reigned as Pope between 67 and 79 AD and after him was Pope Anacletus. The succession has continued unbroken till date with Pope Francis presently occupying the Chair of Peter as the two hundred and sixty-third (263rd) Pope.

122 Canon 1752.

22

The Six Commandments (Precepts) of the Church[123]

The church desires that her members be true and authentic Christians by living up to the expectation of Christ. In other words, Catholic Christians are expected to live lives worthy of the call of Christ. As part of the measures to help and enable Catholics to be true Christians, the Church proffered six laws/precepts, which are often described as "the six commandments of the Church." The Church extols and impresses on all Catholics to adhere to these precepts. These precepts do not replace the Ten Commandments of God, neither do they compete with them nor deplete them. I want to emphasize that the Ten Commandments of God are unchangeable and not subject to human alteration or that of the Church. They are divine and the Church only interprets and explains them. Whereas, the precepts of the Church, which this article aims to explain, are guidelines for Christians to assist and enable them adhere and keep the Ten Commandments. Since they were instituted by the Church, the Church can always amend or even alter them.

In the "Penny Catechism," question 229 asked: "What are the chief commandments of the church?"[124] Note that this question and questions 247 and 248, which deal with the precepts of the church, were revised in 1978. Perhaps this explains why the new Catechism of the Catholic Church (CCC) dropped the term

123 First published in *The Promise Newspaper*, a monthly publication of the Catholic Diocese of Auchi.

124 *A Catechism of Christian Doctrine*, Revised Edition, (London: Catholic Truth Society, 1971), ques. 229.

"commandments" in preference for "precepts."[125] As in the revised edition of the Penny Catechism the precept on the contribution to the support of your pastor is not listed but referred to in the text. These precepts of the Church are:

i. To keep the Sundays and holy days of obligation, holy, by attending Mass and resting from servile works.
ii. To keep the days of fasting and abstinence appointed by the church.
iii. To go to confession at least once a year.
iv. To receive the Blessed Sacrament at least once a year, and that at Easter or thereabouts.
v. To contribute to the support of our pastors.
vi. Not to marry within certain degrees of kindred.

Observation shows that many Catholics are not aware of these precepts, let alone make efforts to keep them. They perhaps know there are certain precepts of the Church, but cannot even list them, not to talk about practice them. Catechumens are taught to memorise these precepts and no sooner have they received the sacraments than they forget the precepts. Even at the time they memorize the precepts they cannot explain them as they are never taught the meaning of some of the operative terms in which the precepts are couched.

The first precept obliges us to keep Sundays holy as a day set aside to serve the Lord. To aid us in dedicating Sundays to the Lord, we are to attend Mass[126] and avoid any strenuous work that would divert our attention from God. This is precisely what "servile works" refer to; any work that brings material benefits. This requires some clarifications to avoid a blind and false interpretation. Such essential services provided by health care workers, social services or humanitarian workers, as well as transporters are not necessarily included here. Thus, a nurse on duty, or a doctor on call, a transporter expected to convey a group to certain destination on a particular mission on a day that

125 *Catechism of the Catholic Church*, nos. 2041-2043.
126 *The Catechism of the Catholic Church*, no. 1389.

unavoidably falls on Sunday or a holy day of obligation may not be bound by this precept. Those who are seriously sick and those saddled with the responsibility of taking care of them are equally exempt from this precept. Therefore, it is not every time one fails to attend Mass on a Sunday or holy day of obligation that he/she has sinned. However, such excuses like; travelling, the Catholic Church was not close by, I did not know where the Catholic Church was in the area as I was a visitor there, I was attending to my relations who came home for a burial, etc. are definitely not good reasons to skip Sunday Mass. This precept also binds parents, guardians and masters, to allow all in their charge to attend Mass on Sundays. There are known cases where masters go to church and ask their wards to stay at home or go to the market or do other things that would not allow them attend Mass that Sunday. Holy days of obligation are days that should be treated as Sundays. These are days of solemnities that may not necessarily fall on a Sunday. Some of such solemnities include; Assumption, the feast of All Saints, and others as stated in the Roman calendar.

The second precept binds all Catholics to keep the days of fasting and abstinence appointed by the Church. These days are; Ash Wednesday, which marks the beginning of the Lenten season and Good Friday, the day Jesus Christ was crucified. Apart from these days, the Church encourages all the faithful to periodically practice abstinence and fasting, especially during the Lenten season and all Fridays of the year.[127] This is to help the faithful develop self-control, discipline and the mastery over the desires of the flesh, which more often than not disposes us to sin.

We have all sinned and fallen short of God's glory (Rom. 3:23). But God, like the father of the prodigal son, is always willing and happy to welcome us back, so we are called to turn away from sin and do penance. Fasting and abstinence are aspects of penance. The Church encourages us to practice them so as to cultivate the good habit of self-discipline that puts our inordinate appetite under check. Fasting and abstinence is recommended for

---

127 *The Catechism of the Catholic Church*, no. 1438. Also see *Sacrosantum Concilium*, nos.109-110.

the physically healthy and those who are within the age bracket of 15 to 65 years old. Those who are sick and are under-aged are not bound by this as it may do them more harm than good.

Fasting and abstinence is not about food and drink alone, but more so about such things that can easily lure us away from God and deceitfully put us on the path of sin. Fasting and abstinence can take the form of suspending our favourite television programme, social entertainment, limiting the consumption of our favourite meal, etc. All these help us to master our instincts and freedom of heart.[128]

The third precept obliges the faithful to go to confession at least once a year. Once a year confession is the barest minimum, otherwise, confession should be a very regular practice for any good Christian. Unfortunately, for various reasons which we cannot discuss within the present scope, it is one of the least utilised sacraments. In most parishes, the number of penitents at weekly confession is ridiculously small compared to the number of communicants on Sundays. I wonder at times if people no longer sin. As the latter is definitely not the case, it is most likely the case then that the faithful do not find it necessary to go to confession. Many wait for Easter to keep the once a year obligatory confession.

Every good Christian is encouraged to go to confession as often as he/she falls into serious sin. Serious sin refers to what we generally call "mortal" sin; a term that has been replaced with "grievous" or "serious" in more recent Church terminology. A serious or grave sin destroys the sanctifying grace of God in us. "Confession is to accuse ourselves of our sins to a priest approved by the Bishop."[129] It is a humble act of asking God's forgiveness that avail us of the forgiving grace of God and the restoration of God's sanctifying grace in our lives. Many Catholics are deceived today by the Protestant and Pentecostal claim that we do not need sacramental confession but we can, on our own, ask God's forgiveness without confessing to a priest.

---

128 *The Catechism of the Catholic Church*, no. 2043.

129 *A Catechism of Christian Doctrine*, Q. 295, p. 51.

Although this possibility is not completely ruled out in certain cases or situations, it is out-rightly mistaken and blatantly untrue that we do not need the priest for the forgiveness of sin. This is not an attempt to glorify the priesthood because I am a priest, the priesthood is already an honoured way of life as the Bible says, "no one takes this honour upon himself ..." (Heb. 5:4). To concede to the Protestant and Pentecostal claim is to allow the evil one play on our sense of human pride against the humility required for the sense of remorse to say sorry to God for our sins.

The act of confession is outwardly an action between a person and another person but one of the two persons is a mediator between God and other persons. So it is indeed an act between a person and God. Remember that the priest is taken from among men to act as a mediator between God and man (Heb. 5:1). Christ has entrusted to the Church the powers to bind and loose, the powers to forgive and retain sins. (Mt. 16:19, 18:18, Jn. 20:23). The Church exercises this power through the ministry of her priests who are ministers of God as empowered by the Church.

Regular confession does not only restore us to the grace of God but it also strengthens us against sin and continually keeps us mindful of the dangers of the temptations around us. It is an observed fact that most of the leaders among the lay faithful avoid confession with the general attitude that it is not meant for them but for the "floor members" of the parish. You hardly see many of the Laity Council executives and heads of societies in the queue for confessions, except, maybe at Easter confessions. This is not a proper thing on their part as it is not leadership by example.

The fourth precept obliges the faithful to receive communion at least once a year and that at Easter or thereabout. I must commend the fact that many Catholics make efforts to receive communion regularly. However, I cannot say for sure if all such reception of the Eucharist is genuinely motivated or just a public show. There is no law that actually says all Catholics cannot be communicants. So, that many Catholics are communicants do not make it enough, others who are yet to be communicants should make the efforts to become communicants.

Communion, which is the same as the Holy Eucharist, is the true body and blood of Jesus Christ, with his soul and divinity, in the appearances of bread and wine.[130] It is meant for the nourishment of the soul as it is the food of the soul. Frequent and regular reception of communion in a state of grace makes our spiritual life robust and strengthens us against sin and negative spiritual forces. We are encouraged nowadays to celebrate reconciliation frequently and receive Holy Communion often to keep us close to God in order to ensure our salvation.

The Church particularly emphasises Easter or thereabout because it is the period when we celebrate the greatest feast of Christianity, namely, the resurrection of Christ. This marks the victory of good over evil, light over darkness, virtue over vice, the crown over the cross, Jesus over Satan, and heaven over hell.

The fifth precept states that the lay faithful should contribute to the support of their pastors. Pastors here refer to the priests in charge of parishes or Mass centres. In recent times, this precept is not stated as autonomous but as an addendum. The CCC added it as an appendage to the precepts thus; "the faithful also have the duty of providing for the material needs of the Church, each according to his abilities."[131] While it is not on the list of the chief commandments of the Church in the 1971 edition of the Penny Catechism,[132] it appears as the answer to question 245, "What is the fifth commandment of the Church? The fifth commandment of the Church is 'To contribute to the support of our pastors.'[133] The answer to the following question, "Is it a duty to contribute to the support of religion?" states that, "It is a duty to contribute to the support of religion according to our means, so that God may be duly honoured and worshipped, and the kingdom of his Church extended."[134]

The obvious impression this gives is that the contribution mentioned by this precept is not to the person of the pastor or

---

130 *A Catechism of Christian Doctrine*, ques. 266, p. 45.
131 *The Catechism of the Catholic Church*, no. 2043, # 3.
132 *A Catechism of Christian Doctrine*, ques. 229, p. 39.
133 *A Catechism of Christian Doctrine*, ques. 245, p. 42.
134 *A Catechism of Christian Doctrine*, ques. 246.

Priest in charge, but for the work he does in the enhancement and building of the kingdom of God in his place of parochial assignment, like, the parish or Mass centre. Therefore, the contribution is not for the priest to buy a new car, change his wardrobe, acquire a new set of electronics, or take care of his family members. It is for him to advance the faith of the people in his charge and attend to the pastoral, liturgical and social needs of the parish and parishioners. May I quickly add that the welfare of the priest is part and parcel of the pastoral need of the parish. A hungry priest, a sad priest and/or a sick priest, cannot minister as he himself will stand in need of being ministered to.

What, however, should not be encouraged is the luxurious and lavish lifestyle of God's ministers, especially from the purse of the parish. Even from the personal purse of the priest, given that he has a personal purse that can accommodate such a lifestyle. This negates the injunction of Christ in Mt. 10:9-10, Lk. 10:7, where Christ directly counsels his apostles against luxurious and outlandish lifestyle.

Parishioners are not to steal to contribute hugely to the growth of the kingdom. They are all to contribute honestly, sincerely and generously according to their means. Such contributions are to be judiciously and wisely utilized for the growth of the kingdom of God under existing Church and diocesan guidelines as approved by the Local Ordinary, the Bishop. This is to be coordinated or supervised by the priest in whose charge or area of jurisdiction the contribution is meant to be utilised.

The last but not the least precept demands that a good Catholic does not marry within certain degrees of kindred. This deals with the very vast and complicated subject of marriage. It forbids that people with very close blood ties be allowed to marry. Such closeness should at least exceed the third degree of consanguinity. This is not a real problem in Nigeria as most, if not all cultures in Nigeria already forbid such. Notwithstanding, limits still have to be specified just in case a situation arises which such restriction does not exist.

This precept encourages all Catholic laymen and women to marry in the Church and raise the offspring of such marriages as good Catholic children. This is one area where there are so many questions to be asked, especially with the very recent and rampart trend of mixed marriages. Mixed marriage is not a new thing in the Catholic Church, but it has assumed a new dimension in recent times. The new trend seems to be one sided. It is most times always the Catholic girl getting married to the Pentecostal young man. I do not want to delve into this beyond expressing my serious suspicion that something seems not right with this new and common trend.

Apparently, these precepts of the Church do not contradict in anyway the commandments of God. They actually guide the Catholic faithful to follow and keep the commandments of God and practically live out their Christian call to the glory of God and the good and growth of the Church here on earth. It will be helpful in the practice of our faith if Catholics familiarize themselves with these precepts and allow their spiritual, moral, pastoral and social life be guided by them.

23

Pentecost and Speaking in Tongues[135]

> When the day of Pentecost came, they were all together in one place. And suddenly out of the sky came a sound like a strong rushing wind and it filled the whole house where they were sitting. There appeared tongues as if of fire which parted and came to rest upon each one of them. All were filled with Holy Spirit and began to speak other languages as the Spirit enabled them to speak (Acts 2:1-4).

Pentecost was one of the greatest feasts of the Jewish calendar originally associated with agriculture. In the latter centuries of the Old Testament, it was celebrated as the giving of the Law to Moses on Mount Sinai. On account of this celebration, many Jews in the diaspora, in countries around the Mediterranean, came on pilgrimage to Jerusalem. According to the CCC, in reference to VC II, especially *Sacrosanctum Concilium*, n. 6 and *Lumen Gentium*, n. 2, declares that, "The Church was made manifest to the world on the day of Pentecost by the outpouring of the Holy Spirit."[136]

The word Pentecost is rooted in the Greek word *pentekoste*, which means, "the 50th day." In Ex. 23:14-17, it was listed simply as the harvest festival, being one of the three festivals listed in these verses of the Old Testament. In Ex. 34:22, Lev. 23:15-21, Num. 28:26-31 and Deuteronomy 16:9-12, it was referred to as the feast of the weeks. The feast of the weeks referred to the first-fruits of harvest, which is calculated by counting seven weeks from the beginning of the grain harvest. Aside these references, the Old

---

135 First published as an article with the title "Pentecost" in *The Promise Newspaper*, a monthly publication of the Catholic Diocese of Auchi.

136 *The Catechism of the Catholic Church*, no. 1076.

Testament only referred to it again in 2 Chron. 8:13, thus, some scholars concluded that it was not an important feast. This conclusion does not, however, enjoy much popularity among scripture scholars. It is definitely one of the three major festivals of the Jews even older than the Passover.[137]

The actual date of the festival was not definite, in the sense that it was not fixed. This is because the beginning of the grain harvest cannot be put on a certain date. Later when the Passover celebration and *Mazzoth* were combined and fixed on a particular date, the feast of weeks was given a regular date; namely seven weeks or fifty days after the Passover. This has remained the date of the celebration of Pentecost to our time. Much later in Judaism, the feast of week – Pentecost, was given a historical motive. It became associated with the anniversary of the giving of the Law to Moses on Mount Sinai.

The New Testament apparently gave more prominence to Pentecost than the Old Testament. The importance that Pentecost enjoys today in Christian belief and liturgy came from the event narrated in chapter two of the Acts of the Apostles, that is, the descent of the Holy Spirit upon the disciples. Three main activities were associated with this event; (i) the gift of tongues, (ii) the address of Peter and (iii) the formation of the first Christian church. The gift of tongues has enjoyed more attention and prominence among these three activities in modern day Christianity.

Along with the prominence and attention the gift of tongues enjoys in modern day Christianity, there is also widespread abuse of its meaning and significance. According to Innocent Amasiorah, "This gift of tongues has done much harm to the Church today than good following the abuses in it."[138] We must admit that the event of Pentecost as described in the Acts of the Apostles provides a complex and difficult scenario for theological interpretation.

---

137 John L. McKenzie, *Dictionary of the Bible*, (London: Geoffery Chapman, 1972), pp. 657-658.

138 Innocent C. Amasiorah, For *This I was Born*, (Lagos: Emmatoha Nigeria Limited, 2001), p. 7.

The gift of tongues at Pentecost seems to already have antecedents in the Old Testament passages like Num. 11:25-29; 1 Sam. 10:5f, 10-19 and 19:20-24. In the episodes described by these passages, the elders and Saul prophesied under the impulse of the spirit. Now, at Pentecost, under the impulse of the Spirit given by Jesus, the same charisma is exercised. More significantly though is the fact that by the outpouring of the Spirit, the Church is empowered to address herself to all nations and to be understood by all nations. It has been argued by some scholars that in the Pentecost, there is an allusion to the story of the tower of Babel (Gen. 11:1-9). At the tower of Babel, humankind was divided by languages and unity was lost. The unity that was lost at Babel is restored in the Church which speaks all languages but is a single unified society at Pentecost.

The idea of different tongues was referred to four times in the entire account of the Pentecost; Acts 2:4, 6, 8, and 11. The last three references; verses 6, 8 and 11, were repetitions. These repetitions provide an insight into the understanding of the Pentecost event and the issue of tongues. It simply indicates that it was not the case that the apostles who were of Palestinian origin started speaking in foreign languages. Rather, it was in fact, the other way round. Namely, that all the foreigners heard and understood the proclamation of the wonderful deeds of God in their own language. "Full of amazement and wonder, they asked, 'Are not all these who are speaking Galileans? How is it that we hear them in our own native language?" (Acts 2:7-8).

The significance of Pentecost has been swallowed up in the overemphasis on the gift of tongues by many Christians in our time. There is a maddening attempt by many Christians to speak in tongues. Speaking in tongues has become a symbol of holiness and closeness to the divine. This is definitely not true; it is mistaken to take speaking in tongues as a sign of holiness or righteousness. And the way, Christians go about it today is suspicious. Day after day, worship after worship, they make the same unintelligible sound, which often is tantamount to noise and claim to be speaking in tongues. Many learn to speak in tongues by memorizing some meaningless expressions, which they claim is the language of the Spirit. Holiness or righteousness is not memorized. Holiness or righteousness is a lived experience of overcoming temptation and saying no to sin with the assistance of the grace of God.

According to George Ehusani, "The event of Pentecost symbolizes a new genesis, a new creation, a new world."[139] It represents the overcoming of the division in humanity occasioned by sin as exemplified in the event of Babel (Gen. 11:1-9). Pentecost is the reversal of Babel; the division of humanity by languages is reversed in the unity of understanding occasioned by the gift of tongues.

At Pentecost, the Holy Spirit transformed common men, ordinary folks, low profile fishermen, cowards and tax collectors, into fearless, courageous, veritable, vocal and powerful preachers of the good news. Pentecost is a confirmation of the universality of the mission of the Church. By the outpouring of the Spirit at Pentecost, "the Church is now empowered to fulfil the mission which was committed to her by Jesus."[140] As recorded in the gospel of Matthew, the mission commands: "Go, therefore, and make disciples from all nations ... and teach them to fulfil all that I have commanded you. I am with you always until the end of this world" (Mt. 28:19-20).

Pentecost is the establishment of a new people with one new language; a language that transcends nations and knows no boundaries, a new language that is understood by all and can be spoken by all, irrespective of race, age, colour, status and gender. This is the language of love. It is the identity by which the world will know those who belong to Christ. "Now I give you a new commandment: love one another... by this everyone will know that you are my disciples..." (Jn. 13:34-35). According to the Catechism of the Catholic Church, "On the day of Pentecost when the seven weeks of Easter had come to an end, Christ is fulfilled in the outpouring of the Holy Spirit, manifested, given and

---

139 George O. Ehusani, *Gospel Reflections for Our Time*, (Ibadan: St. Pauls Pub., 2004), p. 188.

140 John L. McKenzie, pp. 657-658.

communicated as a divine person: of his fullness, Christ, the Lord, pours out the Spirit in abundance. On that day, the Holy Trinity is fully revealed. Since that day, the kingdom announced by Christ has been open to those who believe in him..."[141] Those who believe in Christ are united by one common language, understood and spoken by all as their identity of membership of God's children; this is the language of love.

---

141 *The Catechism of the Catholic Church*, nos. 731 and 732.

24

Prayer (1): Understanding the Concept of Prayer[142]

The topic of prayer is a very wide and interesting one especially in the face of some practices in modern day Christianity where we have all forms and shades of prayer. I intend to carefully, gradually and steadily guide the reader through an understanding of prayer so that at the end of this series, we may have a better appreciation and attitude towards prayer.

Prayer is an indispensable part of our Christian relationship with God. We cannot do without prayers as Christians. It is a means by which we cement our relationship with God, submit ourselves to the grace of God and a channel through which God makes His graces available to us. Traditionally, prayer is the raising of our minds and hearts to God.[143] We do this by thinking of God, adoring and praising him, thanking and begging him for blessings for both our bodies and souls.[144] St. Therese of Lisieux, describes prayer as a surge of the heart, a simple look turned toward heaven, a cry of recognition and love, embracing both trial and joy. Prayer is a phenomenon that enables us live out our vital, personal, conscious and responsible relationship with the One, True and Living God.[145] The CCC further describes prayer as a gift from God that is implanted in our hearts to express the covenant

142 First published in two series with the titles, "Prayer I: Understanding the Concept of Prayer" and Prayer II: Expounding the Concept of Prayer" in *The Promise Newspaper*, a monthly publication of the Catholic Diocese of Auchi,

143 *A Catechism of Christian Doctrine*, ques. 141, p. 23.

144 *A Catechism of Christian Doctrine*, ques. 142, p. 23.

145 *The Catechism of the Catholic Church*, no. 2558.

between God; the divine and us, who are human. It is a form of communion between us and God since it enables us come into the presence of God.[146]

These various definitions and descriptions point out a number of important things about prayer. First of all is the fact that there are possibly four types of prayer:

i. The prayer of adoration, which its immediate purpose is to praise the glory of God.
ii. The prayer of thanksgiving, which gives gratitude to God for His blessings upon us – the Eucharist is the perfect prayer of thanksgiving.
iii. The prayer of contrition, which expresses our sorrow for sin.
iv. The prayer of intercession or petition, which is by far the most popular in the practice of Christianity today. This is asking God for blessings for ourselves and for others.

Another important aspect of prayer noted in the traditional definition of prayer above is that, it is the raising up of our minds and hearts to God. It is interesting to note that this does not include the raising of our voices to or *at* God. This is a very common practice at prayer sessions today. We hear Christians howl and shout in the name of prayer. Some call it charismatic and others call it Pentecostal. There is nothing charismatic or Pentecostal about this. It is simply shouting *at* God, disturbing the peace of others and the environment, and to say the least, it is insultive to the divinity of God. To be charismatic is to exercise an active positive charism attracting to God and attractive to humans and to be Pentecostal is to allow the Holy Spirit use us to the glory of God. The Holy Spirit will definitely not use us to shout at God or be disrespectful and insensitive to the needs of those around us, whose peace and quiet we corrupt at such shouting frenzies we call prayer. There is nothing wrong with being audible or loud when we pray but everything is wrong when it is done in

146 *The Catechism of the Catholic Church*, nos. 2558-2565.

disrespectful manner as it is often the case at many prayer sessions these days.

Prayer is an act of communication with God. As such, it involves some form of language, mostly verbal, but can also be non-verbal. This notwithstanding, it goes beyond language. As a verbal act of communication, it does not depend on the excellence of speech; for the one who stammers and the Professor of oral English can both pray perfectly to God given that all other conditions for a perfect prayer are met.

The attitude of rushing and talking non-stop, without punctuations, in the name of praying is a wrong attitude. Unfortunately, it is one of the "characteristic marks" (mistaken though) of what many contemporary Christians see as "powerful prayer." If prayer is directed towards God, our Father Almighty, why should we address him in that manner! I wonder how many parents will see anything good in their children addressing them as if they (the children) are rap artist, when they come to make request of them. How much more should we then think of that as a proper and respectful way to address God who is the Father Almighty?

If prayer is a gift of God that brings us into His presence, as the CCC rightly tells us, it is only right and proper that we conduct ourselves becomingly and respectfully in God's presence. It is okay to give expressions to our emotions when we pray, like Hannah, the mother of Samuel did (1 Sam. 1:12-16), our emotional expressions should not be aggressive or disrespectful. Stamping of our feet on the floor, hitting on desks and tables, snapping of fingers, clapping of hands, and uttering revengeful statements directed at perceived enemies, which in itself negates the express demand of Jesus Christ that we pray for those who persecute us, (Mt. 5:44) are negative and unacceptable forms of emotional expressions during prayer. When we address authorities here on earth, like when we are in the presence of the state governor, the local government chairman, the Bishop or even the priest, for instance, we conduct ourselves becomingly and tame our emotions so as not to appear disrespectful. Must we then let ourselves lose emotionally in the presence of God?

It is possible for us to mistake Acts 4:24 to justify shouting during prayers. Acts 4:24 says, "when they heard it, they raised their voices as one and called upon God ..." The use of the term "raised" here does not in any way translate as "shouted." The group of believers had just listened to Peter and John who shared with them their experiences with the elders and the chief priest and Pharisees who had arrested them and released them on the strong warning that they should no longer speak in the name of Jesus Christ (Acts 4:1). As one body and group, they prayed in thanksgiving to God with one voice. It is a common experience and expression that people talk about praying as raising our eyes to heaven, or looking up to God, or evening going up the mountain. These are common ways we express our communication with God in prayer. They do not mean shouting as in raising our voices at God, which I insist is wrong.

Absolutely nothing justifies raising our voices at God during prayer. In the pattern of prayer Jesus gave the apostles, the popular "Our Father" (Mt. 6:9, Lk. 11:1), respect and homage to God – "Our Father in heaven, holy is your name" comes first before any other thing. According to William Barclay, "holy is your name" or "hallowed be thy name" interprets as God's name is to be separated from others and given a special reverence as it differs from any other name.[147] There is no conception of this phrase that disagrees with this interpretation. A child never in any way show respect to the father by shouting or raising his/her voice at the father.

In our time, the raising of our voices at God takes a different and worse dimension when speaking in tongues is involved. I do have my deep reservations about speaking in tongues but would rather not discuss that here or now. Suffice to note that at the point of speaking in tongues, most times, not all the times and not by all who speak in tongues, but most of those who do and most of the times they speak in tongues during prayer, the rudeness at

147 William Barclay, *The Daily Study Bible: The Gospel of Matthew*, Vol.1, Chapters 1-10, Revised Edition, (Bangalore: Theological Publications, 1975), pp. 206-207.

God gets into the realm of reckless abandon. What is supposed to be a respectful and docile supplication addressed to a most superior Being becomes a reckless display of "acquired talent" and a show of disregard and disrespect to the divine.

Perhaps at this point, we should look through the scripture in relation to prayer. The idea is to see how the children of God prayed and sift out any noticeable trend as a model of prayer. The Old Testament shows prayer as a dialogue between God and Israel. The Psalms constitute the prayer handbook of the Old Testament. In addition to the Psalms, you have the prayers of Eliezer (Gen. 24:12-14), Jacob (Gen. 32:10-13), Moses (Ex. 3 2:11-14, 34:8, Num. 14:13-19), Gideon (Judges 6:36-40), Samson (Judges 15:18, 16:28), Hannah (1 Sam. 1:10), David (2 Kings 7:18-29), Solomon (1 Kings 3:6-9, 8:23-53), Elijah (1 Kings 19:36). These represent the Israelites' typical form of prayer. The prayers ascribe to Moses are of special interest as they are more like the intercessory prayers we are used to in our own time. This is also the pattern of prayer in the story of Abraham and God's intention to destroy Sodom and Gomorrah (Gen. 18:20-32).

The common characteristics of these prayers are that they are short, dignified and humble. This immediately calls to mind the injunction of Jesus to his disciples when he taught them to pray, "When you pray, do not heap up empty phrases as the Gentiles do, for they think that they will be heard for their many words" (Mt. 6:7). Jesus asked his disciples to go into their rooms, close the door and pray there, the Father who sees in secret will reward them (Mt. 6:6). This is not necessarily a suggestion that prayer should be a secret affair, it definitely goes against making prayer a public show as is often the case these days. Churches turn their public address systems to the houses around them and disturb the entire neighbourhood in the name of prayers. Jesus out rightly condemns those who are unfair and unjust to others and yet offer long showy prayers in public (Mk 12:40; Lk. 20:47). The Old Testament suggests that our prayers should be a humble dignified dialogue with God, not a jamboree or adverts to attract and distract others.

Prayers in the post-exilic books of the Old Testament, like Ezra 9:6-15; Tobit 3:1-6, 13:1-18' Judith 9:2-14; and 2 Macc. 15:22-24, are longer and more formal than what we find in the pre-exilic period. They are often prayers of contrition. The prophetic literatures are replete with prayers and one spirit runs through all the forms of prayer, namely, humility or a humble submission to the Most High. The prophets were not known to command God or hold God to ransom on account of the covenant. The contrast in prayer style is seen in 1 Kings 18:27-29, 36-37. This is the prayer of the prophets of Baal and Elijah respectively. The prophets of Baal shouted, gashed their skin with knives until they bled and raved, Elijah dignifiedly and humbly entreated Yahweh and at once, he was answered.

In the New Testament, Jesus was very critical of pharisaic practices, including their "show-off" method of prayer. He cautioned his followers against such prayer practices (Mt. 6:5-8), which he likened to pagan practice, a fact confirmed by the example of the prophets of Baal above. Note that Jesus did not condemn lengthy prayers because they are long as there is nothing wrong with long prayers. What he condemned was the public show, which to a great extent is the intent behind such lengthy prayers. In today's Christian world, it is like we want people to know we can pray eloquently for a sustained period of time. The Pharisee was eloquent in giving an account of himself to God while the publican was brief, contrite and humble (Lk. 18:10). The publican went home at right with God, indicating he left the presence of God fulfilled and renewed. It was not what was said and what was not said, but how what was said was said; for more than anything else, prayer is the raising up of our minds and hearts to God.

Jesus' own prayer life which dominates the gospels is our perfect example of how to pray. His method of prayer illustrates his recommendation as he often prayed in solitude (Lk. 6:12). The event and prayer in the garden of Gethsemane showed how Jesus controlled his emotions in and through his prayers (Mt. 26:36-46; Mk 14:32-42 and Lk. 22:40-46). He was overwhelmed with the reality of his forthcoming agony, suffering and death and wished it could pass over him. But it was not a matter of "by fire by force" as we are used to today, rather he prayed, "... Yet not what I want, but what you want" (Mt. 26:39, Lk. 22:39 and Mk 14:32). This stands in very sharp contrast with today's Christian practices. Most Christians today will remind God what a faithful God He is and how faithful they have tried to be. They will remind God of His promises to His children and command that the "Holy Ghost fire consume them." "Them" here refers to their real or perceived enemies.

Jesus preferred and indeed most of his prayers were in solitude, but was not against cultic prayer. By "cultic prayer" we mean public liturgical prayers as different from personal, private or family prayers. The New Testament cites various times that Jesus was in the synagogue to worship and share the word of God. For example, Mt. 4.23 talked about Jesus spending much time in the synagogues, he taught in them (Mt. 13:54), healed in them (Lk. 4:33-35, Mk 3:1-5) and debated the Torah in them (Jn. 6: 28-59). A further confirmation that Jesus was part of worship in the synagogue is the fact that he was scheduled to read from the Torah (Lk. 4:16-30).

25

Prayer (II): Our Prayers and the Will of God[148]

Through prayers we establish a link with God whom we duly recognize as the Supreme Being, capable of doing all things. In prayers we express our desires to God and ask Him to grant our needs. Does God always grant those needs? To put it more inclusively, does God always answer our prayers? God answers our prayers always but His answer may not be what we have asked for. The issue most times is whether we always recognise His answers when He answers us? God always answers our prayers but does not always grant our desires. If our desires conform to the divine will of God, He grants them but when they do not, He does not change His will to grant our desires. In other words, our prayers do not change the will of God. We may ask if it is the case that our prayers do not change the will of God, why do we have to pray?

This is a serious theological question that is equally highly sensitive spiritually and pastorally. The theological problem here is the problem of the relationship between divine sovereignty and human freedom. Divine sovereignty refers to the reign of God; the fully independent rule of God over the world, God whose power is beyond and above any other conceivable powers. Human freedom refers to the exercise of free will by humans as granted to them by God. If humans are truly free and have a will of their own, then they should have a right to what they want, which means that God should respect their will and grant their desires. In the absence of

148 The third and last in the three series on Prayer originally published in *The Promise Newspaper*, a monthly publication of the Catholic Diocese of Auchi.

that, it would mean that God has no regards for the free will He has granted humans and that humans are not truly free. Perhaps there is a limit to the exercise of human freedom.

The issue here can be formulated in the following questions; can we change the course of events through prayer? Can we alter God's will and so receive some blessing that otherwise might pass us by? Can we fend off some evil occurrence by specifically imploring God to save us from them?

There are two possible extremes to this issue. For theologians, this is a component of the problems of providence and of evil, since prayer has to do with the interaction between divine sovereignty and human freedom. One extreme will be to conceive prayer as a way of manipulating the mind of God to our human advantage and the other extreme is to see prayer as a completely useless activity. Neither of these extremes is correct.

God's will is constant and God does not err or make mistakes. God knows us and what is best for us at all times and He will never wish us evil or bad (Lk. 11:13). When we ask God in prayers for things that are within His divine plan and will for us, He will graciously grant them. Our human purpose is to do the will of God. In the Lord's Prayer, we say, "Thy will be done on earth as it is in heaven" (Mt. 6:10). Jesus Christ who gave the prayer to his disciples as a model of prayer showed us an example of how to submit ourselves to the will of God. In the garden of Gethsemane, he prayed that his coming passion be averted, which was a candid expression of his desire, but he ended the prayer by saying, "not my will but your will be done" (Mt. 26:42). Thus, while he expressed his desire, he made us realize that much more than his desire is the desire of God. This is precisely where the problem lies.

More often than not, we regard our desires as more important than the will of God for us. But God who created us to know Him, love Him, serve Him, in this world and to be happy with Him forever in the next,[149] above all else desires our happiness and joy both in this world and in the world to come. His divine will and

---

149 *A Catechism of Christian Doctrine*, ques. 2, p. 3.

plan is that we be happy by remaining with Him. If we start making request for and desiring things that will pull us from Him, He is not obliged to grant such request as it negates the very purpose of our being. Given that God grants such request, it would mean that He is acting against His own agenda, or that He is changing His agenda. For God to change His agenda would mean that there is something wrong in His original plan, if God is wrong, then He is not God for God is infinitely perfect and all knowing. To be wrong would negate these attributes of God.

If our prayer does not change the will of God, why do we need to pray at all? First and foremost, prayer is necessary in the Christian life because it follows the example of Christ our leader who by his life style taught us to always pray. According to Ronald Lawler et al:

> Jesus himself lived always in a prayerful spirit that blossomed easily into explicit prayer. He taught such prayerfulness to his disciples also when he asked them to always 'watch and pray.' The Lord seems even to have commended prayer as a constant activity: 'And he told them a parable, to the effect that they ought always to pray and not lose heart' (Lk. 18:1).[150]

The example and the teaching of Christ make it abundantly clear that a Christian should be a person of prayer since the physical and spiritual life of a Christian comes from God, s/he should always be in communion with God and prayer is the means by which we commune with God. Through prayer, the Christian acknowledges his/her weakness and dependence on God and expresses the filial relationship between him/herself and God. The Fathers of VC II acknowledged that prayer is an identifying mark of the genuine Christian.[151]

The importance and effects of prayer in the life of a Christian cannot be over emphasized. According to St. Thomas Aquinas,

---

150 Ronald Lawler, Donald W. Wuerl, and Thomas C. Lawler, (eds.), *The Teaching of Christ: A Catholic Catechism with Study Guide*, (Bombay: St. Paul Publications, 1976), p. 382.

151 Austin Flammery O.P., *Lumen Gentium*, nos. 10, 12, 40 & 41.

there are three distinctive effects of prayers; (i) it merits the graces of God for the Christian, (ii) it obtains other benefits from God for the Christians, and (iii) it brings a certain spiritual refreshment of the mind to the Christian.[152] Prayer has the power of transforming the life of the Christian to fit into the divine plan of God. Therefore, we can only pray well when we are ready to change in our lives those things that hold us back from God.

Every genuine Christian prayer must have the following essential qualities; attention, devotion, confidence and perseverance. In Matthew 6:5-8, Christ taught us to pray with absolute inner serenity and to avoid the hypocritical externalism of the Pharisees. This means that the good Christians should keep their mind on what they are doing during prayer. Distractions should be avoided with as much efforts as would be required. This notwithstanding, we must note that involuntary distraction may come and go because of our human weakness; they do not necessarily destroy the value of prayer.

Prayer should be devotional. It is not just an exercise of the mind; it is a humble submission to the will of God. Genuine devotion should never be confused with a feeling of satisfaction or with emotion. Devotion is properly a total dedication to God. The more devoted one is to God, the closer in friendship one is with God and the more likely one's prayer is heard by God. Mt. 11:24, Lk. 17:5 and James 1:5 tell us to pray with unshakable confidence proceeding from our deep faith in God. We do this by praying through Jesus Christ who is our mediator with the Father. Our confidence is borne out of our faith in his redemptive love and the power of his merits to get for us from the Father what we ask (Jn. 16:23-24). St. James tells us that approaching God with little hope is tantamount to offending God (James 1:6).

As the gospels teach, God will vindicate those He has elected who cry to Him day and night (Lk. 18:7, Mt. 7:7-11). These and other passages in scripture emphasise the quality of perseverance as an essential element of prayer. Christians are not to give up when they pray, especially when it seems their prayers are not

152 Thomas Aquinas, *Summa Theologica*, 11-11, 83, 13.

answered. Rather, they should learn to submit themselves to the will of God instead of wanting God to bend to their own will and desires. Many of us may want to ask how we interpret the passages in the bible that instruct us to ask and we shall receive for whatever we ask of God He will give us (Mt. 7:7-8). Such passages should be interpreted in the context of other passages that tell us that God knows what is best for us (Mt. 7:11). Thus, it is not just what we want, for many a time, we do not know what is really good for us as much as God who knows and sees all.

26

The Lord's Prayer: A Disciple's Prayer[153]

Every disciple is expected to be a great and impressive sample of his master. We are expected to be great disciples who are positioned to follow the Lord with a lot of commitment and trust. The Lord's Prayer, which is popularly known as the "Our Father" is the prayer of a true disciple of Jesus Christ. This is a prayer that Jesus Christ himself taught his disciples as a pattern of prayer. It is a prayer that is so rich in content, meaning and symbolism. It contains the expectations of the Lord from his disciples and the characteristic features of a true disciple of Christ. As some authors maintained, it was one of the principal sources which Jesus Christ used to communicate his message.[154]

In the gospel of Mt. 6:5, Jesus counselled his disciples on prayer and in verse 9 told them, "This, then, is how you should pray…" he went ahead to give them the Lord's prayer or the "Our Father." In Lk. 11:2, Christ told his disciples, "… when you pray, say this …" This was in response to the request of one of his disciples that he should teach them how to pray. Scripture scholars seem to generally agree that the Lucan version is closer to the actual prayer Jesus taught his disciples, however, the Church has adopted the more cordial Matthean version universally. Whichever version we choose to consider, it is clear in scripture that the Lord's Prayer is a disciple's prayer, "a prayer which only one who is committed to Jesus Christ can take upon his lips with

153 Originally presented as a talk to the Knights and Ladies of St. Mulumba, Afemai Sub-Council in 2009 and later published in *The Promise Newspaper*, a monthly publication of the Catholic Diocese of Auchi.

154 Richard McBrien, p. 458.

any meaning."[155] This is contrary to the popular thinking that the Lord's Prayer is a child's prayer or a family prayer. It can be said to be a family prayer if we see the family within the context of 'the family of the Church.' The Lord's Prayer is specifically and definitely a prayer that attains its full meaning and import on the lips of a disciple, because only a true disciple can really appreciate what it states. Until one enters into full discipleship with Christ, one cannot properly pray this prayer.

This is however, not what we see and hear every day. The Lord's Prayer, to say the least, is rushed over and commonized when it is prayed, so much so that more often than not, its meaning and implications are lost. For this very reason, it is necessary and good that we remind ourselves of the true meaning of this prayer so that when next we utter the words of this great and beautiful prayer, we enter into a deeper communion with the Father, Son and Holy Spirit. In this way, we bring our entire being in its past, present and future, to the Godhead.

The Lord's Prayer is easily divided into two parts. The first part, which contains three petitions, is dedicated to God and the second part, which also contains three petitions, is about us in our relationship with God and one another. In all, the Lord's Prayer contains six petitions. Thus, it is a prayer that from the beginning prioritizes the Christian character. It is primarily, vertically directed to God and then secondarily, horizontally directed to us and our neighbours.

Using the Matthean version as our reference, it begins with, "Our Father, who art in heaven; hallowed be thy name, thy kingdom come, thy will be done on earth as it is in heaven." This first part gives to God His proper place in the life of every true disciple of Christ. It acknowledges God as taking the number one position in the life of a true disciple before any other thing. As Barclay puts it, "It is only when God is given His proper place that all other things fall into their proper places."[156]

---

155 William Barclay, Vol. 1, Chapters 1-10, p. 198.
156 William Barclay, p. 199.

The prayer begins with "Our," which establishes the community and communion and the universal Fatherhood of God. God is a Father to all irrespective of race and colour. The opening phrase; "Our Father," summarises the relationship between the one praying (the disciple) and the one prayed to (God). When Jesus himself prayed in Mk 14:36, he said, "Abba, all things are possible for you; take this cup away from me. Yet not what I want, but what you want." In Rom. 8:15 and Gal. 4:6, Paul tells us that we too can call God "Abba." According to Paul, "And because you are sons, God has sent into your hearts the Spirit of His son which cries out 'Abba' that is Father" (Gal. 4:6). Thus, in this prayer, Christ recommends that we call God "Our Father."

"Abba" is the Aramaic word for Father and it is quite common to hear the little Jewish boy or girl running around the house shouting "Abba" as s/he seeks the attention of the father. It would be ordinarily translated as "daddy" today in English language. There is a familiarity and closeness associated with the use of this term. So to call God "Our Father" is to begin a communication with one who is close to us and not some remote, far away and strange deity.

God is not just "Our Father," He is, "Our Father who art in Heaven." It means besides being close and familiar with us, God is the holy and mighty one; full of majesty and power. For us, it is an expression of an implicit trust in a Father who has the power to do whatever He wants and the majesty or authority to do it. It is one thing to have the power to do something and another to have the majesty to do it. Majesty here includes the goodwill, the integrity and the authority to do it.

Immediately following the acknowledgement of the magnanimity of God is the first petition that recognizes God in His uniqueness; "Hallowed be thy name." The word "hallowed" is from the Greek verb; *hagiazesthai*, which is connected with the Greek adjective; *hagios*. The adjective, *hagios* is often translated as "holy" but it's real and basic meaning is "different" or "separate." A person who is *hagios* is a person who is separate from other people on the basis of his/her difference from the others. Applied to God, it means, God's name should be treated differently from other names as it is separated from other names; it should be given a unique position. "Hallowed be thy name," therefore, means to treat the name of God different from other names, separate it from other names, and give it a unique place among other names. It literally means that God's name should be sanctified or held holy.

Let us note that the Hebrew understanding of 'name' goes beyond the noun that designates someone, like, John, Andrew, Peter, etc. It actually implies the nature, character and personality, of the one such noun designates, insofar as it is revealed to us. This explains why Hebrew families and indeed, African families, would not just give a name to a child without first making preliminary investigations as to what they expect the baby to grow into. We see this playing itself out in the naming of John the Baptist in Lk. 1:59-66. It is also within this context that we understand the Psalmist in Ps. 9:10 saying, "Those who know thy name put their trust in thee." And again, "Some boast of chariots and some of horses, but we boast of the name of the Lord our God" (Ps. 20:7).

If we therefore, put *hagiazesthai* as "different" with the Hebrew understanding of a name together, it means when we pray, "Hallowed be thy name," what we say is, "Enable us to give thee the unique place which thy nature and character deserve and demand."[157] Therefore, "Hallowed be thy name" means to treat God as different from everyone else; to put him in a unique place in our lives and reverence him. To reverence means to obey, please and allow the one reverenced control our lives. We surely cannot reverence someone we do not know to exist. So to reverence God means we already believe that He exists and that we understand the nature of His character and personality enough to command our respect for Him. What is this nature of God that we understand? That He is just, holy and loving.

To confirm the interpretation of the last petition, the second and third petitions say, "Thy kingdom come, thy will be done on earth as it is in heaven." I put these petitions together, even though they are separate because they express the same fact and

157 William Barclay, p. 206.

are variations of the same desire. To pray for the coming of God's kingdom is to pray to do the will of God. This is because in the kingdom of God, only His will is done, so if His kingdom is to be established here on earth, it would mean His will is to be done on earth. The New Testament is about the coming of the kingdom of God. The gospel of Mk 1:14 records that the first appearance of Christ as a public preacher was all about preaching the good news of God's kingdom. In Lk. 4:43 and Mk 1:38, Jesus specifically declared that he has come to preach the good news of God's kingdom. "But he said, 'I have to go to other towns to announce the good news of the kingdom of God. That is what I was sent to do" (Lk. 4:43).

It is interesting and very tempting to attempt an understanding of the kingdom of God here, but it will be way too elaborate for our purpose, so suffice to just note that, "the kingdom of God is a society upon earth where God's will is as perfectly done as it is in heaven."[158] To be a member of God's kingdom is to obey the rules and abide by the regulations of His kingdom. A Christian who truly desires and makes honest efforts to follow the Lord is a disciple who never again does what s/he likes. S/he would rather do what God likes. A perfect example of this is given in the life of Paul. When he encountered Jesus Christ, his first question was, "What shall I do Lord?" (Acts 22:10).

A true disciple is one who seeks the will of God in all things and in all situations and circumstances of life. Unfortunately, however, what we observe today are Christians who seek that God should change His will and do their will. More often than not, we pray that, "Thy kingdom come, our will be done on earth as yours is done in heaven." Many so-called Christians of today are not disposed to do the will of God. A lot of the prayers we hear these days are phrased to *blackmail* God. We hear people in their prayers holding God to ransom on his promises, to do for them what they want. We want God to fulfil His promises in our lives but we are not ready to follow the path that makes us worthy beneficiaries of such promises.

---

158 William Barclay, p. 211.

The second part of the Lord's Prayer is about our needs and necessities. "Give us this day our daily bread, and forgive us our trespasses as we forgive those who trespass against us. Lead us not into temptation but deliver us from evil." Embedded here are three petitions; the first is a request for one of the basic necessities for the sustenance of life, food. The request for food is a request for basic necessity and not a request for luxury. A Christian is called to live well and not to live luxuriously. This is where we need to question the modern day craze for economic and financial "breakthrough" by Christians that keep them jumping from one revival today to another crusade tomorrow. It questions particularly the excessively flamboyant lifestyle of some so-called men of God, especially in the Pentecostal fold and now steadily becoming common among Catholic priests. Christianity does not forbid living well and comfortably, but it frowns at materialistic, flamboyant, and worldly living.

It is a biblically proven fact that God cares about the basic necessities of human life. This is abundantly shown in the life and ministry of Jesus Christ. He cared about the bodily needs of the crowds that always gathered around him. Several times he fed them, cured their diseases, and brought consolation to the afflicted. In Lk. 4:18, he declared that he had come to bring relief to the needy and proclaim the Lord's year of favour.

This petition also teaches us to take one day at a time and to give God the provider of all living things His proper place. Modern science can talk about the improvement of seeds for better yield, but it cannot create seeds that will grow and yield a harvest. We can only work on what God has given us, and all living things come from God alone. We, however, have to note something else here; we need to work on what we have for it to yield a harvest. So this petition teaches also that prayer and work go hand-in-hand. When we pray, we have to work to make our prayer come to pass. Thus, this petition reminds us that without God we cannot do anything and without us God will not do anything for us.

Finally, this petition brings out a salient issue that has been hidden inside the Lord's Prayer from the very beginning; the use of the collective pronoun, "us." At no point did the Lord's Prayer use the individual "I" or "me," it is always "our" and "us" to indicate that it is not a personal prayer asking for a personal thing. It includes everyone because there is enough for all. In this light, it discourages the disciple from selfishness and self-centeredness.

"And forgive us our sins as we forgive those who sin against us." This is no doubt the most frightening petition in the Lord's Prayer and the most demanding of the six petitions. It literally means, forgive us to the degree we forgive others. If we rephrase this negatively, it would mean, "Do not forgive us if we do not forgive others." This line of thought runs through the entire New Testament. In Mt. 5:7, Jesus specifically states that it is the merciful that is entitled to mercy, and in Mt. 18:23-35, he tells the story of the servant who has been forgiven much by his master but could not even forgive his fellow servant over something so little. The story ends with the unforgiving servant forfeiting the forgiveness he had earlier been granted. James 2:13 concludes this trend when he writes, "Judgment is without mercy to one who has not shown mercy." Our forgiveness of one another is an imperative for receiving forgiveness from God.

"Lead us not into temptation but deliver us from all evil." In this final petition is the subtle suggestion that God can actually tempt us; for to say "lead us not into temptation" is to say "you can tempt us but please do not tempt us." If we understand temptation as an attempt to persuade somebody to do what is wrong, it definitely will sound out of place that God will be involved in this. A look at Gen. 22:1, where some Bible translations state that God tempted Abraham, would leave many of us puzzled. Scripture scholars however, hold that the word "tempt" is not used here as we generally understand it, but as a "test." The Revised Standard Version (RSV) of the Bible, which many scholars think is a more accurate translation than most other versions actually used the word "test." Within the context of this understanding therefore, when we pray that God should not lead us into temptation, what are we praying for? We are simply asking that God should not subject us to severe test, that is, He should not test us beyond our ability. And to add, "But deliver us from evil" is to say that even if such severe test comes our way, help us to come through it safely.

It is worthwhile to note that no test is ever meant to break someone down, but to make the person tested stronger and fitter. There is a saying among my people that, "What does not kill a man makes him stronger." This applies both in the circular and religious world. Every test is to ascertain one's ability and prompt more efforts on the part of the one tested.

On the whole, as we see, the Lord's Prayer has six petitions in it, each making its own demand on the disciple who prays the prayer. The first part of the prayer, with three petitions pertains to the glory of God, while the last three have to do with us and our needs. A closer look at the petitions shows an amazing unity of our entire life with the Godhead. It reveals that the petitions contained in the second part of the prayer deal with our past, our present, and our future, as well as invoke God the Father as creator, sustainer and provider, the Son as saviour and redeemer and the Holy Spirit as comforter and guide. In asking for bread for this day, it brings the present into the presence of God, in asking for forgiveness, it brings the past into the presence of God and in asking for deliverance from temptation and evil, it entrusts the future into the hands of God. As Barclay puts it, "In these three brief petitions, we are taught to lay the present, the past and the future before the footstool of the grace of God."[159]

The Lord's Prayer brings the whole of our life before God and in a marvellous web of unity brings the whole of God to our lives. When we ask for bread, our thoughts go to God the Father, who creates and sustains life. When we ask for forgiveness, our thoughts go to God the Son, the saviour and redeemer of the world and when we ask for help to handle temptations and avoid evil, our thoughts go to God the Holy Spirit, the comforter, who strengthens us, guides us and enlightens us. Therefore, the Lord's Prayer puts together in the most amazing way, our present, past and future, the whole of our life, and presents them to God the Father, God the Son and God the Holy Spirit, to God in all his

159 William Barclay, p. 199.

fullness. We can say that Jesus teaches us in the Lord's Prayer how to bring the whole of our life to the whole of God and to bring the whole of God to the whole of life.[160]

We see that the Lord's Prayer is indeed a disciple's prayer for only a disciple can commit his/her whole life; past, present, and future, to God. Only a disciple can give God the true and rightful place in his/her life, trusting and committing self to doing the will of God in all things and at all times. "The simplicity and brevity of this prayer suggest a very special, intimate relationship between the petitioner and God. For the person who can pray the Lord's Prayer, the kingdom has already come."[161] We should therefore, be careful when next we pray the "Our Father" and ensure that we pray it properly, taking notice of its meaning and implication and meaning everything we say as we pray it.

---

160 William Barclay, p. 200.
161 Richard McBrien, p. 453.

27

About Tithes in the Church[162]

The issue of tithe is a controversial one in the Catholic Church because it is not properly understood by most Catholics. For many Catholics, it is a practice of the Pentecostal churches, and therefore, not catholic. For others, the Catholic Church does not encourage it as it belongs to the Old Testament. For those who agree that it is a valid and acceptable present-day practice not exclusive to the Pentecostals but to all Christians, there is still this confusion between tithes and development levies, dues, and contributions in the Church. Thus, different questions like the following are generated: What is the stand of the Church on tithes? Is it encouraged in the New Testament? Does it replace Church development levies/contributions? How can a trader/farmer/artisan calculate his/her tithes, and many more?

The term 'tithe' is a variation of the word, *teogopa*, which means 'tenth.' In this context and as it is used till date, it is a one tenth part of something paid as a usual voluntary contribution or as a tax or levy to support a Jewish or Christian religious organisation. Therefore, tithe could either be a voluntary contribution or a tax. When it is voluntary, it depends on the one who pays it, and when it is a tax, it is mandatory or compulsory, which means that it is binding on the one who pays it.

Some biblical interpretations contend that tithing was though an extensive practice in the Old Testament, it was not taught in the first century Church. And that the New Testament encouraged the concept of a 'freewill offering' as a means of supporting the

162 This was original published with the title "Catholics and Tithes" in *The Promise Newspaper*, a monthly publication of the Catholic Diocese of Auchi.

Church rather than a compulsory one-tenth of your earnings as a monthly or yearly tithe (1 Cor. 16:2, 2 Cor. 9:7). The practice of Acts 2:44-47 and 4:34-35, however, suggests otherwise. Early Christians sold all they had to contribute the proceeds to a common purse for the use of the Church. A couple, Ananias and Sapphira, who tried to cheat on this practice was struck dead immediately. Note however, that it was not because they kept part of the proceeds from their sales that they were struck dead, it was because they lied to the apostles, and therefore, to God. As Peter pointed out, they were not compelled to sell their land or submit the proceeds, which indicate that such offering is premised on the whole-heartedness of the giver who makes it. In fact, it is an indication of the freewill offering pointed to by Paul in the Letters to the Corinthians.

Tithe is first mentioned in the Bible in Gen. 14:18-20. This was when Abram, returning from a battle by the Dead Sea, was hailed by the King of Jerusalem, Melchizedek, who was also the priest of El Elyon (the 'Most High God'). Tithes were exchanged here but it was not specific who gave who tithe. The conclusion that Abram paid tithe to Melchizedek is drawn from other specific instances in the Old Testament that indicate that tithes were paid to priests. Such specific instances include Deut. 18:1 and Num. 18:24. The Letter to the Hebrews was, however, categorical in saying Abram paid tithe to Melchizedek (Heb. 7:2). And Heb. 7:5 talks of tithes received by priests and high priests. Jacob, the grandson of Abraham promised God one-tenth of his increase in Gen. 28:22.

Historians of scripture say that the oldest certain prophetic allusion to tithes is found in Amos 4:4, which talks about tithes paid at Bethel. Amos 4:5 alludes also to freewill offering. The point in this prophecy is not about tithe but the fact that rituals do not absolve one from misdeeds in the sight of God. The same fact characterizes most of the references in the New Testament to tithes. Deut. 14:22-29 outlines the law on tithes, which is here defined as one-tenth part of the crops to be offered to God. Generally, the book of Deuteronomy makes tithe offering the foundation of a believer's faith. For instance, Deut. 26:12-15 makes specific prescriptions of annual tithes, which went through different stages of reforms from Num. 18:21-32 to Neh. 10:37.

Under the Mosaic Law, tithe is discussed in Leviticus, Numbers, and Deuteronomy. The idea of tithing presented in these books is that tithes are organized in a three-year circle and what we have today is more like the third year, which is the tithing year (Deut. 26:12-14). On this tithing year, ten percent of the people's earnings were paid to the Levites, strangers, orphans, and widows. They were more like taxes, which were mandatory. Among the minor prophets, Malachi has the most quoted verses on tithe. It refers to the cause and effects of paying tithes. Namely that if you give to God, you will be blessed and if you refuse to give, you are cursed (Mal. 3:8-12). All these belong to the cultic practices of the Old Testament.

Payment of tithes in the New Testament was portrayed in the gospels as a proof of pharisaic piety (Lk. 18:12). Though the Old Testament tithes were levied on the produce of the grains, vines, and flocks, the Pharisees extended the obligation of tithe to even the smallest herbs (Mt. 23:23, Lk. 11:42). Based on Abraham's tithes to Melchizedek, Heb. 7:1-10 argued extensively that tithes are paid by the lesser to the greater, and the priesthood of Christ is greater than that of Aaron.

According to 1 Cor. 9:13, those who serve at the altar should live by the altar. This seems to suggests that some kind of provision should necessarily be made for the Sacred Ministers. Initially, such provision took the form of spontaneous offering of thc faithful but ovcr timc, as the Church grew and expanded, various institutions arose. Thus, it became necessary to make laws which would ensure the proper and permanent support of the clergy – Deacons, Priests, and Bishops. Many Christians (Catholic and Protestants) support their church ministers with monetary contributions of one sort or another. These supports are often called tithes, whether or not they represent ten percent of their earnings.

For Catholics, tithe was adopted from the Old Testament and early Catholic writers speak of tithes as a divine ordinance and an obligation of conscience, rather than a direct command by Jesus

Christ. Mt. 23:23 and Lk. 11:42 are often cited as support for tithing. These passages show that Jesus endorsed the payment of tithes and clearly stated that tithes do not cover for moral and religious bankruptcy. Let us not overlook the fact that most New Testament discussions seem to give up tithe as an obligation while encouraging freewill offering, cheerful giving, and voluntary support donations. 2 Cor. 9:7, 2 Cor. 8:3, 1 Cor. 16:2, 1 Tim. 5:18, Acts 11:29 and James 1:27 are all parts of such passages.

For about seven centuries after the beginning of the Church, it was thought that the Catholic Church does not adopt tithe, it was in fact, initially rejected, but mentioned in the councils of Tours in 567 and Macon in 585. Officially, it was formally recognized under Pope Adrian 1 in 787 AD.

Although tithing as a religious obligation does not enjoy a pride of place over and above other voluntary and freewill donations for Church development. All honest donations in the house of God are duly recognized as contributions to the spreading of the word of God and His kingdom here on earth, the maintenance and upkeep of the Church, and her ministers. Payment of tithes does not exempt the faithful from other developmental levies and contributions. Those who are selfish would often use tithe as excuse not to participate in fundraising in the Church, which also shows that even the tithe they pay, they only do as obligation, making it lack its religious and moral value. Jesus Christ would say to such persons, "Do the pagans not do as much?"

Some persons ask a question that I consider absurd, questions like, how does a trader or farmer or artisan calculate tithe. Everyone who earns, either by trading, farming or handiwork, knows how much s/he earns. The trader knows how much profit she makes, as the farmer or artisan knows the worth of her produce and handiwork. If you know the worth of your produce and handiwork, then you can find out the ten percent of it. It is left for anyone to choose to lie to God by pretending not to know the worth of his/her business, farm produce or handiwork.

PART FOUR

SELECTED HOMILIES

These homilies have been selected at random and do not take any particular order as they do not cover any particular circle of the liturgical seasons. They are mainly Sunday homilies and each has a theme that constitute the title of the chapter they appear as, and the themes are formulated from the readings of the Sunday.

28

Marriage: What God Has Joined Together (Mt.19:3-6)

As Msgr. John Anaigwu identified in one of his great homilies, people often refer to Christian marriage as “holy wedlock,” “holy matrimony” and talk of Church marriage as “solemnising ...” They do this because they recognize that Church marriage or Christian marriage is something holy and distinct from a merely social or legal activity. If it were any of the latter, couples marrying would not come to church to do their marriage, rather, they would go to a banquet hall, an event centre or the registry.

Indeed, Christian marriage is something holy because it was made so by God. For the word of God tells us in Gen. 2:23-24 that having made man, God found him to be lonely and therefore decided to give him a help mate in the form of a companion. Making him fall into a deep sleep, God removed from his side a rib from which he fashioned woman and on seeing her, man exclaimed, here at last is bone of my bones and flesh of my flesh.

More than just being holy, Christian marriage is also a sacrament. It is a sign; an outward sign that bestows inward grace. It is a sacrament for Christ made it so. Confronted with the Scribes and Pharisees, Christ reminded them that from the beginning, God made man and woman to be together. Thus, he, who had come not to abolish the law but to complete it (Mt. 5:17), confirmed what had already been made holy, if you like, he made it doubly holy. In reference to this, Paul, in the letter to the Eph. 5:21-23, specifically said that marriage should be seen as a sign of the relationship between Christ, the head of the Church and the Church, the body of Christ.

What is the purpose of Christian marriage? Against the idea held by some Christians that it is to help avoid fornication and adultery, Christian marriage is actually to sanctify and make holy the Christian family as the other sacraments do. The objectives are for companionship, unity, and procreation. This being the case, Christian marriage should be built on love. By love, I mean Christian love which Paul describes in 1 Cor. 13:4-7 as patient, kind, never jealous, never boastful, never seeking its own advantage, does not rejoice in doing wrong, always ready to forgive, make allowances, to trust, hope and endure all things. We may call these the attributes of love, they also point to the essence of love as that which accommodates all that is good and work for the growth of the other person.

It is important that we enter into marriage for the right reasons. These days, people enter into marriage out of convenience, to gain political affiliation and power, to boost their social status and to maintain economic and financial stability. While these could be some benefits that come with marriage, they do not discern who one's appropriate partner is or should be. The institution of marriage was not intended for this. Marriage should be between persons, male and female, not two males (gay-marriage) or two females (lesbianism) who love themselves and want to share their future lives together as companions and co-creators with God, through procreation and education of their off-springs. In this wise, love should be the bedrock and foundation of the marriage covenant.

Love is a verb and a verb is an action word, which means that love is not a theoretical phenomenon but something practical. It is not what we theorize, profess or explain to each other, it is what we do to each other. Authentic practical love, which is expected to be the binding force of every marriage transcends language and culture. It is not spoken but expressed in our actions. And it is only the beloved who can claim that he or she is loved. This kind of love bears and endures all things without feeling any burden.

Marriage is not an affair to be rushed into, it is a life-long commitment that requires careful discernment and proper preparation. A lot of young intending couples these days trivialize the very important aspect of marriage preparations. This is partial due to their misunderstanding of marriage as a social affair. They take their time and commit a lot of resources and energy into making the arrangements for a perfect social outing and neglect the very aspect needed to live the married life. This is what proper preparation is about, what we learn in marriage courses.

We all have a part to play to ensure a happy and successful marriage. Beginning with the bride and the groom marrying each other. Notice that it is not the groom marrying the bride or the bride marrying the groom, both of them are marrying each other. It is a complementary activity, which implies that both the groom and the bride have equal stake in the marriage covenant. Therefore, both bride and groom must work hand-in-hand to ensure that they sustain and live out their marriage vows by supporting each other. Such support is built on love, the love that understand, that tolerate, that is patient, that is forgiving. These virtuous practices are possible if there is communication between the bride and the groom, both of you must learn to communicate your feelings and promptly too.

Share your ideas and discuss matters about your life together as husband and wife. The husband should always be a priority to the wife as the wife is a priority to the husband. Respect each other's feelings and appreciate each other's concern. Never talk down on each other, especially in public. By public, I mean in the presence of someone else, whoever the person may be. Respect each other in the presence of everyone, including the children. Show your love for each other, make sure you take one of the day's meal together. It affords you the opportunity to share a lot of your thoughts. Buy each other gifts, take time out together, do not keep hidden or secret friends – not known to your spouse, avoid friends that want to interfere in your marriage by teaching how to treat your husband or wife. Learn what your wife or husband wants and give it to him, as long as it is not something immoral. The husband should be alive to his responsibilities of protecting and providing for the family, treating the wife as his queen, which she is. The wife should, likewise be alive to her responsibilities and making sure all is well in the home front. Avoid hard and fast rules about who does what, you should assist each other in doing what has to be done. Be attached to each other. Above all these, pray together. A family that prays together stays together. Never let a day pass by without saying a prayer together.

Complains are the beginning of cracks in marriages. Not to complain does not mean married couples should hide their feelings and repress their displeasures, but it means to be generous and tolerating, patient and understanding, above all, to be forgiving of the shortcomings of the other. Be always ready to excuse the weakness of the other, while patiently and lovingly share your thoughts with each other so as to build stronger and better ties of understanding. If you are not pleased with something about the home or your spouse, do not go and share it with someone else, discuss it with your spouse. Try to understand it from his/her perspective and share your perspective on the issue. Resolve it between yourselves; in that way, the cracks are mended before they expand.

All of us who witness to their marriage and public declaration of love for each other have the responsibility to support them. What God has joined together, let no man or woman put asunder. We should never, ever, counsel them against each other. If we are privileged to have the opportunity to settle a misunderstanding between them, never take sides, let your counsel be aimed towards one end only – to help them resolve issues and get back together. Never be a dividing force between them. Support them always to be loving husband and wife and pray for them.

29

Christianity: A Call to be There for Each Other

(The Sign and Message of the Wedding at Cana – Jn. 2: 1-11)

There was a wedding, and at one point Jesus was discreetly informed by his mother that the wine had run out. Miraculously Jesus produced a vast quantity of new wine. This is a simple summary of the events that took place in Cana, at the wedding feast to which both Jesus and his disciples and his mother were invited. This summary makes the affair sound so simple, especially when compared to other signs that we find in the scripture. But is it really that simple?

The fact that this sign is found in the gospel of St. John gives one the feeling that it is not as simple as we may think. The keen reader of the gospel of John would know that beneath the simple stories of John, there is always a deeper meaning. Every little detail in the gospel of John carries some significance. According to Barclay, "In all his gospel John never wrote an unnecessary or an insignificant detail. Everything means something and everything points beyond."[163]

The wedding at Cana in Galilee, according to St. John, was a sign and the first of the signs given by Jesus. Only seven such signs were recorded in the entire gospel of St. John, and this miracle of turning water to wine is the first of them all. That he narrated this one first means that he accords some prominence to it. So we might rightly conclude that this sign is a very special one in the opinion of John. John chose and recorded only the signs that best

163 William Barclay, p. 103.

explain who Jesus was. He saw a sign by Jesus as a revelation about the mystery of Jesus, rather than a marvellous act of power. Thus, the signs recorded in John are symbolic and representative. No wonder John calls this a sign.

The setting of this sign provides an insight into what it reveals about the person of Jesus. It was a wedding banquet. The theme of a wedding banquet is very important in the history of Israel. And a banquet is used at various times in the Bible to portray the happy future, which the Messiah was to bring. This future consists of a banquet with lots of good food and abundance of wine. Is. 25:6 says, "Here on mount Zion the Lord Almighty will prepare a banquet for all the nations of the world; a banquet of the richest food and the finest wine." Using the same images of wedding banquet, Christ, many times, spoke of God's kingdom, which he has come to inaugurate as a banquet. He compared himself to the bridegroom in Mk 2:19 when he says the wedding guests cannot fast while the bridegroom is with them. And in verse 22, he compared his teaching to the new religious order he was bringing to new wine, which no old wineskin could contain.

In Cana, we see a bridegroom who could not provide enough wine at his own wedding banquet. And Jesus Christ, the real bridegroom of humankind was invited in. And what did he do? He turned water into wine, wine so much in quantity and so fine in quality! Why did Jesus turn water into wine, even after telling his mother that his "hour" had not yet come? He acted in sympathy, in kindness, and in understanding towards the couple. When invited to big occasions where we would be expected to play a role, we take our time to prepare and shine; only "a Jesus" can take his time to shine on simple and homely occasions by doing a big thing like turning water to wine. He used his power to save a simple Galilean couple from humiliation and shame. It is by such simple kindness, understanding, and loving deeds that we too can show that we are Christians, followers of Jesus.

There are a few more significant little details in this sign that give us a fuller appreciation of our mission and call as Christians. John tells us that there were six stone water jars. The specific mention of six is in contrast to seven. Seven among the Jews is a complete number, therefore, a sign of perfection. Six in contrast is an indication of something unfinished and incomplete, therefore, a sign of imperfection. The six stone water jars are pointers to the imperfections of the Jewish law and these are the imperfections that Jesus came to do away with. In their place he puts the new wine of his grace. So, he turns the imperfection of the law into the perfection of grace. The insufficiency of wine to superabundance and enough for everyone.

The six stone water jars are capable of holding twenty to thirty gallons of water each. That will give a minimum of one hundred and twenty and maximum of one hundred and eighty or perhaps an average of one hundred and fifty gallons of water. Where a full gallon is an equivalent of five litres we would be talking about a minimum of six hundred and maximum of nine hundred or perhaps an average of seven hundred and fifty litres of wine. The emphasis here is the abundance of wine, which John uses to point to the abundance of the grace of Christ, a grace that is unlimited and sufficient for every need.

Earlier we mentioned why Jesus came to the rescue of the wedding couple, he was sympathetic, he was kind, and understanding towards their situation. In this same gospel of John, he says, "I have given you an example that you should follow" (Jn. 13:15). His example is one of love hence, in Jn. 15:12, he says specifically, "This is my commandment: love one another, as I have loved you." This is what the Christian mission is all about, to take a little extra step and be nice for the sake of Christ.

The role of Mary in this miracle is interesting; she was the one who noticed that there was no more wine, not Jesus. She felt concerned and felt the urge to help but she cannot do anything as such. She however, knows someone who can do something, so she took the case to him. She did not ask him to do anything really. All she did was to present the situation to him leaving him to do whatever he wills. Somehow, however, she had the implicit trust that he will do something. Hence she asked his disciples to 'do whatever he tells you.'

Many of us often walk away from unpleasant situations refusing to be a part of it, not to talk about offering a helping hand to alter the situation. Very often we laugh and jeer at others in their misfortune, enjoying their disgrace and verbally analyzing what should have been done that was not done. We would not do it ourselves though. Mary however, saw the shame and disgrace coming to the couple, she did not laugh at them or make mockery of their inability to provide enough for their guest. She did not excuse herself from the party, but took steps to help amend the situation. This is what Christians are called to do.

At Cana, we see Jesus and Mary in their respective ways come to the rescue of those who could not help themselves. It is a sign of what we Christians are called to do, help the needy. The message of Cana is therefore, "Be there for your brother and sister who are in need."

30

Christmas: A Festival of Love[164]

Christmas is, no doubt, the most widely known and celebrated Christian festival all over the world, celebrated by Christians and non-Christians alike. What exactly does this festival entail? How can we trace the origin and what implication does it hold for Christians? These are some issues that would engage our attention in this reflection.

Christmas is the celebration of the birth of Jesus *who is Christ*. I emphasize, "Jesus *who is Christ*" here because Jesus Christ who is the most important figure that has ever walked the paths of life on the earth is that important not merely because he is the Son of God, but because of what he came to do on earth as the Son of God. In Lk. 4:18, Jesus said, "The spirit of the Lord is upon me, for he has anointed me to bring the good news to the afflicted. He has sent me to proclaim liberty to captives, sight to the blind, to let the oppressed go free, to proclaim a year of favour from the Lord." Jesus himself declared his own mission at Nazara in the presence of the faithful of Yahweh. He echoed the prophecy of Is. 61:1-2 and declared that, "This text is being fulfilled today even while you are listening" (Lk.4:21).

Jesus' mission on earth was to proclaim peace, joy, happiness, liberation, and general well-being for all. He did not come for a political, economic or social revolution; he came for a moral and spiritual revolution. Thus, he had to build on a foundation that is required to sustain such revolution. He chose the foundation of

---

164 Original dilivered as a pre-Christmas reflection to a group of couples gathered for a one-day Christmas get-together at Engr. Charles Osezuwa's residence in Uhiele, Ekpoma in December, 2001.

love, which is the best of all. Authentic Christian love, which Christian theology call *agape*. *Agape* is different from filial and erotic love, it is the love that vertically proceeds from God to humankind and distributed through human co-operation amongst humankind in a horizontal manner. Christmas is the beginning of this network of love.

The association of *Santa Claus* with Christmas, and not with any other festival or celebration is not strange. It vividly expresses the belief that Christmas is when we remember our loved ones, a time to display some generosity and exchange gifts as our sign of love. The issue, however, is how deep this consciousness is in us? Is it just one of those social functions? Of course, it is not and should not be made to look like so.

Far from being a mere social function, Christmas is a period of sober reflection. This is not to suggest that we are to cut out of the social aspect of this beautiful festival, rather it is a call to be fully aware of what Christmas is all about. Our people say that, "Tears do not prevent the eyes from seeing." In other words, that we should not be blinded to the real meaning of Christmas because of the superfluous aspects.

Christmas is a period for us to evaluate our Christian love, a time to assess how we have practiced and lived out our Christian call to love one another as Jesus loved us. I am not saying that Christian love is to be based on and exercised at Christmas alone, but that Christmas provides us an opportunity to evaluate how far we have been able to participate in the horizontal distribution of the divine love that has come to us. God's divine love comes to us in different forms and shades; it could be our rich sense of humour, a gentle manner of speech, a clear sense of direction and organisation, a positive attitude towards life, financial strength, political power, etc. Christmas is a time to evaluate; how have we affected the lives of others positively, with any of these gifts, between the last Christmas and now?

Christmas is essentially a celebration of the love of God for us. At creation, God made everything blissful. But humanity lost this grace when our first parents sinned, death became our portion. God was not going to destroy humanity without offering us an opportunity, so He decided to send us a Saviour, Jesus Christ, His only begotten Son (Gen. 3:15). Jesus' declaration in Lk. 4:18 (mentioned above) is a confirmation that he is the Saviour God has sent into the world. Therefore, the celebration of the birth of Jesus Christ is the celebration of the coming of the Saviour. The amazing truth is that, we are not worthy of this act of God, it is simply out of love that God chose to save us. The whole story from start to finish is one of God's love for his creature.

Christmas is therefore, the period to celebrate the love of God for us. What does love entail? The popular parable of the "Good Samaritan" in Lk. 10:30-37 readily comes to hand in answer to this question. Love entails that we are nice to all and sundry, irrespective of colour, race, financial, political, social, and religious, and in fact, moral status. Love is the extension of a hand of fellowship to all who are in need, here and now. The life of Christ; his words and deeds, epitomizes this love. Jesus knew neither Jew nor Gentile – he did not distinguish between persons in his ministrations, he saw all as equal. The sun and rain from his Father is for all underneath the sky.

Love entails a little time for others, a little of all we have for those who do not have, particularly those whom society seems to reject. Such love that does not discriminate is based on the realization that we are all brothers and sisters. To buttress this point further, let us borrow from Anthony de Mello's story about a spiritual guru who analogically explained the value of not being discriminatory as Christians. According to De Mello, a spiritual guru, in cxplaining to his disciples the difference between day and night said that until we begin to see each other as brothers and sisters, we still are in the dark. The guru asked his disciples how they could tell when the night had ended and the day begun. One said, "When you see an animal in the distance and can tell whether it is a cow or a horse." "No," said the guru. "When you look at a tree in the distance and can tell if it is a neem tree or a mango tree." "Wrong again," said the guru. "Well, then, what is it?" asked the disciples. "When you look into the face of any man and recognize your brother in him: when you look into the face of any woman and recognize in her your sister. If you cannot do this, no matter what time it is by the sun it is still night."[165]

To practice Christian love is not a tedious task, the problem is that, most times, we are too busy to make time for one another. We are too busy running after our businesses, trying to make more money and more connections. If only we can spare a little time for other creatures of God around us, our fellow human beings. It is not as if we have to look too far or keep turning our heads around in search of those in need, they are always around us, if only we would be more perceptive of the situations of others and look beyond ourselves just as Christ did.

As the saying goes, "Charity begins at home," let us begin from our immediate family. According to sociologists, the family is the smallest unit of the society. The Church proclaims also that the family is the first Church. We should therefore, begin the practice of Christian love in our homes. How much of love does the husband have and show to his wife? Maybe, he is busy making money for the family. Perhaps, it is good to remember that the family, particularly the wife needs you, the husband, much more than the money. If this is not the case, then we should put a question mark on the love of the wife for the husband. Christmas is an opportunity to turn to your wife and reassure her of your love for her. Same goes for the woman.

What about the children? The love between the husband and wife provides the invisible but firm foundations for the children to learn authentic love. It guarantees good upbringing for the children as their lives as husband and wife (daddy and mummy) speak volumes to the children. A Chinese proverb states, "What you are doing is so loud that I cannot hear what you are saying." The English, which we are more familiar with puts it thus; "Action speaks louder than voice." Christian love is in Christian action, what we do shows how much we love one another. Christmas is a time to gather your family together and celebrate the love of God in his Son's coming. Let the love so bubble in the family that it

---

165 Anthony de Mello, *The Prayer of the Frog*, Vol. 1, (India: Gujarat Sahitya Prakash, 1988), p. 227.

reaches out to others who do not belong to the immediate earthly family. After all, we all belong to one large family where God is our Father, Mary our mother, and all of us brothers and sisters.

Christmas is here again; God has given us his Son as a gift that we may live. What gifts have we for God as our sign of gratitude? I tell you as a man of God and a minister of His word that the best gift to give to God is the gift of our Christian life of love.

31

Christmas: A Symbol of Change in Human History[166]

Christmas is a season of celebration and rejoicing, a time to eat and drink and be merry with one another. It is a great opportunity in our human history and annual life. Though, it is not the greatest feast in the Christian tradition and life; Easter is, it is however, the most widely celebrated by both Christians and non-Christians alike.

The prophet Isaiah calls on Israel to, "Rejoice and be glad for light has come and darkness is forever gone. Be glad for the Saviour has been born, he is the wonder-counsellor, the mighty God, the prince of peace" (Is. 9:2-7). The same theme of joy is found in Lk. 2:1-14. Here the simple and humble birth of Jesus, who is the Christ, is recorded. The shepherds who were watching their flock by night were the privileged ones to hear the news first, accompanied by the beautiful songs rendered by the wonderful voices of the angels as they chorus, *Glory to God on high, hosanna in the highest*. Thus, in his letter to Titus 2:11-14, Paul calls on us to rejoice and be glad and sustain our joy by giving up everything that does not lead to God and live good and religious lives here on earth.

We have every cause to rejoice and to be glad at Christmas, for the coming of God into human history properly calls for joy. But while in the celebratory mood, we need to spare moments to remember why it is a period of rejoicing and gladness, for we do not just rejoice and celebrate without a genuine cause.

---

166 Originally delivered as a homily in St. Maria Goretti Catholic Church, Benin-City, at the Christmas Mid-night Mass on 24th December, 2002.

We celebrate and rejoice because the presence of Christ in our human history is a symbol and the beginning of a change in human history. A change from slavery to sin, to freedom of "heir-ship." From the biblical accounts of human creation and fall in Genesis, it is obvious that humanity was doomed for damnation, having chosen to exercise God's gift of freewill selfishly and wrongly, but the promise of Gen. 3:15 began to be fulfilled with the birth of Christ.

Heb. 1:1-2 shows that God had made efforts to return Israel, His chosen race, the symbol of God's people, to Himself, by sending them prophets but now in the last days He has decided to come Himself in the form of His son Jesus Christ. If you like, He has now given us everything that is left so that we can, in fact, be saved. This is precisely the beginning of the change from damnation to life in abundance, which Christ talks about in Jn. 10:10. "I have come that you might have life and have it to the full."

The coming of Jesus Christ to the world creates a ladder of some sort by which humanity may and should ascend to the divine and by which the divine comes down to humanity. In Jesus Christ we have the union of the human and the divine, which Catholic theology appropriately describes as the hypostatic union, that is, the union of two natures, the divine nature and the human nature, in the one person of Jesus Christ. Christmas therefore, is a period when we celebrate the beginning of the great change in the course of human history, the change from a road to death to the route of life, the change that is marked by the conquering of Satan and the victory of the children of God.

Christmas presents us with the golden opportunity as individuals to effect a change in our personal lives. Hence, the Advent call of John the Baptist takes on a renewed relevance, "Prepare a way for the Lord, and make his paths straight" (Mt. 3:3). Paul's letter to Titus (Titus 2:11-14) provides for us how to prepare the way and how to make the path straight. According to him, we should give up everything that does not lead to God and live good and religious lives here on earth.

Every Christmas we need to ask ourselves what changes have we made between the last Christmas and this Christmas. We need to also ask whether we should let another Christmas go without at least a change in our lives. Should we let our lives remain on the same course even after another Christmas? The answer should be "No." If Christ's coming into the world marks the end of an era and indicates the beginning of another era in our relationship with God, each Christmas should mark the end of an era in our lives and indicate the beginning of another era in our lives. Specifically, each Christmas should mark a change from sin to a life of grace, an indication of a renewed effort to say "no" to anything that does not lead to God and "yes" to a renewed effort to living a life of grace. We should replace our evil ways with good.

How do we do this? It is common knowledge that evil and good cannot co-habit, one would necessarily have to give way to the other. Therefore, our efforts to do what is right would necessarily eliminate efforts to do what is wrong. The argument is that, when we are preoccupied with thinking, planning, and executing what is right and good in the sight of God, we would not have the time to think, plan, and execute evil or things that lead us away from God.

We have to acknowledge the fact that we live in a world full of distractions. In today's society, we are defined by what we have and not by our character. Our successes are measured by what we have to show materially and the wasteful abandon by which we live. In such a society as this, it becomes extremely difficult to live a life of virtue, but then, it gives us a great opportunity to prove our Christianity. By this, I mean the more hostile our environment gets, the more chances and opportunities we have to demonstrate our faith. All these however, depend on whether we see the hostilities as distractions or as opportunities. If we see them as opportunities to practice our Christian faith, they become for us sources of inspiration and strength.

32

The Presentation of Jesus in the Temple: Purification Time (Lk. 2:22-39)[167]

It is forty days after Christmas! Joseph and Mary, and the baby Jesus make their journey from Bethlehem to Jerusalem to fulfil the law. What law were they exactly going to fulfil? They were going to fulfil two laws in one ceremony:

i. The redemption of the first born who is supposed to be consecrated to the Lord as required by God in Ex. 13:1-2. This redemption is done by paying five shekels to the temple priest as stated in Num. 18:15-16.
ii. The ritual purification of the mother after the birth of a child. According to Lev. 12, if the child is a boy, this purification is done forty days after his birth and if the child is a girl, it is done eighty days after her birth.

The Holy Family of Jesus, Mary, and Joseph, travelled to the temple in Jerusalem to fulfil these two laws. Although they could have done this in their local synagogue, they chose to go to the temple in Jerusalem. By that very choice, they fulfilled the prophecy of Malachi, which among other things, states that suddenly the Lord, whom you seek, shall come into his temple (Mal. 3:1-2).

What is the rationale behind the redemption of the first born and ritual purification of the mother? This question is particularly pertinent in the case at hand; namely, the case of Jesus as the first born of Mary. Honestly, I think it is safer to leave this to our

167 Homily on the feast of Presentation of Jesus in the Temple given at SS. Peter and Paul Seminary Chapel on the 2nd February, 2013.

scripture scholars to explain to us in the classroom. It is however, not out of place to state the issues involved here, these include; whether there was any need to redeem Jesus, the Son of God, who is himself God, from God. And what purification does the Blessed Mother Mary need? She is purity personified; virgin before birth, virgin during birth, and virgin after birth.

Perhaps, more beneficial to us here and now, is the lessons we can learn and the path we can draw from the Lucan account of the Presentation story, rather than trying to resolve these theological questions. Two issues summarize the Lucan account of the Presentation story:

i. The fact that the Holy Family's trip to the temple in Jerusalem was to fulfil the law.
ii. The fact that in the process of fulfilling the law, Jesus was presented to God.

The trip of Jesus, Mary, and Joseph, to Jerusalem exemplifies humility. That exulted as they are, to the enviable status of the Holy Family, they still found reasons to be submissive to the law. This is what Christianity is about, to be law abiding citizens. Unfortunately, in our country, what we see is the reverse. People reach certain positions and begin to feel and act above the law. Those who are supposed to maintain law and order, are the first to break such laws and cause confusion as we see on our roads when there is heavy traffic. In fulfilling the law, Jesus was presented as the acceptable, unblemished offering/sacrifice to the Lord. We too are called to present ourselves to the Lord as acceptable sacrifices. We can only be acceptable when we have purified ourselves of our sinfulness.

Other than the framework of the Lucan context of the Presentation story, there are other nuances in the Presentation account that call for our attention. These include:

i. The personalities of Simeon and Anna.
ii. The prophecy of Simeon.

In Simeon and Anna, we see two people who had devotedly served God, putting their hope in God, and disposing themselves to the promptings of the Holy Spirit. The emphasis here is that they were not serving God at their conveniences, or according to their own preferences and styles. This is contrary to what most of us contemporary Christians do. In our case, going to Church is when we find it convenient, so much so, that at the slightest inconvenience, we have reasons to excuse ourselves and justify our excuses. The reward of their unalloyed dedication to God is the fulfilment of their hopes and the great joy and happiness this brought them, which is lucidly expressed in the praise of Simeon.

The prophecy of Simeon aptly proclaimed Jesus as the light to the nations. The implication of this for us, especially as priests and seminarians (priest to be), is to query ourselves if, we, as *alter Christus* or as persons acting *in persona Christi*, are light to the nations? This question borders on; whether in our daily lifestyle, the way we dress, the way we talk, the way we act, the way we relate, do we lead others aright or astray? Do we, by our actions, speeches, and relations, enlighten the paths of the people of God or, to the contrary, we scandalise, oppress, and derogate them?

The feast of the Presentation of Jesus, therefore, confronts us with the following:

i. The humility of the parents of Jesus in their law-abiding attitude.
ii. The genuine devoutness and trust required of a true child of God as exemplified in Simeon and Anna.
iii. The challenge of the prophecy of Simeon, which Jesus applied to us when he told us: "You are the light of the world..." (Mt. 5:14-16).

On this feast of the Presentation of Jesus in the temple, it is purification time for all of us. It is a time to throw off the garment of pride and stop thinking we are better than the system, institution or society. It is a time to reverse our thinking that we know more than the others on how best things should be done. It is time to be humble and law-abiding. It is time to purify ourselves of pretentious spirituality, to be genuinely trusting in God and open to the Holy Spirit and avoid relying unnecessarily on what we think we are worth; either intellectually, financially, by our position, or otherwise. It is time to face the challenges of our call to be light of the world, so that we can burn brightly that others may see and be guided. It is time to purify ourselves of all that is not worthy of our status as priests, seminarians, and indeed, children of God. It is time to make ourselves presentable to the Lord, purified as we are, in the sight of God.

33

Pentecost: Kindling the Fire of God's Love in Our Lives (Jn. 20:19-23)[168]

The coming of the Holy Spirit on Pentecost day marks the official take-off of the Church. It represents the birth of a new single family of humanity. It is the reversal of the disunity occasioned by the event of Babel. The narration of the event of Babel begins by telling us that, "The whole world had one language and a common speech" (Gen. 11:1). With the noble intention of remaining united and not to be scattered, they decided to build themselves a city and a tower that would reach up to heaven. In His wisdom, God saw this as the foundation of something that would be eventually abused as the success of such a project will pitch humankind against Him. Thus, He decided to remove the uniting factor of language, which will ultimately make their project impossible (Gen. 11:1-8).

Working on the premise that God can never be wrong, there must be something not right with the intention of the Babel project. This is connected with the motive of being great, for definitely, the intention of being united is noble. Even Jesus himself, prayed that his followers to remain united: "Holy Father, keep them in your name (that which you have given me), so that they may be one, just as we are" (Jn. 17:11). Further on, he prayed, "May they all be one as you Father are in me and I am in you. May they be one in us; so the world may believe that you have sent me" (Jn. 17:21).

---

168 Homily on Pentecost Sunday, given at St. Thomas Moore Catholic Church, Sobe, on 27th May, 2012

Jesus' prayer for the unity of his followers is premised on the unity between himself and the Father and for the glory of, and faith in God. The motive for the desired unity of the Babel episode is premised on the greatness of the humans concerned. So, Babel represents the desire for human greatness, without a corresponding acknowledgment of the greatness of the creator. It is an ambition that circles out God. It is a product of humanity trying to overstep its bounds.

At Babel, humans decided to build a tower that would reach up to heaven, the seat of God. At Pentecost, God decided to build a bridge to connect with humans. At Babel, understanding died. At Pentecost, mutual understanding was restored. At Babel, there was disintegration. At Pentecost, there was unification. Thus, Pentecost is, in this wise, a redirection and reunification of humanity. It is a call to be united by the power of the Holy Spirit and not simply by human achievements and designs. A call for oneness in God.

At the Pentecost event, by the power of the Holy Spirit, everyone present heard the apostles speaking in their own native languages (Acts 2:7-8). This is a testimony to the fact of reunification; the barrier of language has been removed. That even though they were speaking in different languages, everyone was able to hear them in their own native language. This is only possible with the presence of the Holy Spirit; the unifying factor that joins us to God as one family. God is the Father and we are the children, with Jesus Christ as our brother.

Pentecost is a celebration that calls on all of us to rededicate ourselves to the active and faithful participation in God's kingdom as members of God's single family, which is the Church. According to Fulton Sheen, "Though we are God's chosen people, we often behave as God's frozen people." We are frozen in our prayer life, we are frozen in our relations with one another, and we are frozen in active participation in activities in God's house. Pentecost opens us to the power of the Holy Spirit that thaws us off our lethargy and gives warmth and life to our otherwise frozen souls.

Pentecost is the day we call on the Holy Spirit to rekindle in us the fire of God's love. The fire that will melt our frozenness and set ablaze in our hearts the love and service that characterized the life of Jesus, his Son, our perfect example of followership. Pentecost provides us, yet another opportunity to submit ourselves to the promptings and directions of the Holy Spirit, an opportunity to allow the Holy Spirit bring out in us the life of God that we have frozen by our waywardness and sinfulness. It is Pentecost, it is time to be rekindled by the fire of the Holy Spirit, it is time to live out the grace of God in our lives again.

34

The Lord Is My Shepherd (Jn. 10:1-10)[169]

On Good Shepherd Sundays, the Church encourages us to pray for vocations and for God's strength and grace upon those who have embraced the special call of God to dedicate their lives to Him in the ministry of priesthood and religious life. We therefore, commit our entire formation team and student body to the special care of God. May his divine assistance and mercy always be with us and keep us in his love and protection. Amen.

Scripture is replete with the image of the shepherd. From the popular Ps. 23, "The Lord is my shepherd..." through the prophecies of Isaiah, Jeremiah, and Ezekiel, the gospels of Matthew, Mark, Luke, and John, to the epistles of Paul, John, and Peter, the image of the shepherd resounds. The shepherd portrays the image of leadership, thus, the Good Shepherd is a reference to good leadership.

In the gospel passage cited above, Jesus refers to himself as the door of the sheepfold. Four times in this passage Jesus mentions the door to the sheepfold (Jn. 10: 2-3, 7-8). The first two references are slightly different from the last two. Jn. 10: 2-3 refer to the door of the communal sheepfolds you have in the villages and towns, to which the village flocks return at night. The door is usually very strong and only the guardian holds the key. He opens and locks the door as necessary, when required. Jn. 10: 7-8 refer to the opening in the sheepfolds in the hillsides where the sheep gather at night during the warm season, as they usually do not return to the village. These sheepfolds have no doors as such but

169 A homily on the 4th Sunday of Easter, Year A, in the Seminary Chapel of SS. Peter and Paul, Bodija, Ibadan, on 11th May, 2014.

openings where the shepherd lies across at night, such that a sheep cannot come out except going over the shepherd. Jesus's reference to himself as the door to the sheepfold is in this second respect.

When Jesus refers to himself as the door to the sheepfold, he means that it is through him alone we have access to God. This is consistent with his claim that "I am the way, the truth, and the life; no one comes to the Father but through me" (Jn. 14:6). Paul makes the same claim when he said, "Through him, we have access to the Father" (Eph. 2:18). We find the same claim in the Letter to the Hebrews, "He is the new and living way" (Heb.10:20).

Apart from this analysis of Jesus as the door to the sheepfold, there are other salient aspects of the Good Shepherd in the passage above that call for further reflection in relation to our daily Christian life.

i. He calls his sheep by name, they hear his voice, and they follow him.
ii. He goes before his sheep and leads them.

The Good Shepherd calls his own sheep by name because he knows them. He is interested in them and cares for each one of them in their individual capacity. When the Good Shepherd calls his sheep, they hear his voice, and recognizing it, they follow him. For the sheep to hear, recognize, and follow the voice of the Good Shepherd means the sheep is attentive and positively disposed to the voice of the Good Shepherd.

Today the Lord continues to call us, even in the midst of other many voices in our world, some of which are even louder than the voice of the Lord. We have the voice of materialism, which is extremely loud in our day. We have the voice of insincerity, which is getting louder even among the children of God. We have the voice of sexual misconduct, with its ever increasing crescendo. We have the voice of pastoral ineptitude and general disinterest, carelessness, and spiritual laziness. And we have the voice of indifference that characterizes the modern world. If we are not attentive, we will not hear or be able to identify the voice of the Lord in the midst of all these other voices.

When we hear the voice of the Lord, if we do hear his voice, do we dispose ourselves positively to it and respond as the Good Shepherd expects us to? When we choose to respond, do we respond on our own terms or follow the guidance of the Good Shepherd?

The Good Shepherd goes before his sheep and leads them. Two things are implied here: (i) he goes ahead to make sure the path is safe and cleared of danger, and (ii) his action of being ahead of the sheep expresses his trust in the sheep to follow him. As priests, seminarians, and Christians, do we, in our actions, trust in God's divine guidance and justify the trust he reposes on us to follow his directions, especially in our superiors? Or we grumble always against authority, and always think we know better than those in charge? Run down the efforts of others simply because it is not ours?

The Good Shepherd is the image of an able, humble, and committed leadership. The life of the shepherd is hard: no day off, no off duty, constant and dangerous, because he is always on guard against wild animals, thieves and robbers. He is constantly vigilant, fearlessly courageous, and patiently loving.

This is the life we all, as Christians are called to as ordinary Christians who should be there for our brothers and sisters always, showing good examples at all times, and nursing each other's injuries and pains back to health; as seminarians, being positively disposed to formation, willing and ready to commit yourselves to a lifelong self-sacrificing leadership; as priests, whose joy is not in what appointments we get but in how much we are ready and able to uplift and better the lot of God's children.

The Lord is my shepherd, I shall not want. May the Lord not allow us to be shepherds whose sheep will be in want, Amen.

35

Jesus the Good Shepherd (Jn. 10:11-18)[170]

Jesus paid the ultimate price of his life to save the human soul, which shows how much we mean to him. He attaches ultimate value to the human soul. In this respect, he declares himself as the Good Shepherd. This declaration was in contrast to the bad shepherds that the leaders of Israel have become.

Ps. 100:3 says, "Know that the Lord is good, he created us and we are his people, the sheep of his fold." The use of the word 'sheep' to refer to the people of God by scripture has great significance. Wild animals like wolves, lions, hyenas, etc., were not used to depict the people of the Lord. Maybe because in the jungle, they can pretty much take care of themselves. Domestic animals however, are easy prey to wilder ones and as such require protection and care. And Jesus declares himself as the protector and caretaker of his people, that they may not be sheep without a shepherd.

As the sheep of the Lord, God has never left his people untended. He had always given them a shepherd. He appointed Moses in Midian to go and ask the Pharaoh of Egypt to 'let my people go.' "Go now! I am sending you to Pharaoh to bring my people, the sons of Israel, out of Egypt" (Ex. 3:10). After Moses was Joshua, the son of Nun (Joshua 1:1-15). Then came the Judges and the Kings, before the prophets. Kings in ancient times were both political and religious leaders, so the king was the chief pastor and shepherd of the people under his domain (2 Sam. 6:12-

170 Originally preached as a sermon at Sacred Heart Catholic Church, Agenebode, on Good Shepherd Sunday, 2007.

22; 1 Kings. 12:25-33). In the exercise of their duties, they assumed a larger than life attitude; they became bad, corrupt, arrogant, and insensitive to the people.

By the time of the Prophet Ezekiel, God could no longer stand their attitude. Thus, through the lips of Prophet Ezekiel, he denounced the evil of the shepherds of his people who have turned themselves into wolves and feeding on the flesh of the very ones they ought to protect. They dress themselves in sheep clothing, while inside they are ravenous wolves, sacrificing the fattest sheep, failing to bandage the wounds of the injured, and refusing to bring back the strayed. (Ezk. 34:11). Thus, the Lord stated in Ezk. 34:10-12, "Look, I am against the shepherds. I shall take my flock out of their hands and henceforth not allow them to feed my flock ... I myself shall take care of my flock and look after it. As a shepherd looks after his flock ... so shall I look after my sheep."

Christ came that we may have life in abundance (Jn.10:10). For the abundance of life, he made himself our shepherd. As our shepherd, he came not only to restore the dignity and work of the shepherd but to show its divine origin. He declared in Jn.10: 11-16: "I am the good shepherd. The good shepherd gives his life for the sheep. Not so the hired hand of any person who is not the shepherd and to whom the sheep do not belong. They abandon the sheep as soon as they see the wolf coming; then the wolf snatches and scatters the sheep. This is because the hired hand works for pay and cares nothing for the sheep. I am the good shepherd. I know my own and my own know me, as the Father knows me and I know the Father. Because of this I give my life for my sheep. I have other sheep that are not of this fold. These I have to lead as well and they shall listen to my voice. Then there will be one flock since there is one shepherd." The shepherd-hood of Christ implies the following:

(i) That he gives his life to the sheep so that the sheep would have life to the full. God has always invited his people to the fullness of life as in Is. 55:1-3 where he calls all to come and partake of him. "Oh come to the water all you who are thirsty; though you have no money, come! Buy and eat, come buy wine without money, free ... Listen carefully to me and you will have good things to eat and rich food to enjoy." In Mt. 11:28-30, he repeated the same thing saying: "Come to me all you who labour and are overburdened and I will give you rest. Shoulder my yoke and learn from me, for I am gentle and humble of heart, and you will find rest for your souls." No wonder St. Augustine noted that "Our hearts are restless until they find rest in the Lord."

(ii) That Christ would lay down his life for the sheep. He taught us the path of truth and love, won back those who strayed, and defiled those who want to defile the Lord's temple. For these, he suffered death on the cross. "No greater love than this to give one's life for one's friends" (Jn. 15:13). According to St. Paul, was it that we were justified and therefore, worthy of his loving self-sacrifice? No! For we were yet sinners when he gave his life for us. "Consider, moreover, the time that Christ died for us: when we were still sinners and unable to do anything" (Rom. 5:13).

(iii) That he should show care and concern for his sheep. In the Sermon on the Mount, he repeatedly emphasized that the care of the sheep is the priority of the Lord. To avoid our misinterpretation or misunderstanding of his intention, he said, "That is why I am telling you not to worry about your life and what you are to eat, nor about your body and what you are to wear ... your heavenly Father knows you need them all. Set your hearts on his kingdom first and on God's saving justice, and all these other things will be given you as well" (Mt. 6:25-33).

(iv) That he leads the sheep. He will surely lead the sheep aright because he knows the way as he himself is the way, the truth, and life. At the last meal with his apostles, he displayed that he has come to lead and left the apostles in no doubt as to his method and style of leadership. He is not the leader who will lord and boss others around, neither is he the leader who will misappropriate and embezzle their funds. He is not the leader who will pick quarrels with his subjects and dismiss their concern. He is the leader who cares and not only wishes, but works to actualize his wishes of good and well-being for his people. And after that he told his disciples that he has given them an example that they should follow (Jn. 13:15).

In appreciation of this distinctive shepherding style of Jesus, we begin to understand and fully appreciate and comprehend the wisdom of Ps. 23, "The Lord is my shepherd ..." this is indeed:

i. A hymn of praise.
ii. A joyful response to God's caring invitation to the fullness of life.
iii. A song of complete trust and dependence on God.
iv. A psalm of total surrender, abandonment, and resignation to the will of God.

The Good Shepherd assures us that our trust in him is not misguided. "Do not let your hearts be troubled, trust in God, trust also in me. In my father's house, there are many places to live in; otherwise I would have told you" (Jn. 14:1-2). For he is with us always even to the end of time (Mt. 28:20).

For every privilege, there is a corresponding responsibility. Therefore, we, as the sheep of Christ, have obligations towards the Good Shepherd. He himself stated this when he said, "The sheep that belong to me listen to my voice; I know them and they follow me" (Jn. 10:27). The great promises of eternal life, protection, and security, given by Jesus as the Good Shepherd are based on the corresponding fact that the sheep would follow him. If the sheep refuses to follow the voice of the master, the master would have no responsibility for any misfortune that comes their way.

Fr. Arthur Tonne reported the experience of an American tourist in Syria. The tourist observed as three shepherds led their flocks to drink from a common pool. The flock were mixed up as would be expected and while the American pondered and watched to see how the shepherds would sort out their flock, he was amazed when one of the shepherds started walking away and called on his flock to follow him. At once, his own sheep left the larger group and followed him. The second did the same and at once his own sheep followed him. Walking up to the third shepherd, he asked that he be allowed to play the shepherd and called on the sheep to follow him, but none would move. He then asked the authentic shepherd, "Will your sheep never follow anybody but you?" With a smile, the shepherd replied, "Oh yes, sometimes a sheep gets sick, and then it will follow anyone."

The response of the shepherd to the tourist captures exactly the phenomenon playing out itself when we refuse to follow the voice of the Lord. It means we are sick. It means we have separated ourselves from the sheepfold. And we have decided to play a discordant tone. This is when we take to the way of sin. We act like the prodigal son by abandoning our true and exulted position as the Father's child and wonder into foreign land where we do not belong. The only thing that awaits us there is misery after a brief and temporal moment of earthly joy and enjoyment. Let us strive to always be under the guidance of the Good Shepherd and we shall never want.

36

Harvest: Let us Give Thanks to the Lord (Luke 17:11-19)

At the beginning of every year, a priest would publish an inventory of the parish, including the names of the parishioners. On the inventory of a particular year, he wrote "9 missing parishioners." Some parishioners who did not understand what he meant by "9 missing parishioners" approached him for clarification. In response, the priest told them that last year twelve sailor parishioners came to him for prayers as they were about to set sail, he prayed for them, three of them had since then come to give thanks for the success of the voyage, and that he has not heard from the other nine ever since. Therefore, he has concluded that the remaining nine that have not come to give thanks are missing.

This story illustrates, not just the need, but also the appropriateness of thanksgiving to God for his mercies in our lives. Today, in most Christian churches, this has taken the form of annual harvest/bazaar thanksgiving. I cannot say specifically the origin of this in Nigeria. However, it has been argued by some persons that it is an import into the Catholic Church from our Protestant brothers. I am not interested in that actually, instead, I am more interested in whether we have any justification for it, particularly in the scripture. There is definitely justification for harvest thanksgiving in scripture.

Gen. 4:3 talks about the thanksgiving offering of Cain and Abel. Cain who was a farmer, brought before God the wretched fruits of his farm and Abel, a cattle breeder presented the best animals in his flock, as scripture puts it, the ones with fat. God accepted the offering of Abel and rejected that of Cain for obvious reasons. In like manner, Gen. 8:20 talks about how Noah offered the clean birds and animals that survived the flood; Noah offered to God a thanksgiving from the clean birds and animals. Gen. 22 provides an account of Abraham's extraordinary faith, which today testify to him as our father in faith. He was a man whom God has promised to be the father of many nations and consequent upon the promise, he was given a legitimate son in the person of Isaac. The same God who gave him Isaac, called him again to go to the mount of Moriah and offer that same son, Isaac, as a burnt offering to Him. Abraham did not hesitate to answer God's call to offer Isaac in sacrifice to Him. Rather than ask God how He was going to become father of many nations if He takes away his only son, Abraham set out immediately to obey God.

Yet another account about thanksgiving from the Old Testament is the pathetic story that ended beautifully. The story of the widow at Zarephath (1Kings 17:11f). Elijah was sent to this widow whom he met gathering wood for fire and asked her for a drink. She proceeded to get the drink for Elijah, but Elijah further asked for some corn and oil. At this point, the widow informed Elijah that as the Lord our God lives, she has a little jar of corn flour and a jug of oil which she was gathering wood to prepare for her son and herself after which they will wait for death through starvation, because that was the last they had and do not have hope for anything from anywhere at the time because of the famine. The prophet of God ministered to her and said; As the Lord our God lives, neither will the jar of corn be emptied nor will the jug of oil be spilled, go and do as I have said. Poor widow, she did what the prophet commanded and truly, the jar of corn was not emptied and the jug of oil was not spilled.

The New Testament also provides instructive teachings about thanksgiving. Arguably the most prominent of these teachings is the Lucan account of the ten lepers healed by Jesus, which happens to be the subject of our reflection here. This is the story of ten sick people whom society rejects on account of their contagious skin disease. From a distance they called on the Lord of life to give them again a normal life and indeed he gave them back a normal life (Lk. 17:11-19). The significant thing at the end of this story is that only one of the lepers came back to thank Jesus.

In addition to being physical cleansed of leprosy, the healed leper who came back to give thanks gained the grace of eternal life. But Jesus wondered about the remaining nine. Were they not cleansed two, why particularly is it that it is this foreigner that has come back to give thanks?

The allusion of Jesus Christ to the cleansed leper who came back to give thanks as a foreigner gives the impression that the other nine who did not come back to give thanks were Jews. Being Jews, they are members of the chosen race whom sickness united with a foreigner that they would ordinarily not relate with. Also, as Jews, they, perhaps, had a sense of right to God's blessings, which means they have only been given what is their due by right. The foreigner, who perhaps, considers his cleansing a privilege, found it necessary to return and show gratitude. Very many of us, consciously or unconsciously think and act in like manner as the other nine cleansed lepers. We think that because we are Christians, and some even drag it further, that because we are Catholics, or even because we have prayed hard, we deserve certain things we get from God. That God is obliged to make certain things available to us, and when they are not available, we think God is not present in the Church, and we start looking for Him elsewhere.

Thanksgiving is an obligation we owe to God. All that we are, all that we have, come from God. God really has no need of our thanks, but as the Common Preface IV during weekday Masses says, "For, although you have no need of our praise, yet our thanksgiving is itself your gift, since our praises add nothing to your greatness, but profit us for salvation..." The physical gifts presented to God are received by the Church and her authorized representatives on behalf of Christ, the Chief Shepherd of the Christian community. Some persons because of this, thinking that it's the priests they are giving their thanksgiving gifts to, withdraw and/or hold back in giving thanks. Some have also complained that they do not like what use their gifts are put to. Why don't you leave that to God to determine? Or do you want to give to God and tell God what to do with what you have given to him? God has His authorized representatives who have the responsibility to account of what is given to God through them. Let them settle that with God.

Some persons have become laid-back in generously giving because they think others are not doing enough or not even doing anything. Should others condition what you do? Let us consider one of Anthony de Mello's stories: "Once upon a time the members of the body were very annoyed with the stomach. They were resentful that they had to produce food and bring it to the stomach while the stomach itself did nothing but devour the fruit of their labour. So they decided they would no longer bring the stomach food. The hands would not lift it to the mouth. The teeth would not chew it and the throat would not swallow it. That would force the stomach into doing something. But all they succeeded in doing was make the body weak to the point that they were all threatened with death. So it was finally they learnt the lesson that in helping one another they were really working for their own welfare."[171] The idea is that whatsoever we contribute for the common good, we actually contribute for our own good. And in the case of God, whatever we give to God, we are really sowing for our own benefit. The leper that came back to thank Jesus did not in any way add to the ministry of Jesus, but rather, he got something much more than the other nine got. In addition to his healing, he got salvation, which the other nine may probably not get, because they could not come to say thank you for the little they had received.

Love begets love and giving begets receiving. The class teacher handed five coins each to a girl and a boy in the class and asked them to walk around the school giving a coin to anyone who smiles at them. The boy walked around and came back with his five coins intact, while the girl came back without a coin. The boy claimed no one smiled at him so he had no one to give a coin to. The girl said everyone she met smiled at her and she even ran out of coins to give out. On further inquiry on how come the girl got smiles and the boy did not, the girl explained that she smiled at everyone she met and they in turn smiled back at her.

---

171 Anthony de Mello, *The Prayer of the Frog*, Vol. 2, (India: Gujarat Sahitya Prakash, 1993), p. 174.

37

Gratitude and Salvation (Lk. 17: 11-19)[172]

Today's readings challenge our sense of appreciation and gratitude and draws a connection between gratitude to God and our salvation. The first reading tells us the story of Naaman, the leper. It provides us a typical example of how we should express our gratitude to God and to one another. It also teaches us that God does not come to our help because of what he will receive from us. After all, what is in the world that we want to give to God that is not already His? "All the silver and gold in the whole world are mine" (Haggai 2:8-9). The common preface, number IV of weekday says, "For, although you have no need of our praise, yet our thanksgiving is itself your gift, since our praises add nothing to your greatness, but profit us for salvation, through Christ our Lord." The gospel passage of today (Lk. 17: 11-19) is a demonstration of what is stated in this preface. Jesus tacitly expressed the intrinsic relationship between being grateful and being saved when he told the Samaritan leper "Rise and go your way; your faith has saved you." The story of the ten lepers shows that God expects us to be grateful and that He rewards our gratitude.

Can we say that gratitude to God is a requirement for our salvation? Hypothetically, yes, it is. The weekday preface cited above says our praises add nothing to God's greatness, but profit us for salvation. Gratitude is an awareness of, and an appreciation for, the good things in our life. It is the attitude of not taking the good things in our life for granted. It is a spiritual attitude by

172 Homily for the 28th Sunday of Ordinary Time, Year C, at SS. Peter and Paul Catholic Major Seminary. October, 2019.

which we accept whatsoever God offers us. Horizontally, it is the acknowledgment of the role of other people in making our life possible and enjoyable. It is a Christian virtue that demonstrates our humility. Humility is the basis and foundation of all Christian virtues, and we do the will of God when we practice the Christian virtues. To do the will of God is to be on the path of salvation. St. Paul links gratitude with doing God's will when he tells us to "Give thanks in all circumstances; for this is the will of God in Christ Jesus for you" (1 Thess. 5:18; Col. 3:17). Gratitude opens us, in greater measure, to the graces of God.

We find some extraordinary similarities between today's first reading (2 Kings 5: 14-17) and the gospel passage. They are both about persons afflicted with skin ailments, which the readings describe as leprosy. Both readings talked about the expressions of gratitude, and the principal characters; Naaman the Syrian and the leper who returned to thank Jesus, a Samaritan, were both foreigners. Does their being foreigners have anything to do with their gratitude? To some extent, Yes. Although, not explicitly stated in the readings, but the explicit reference to the fact that they are not Jews gives us grounds to think that they considered their healing as privileges for which they owe gratitude.

The background to today's first reading is the narrative of 2 Kings 5: 1-17. Naaman, a great and powerful general of the Aramean army, took the part of the powerful and influential in seeking solution to his skin ailment. Going through his own king to the king of Israel, so that he could get to the prophet of God; Elisha ministered to him. It took the advice of a humble servant of his to moderate his pride and do as the man of God instructed. Amazed at the result of following the prophet's instruction, he was full of gratitude, because he was humbled by the simplicity of the process. He wasted no time, as we read in this reading, in expressing his gratitude. If Naaman had not swallowed his pride and come down from his high and mighty position, he would not have followed the prophet's instruction and even if he was cleansed, he would see it as something he deserved perhaps, he would not have seen the need for the thank-you. Pride is a stumbling block to gratitude and humility is the gateway to the faith of giving thanks.

There are some interesting details in the gospel passage that can help us to reflect deeper on gratitude as a Christian virtue. Take, first of all, the point at which Jesus met the lepers; it provides us a better understanding and appreciation of the condition of the lepers. Jesus met them at the border between Samaria and Galilee, the fringes of both cities. Because they were stigmatised and considered as outcast, they were forced to live outside the city (Lev. 13: 45-46; Num. 5: 2), away from others so that they do not contaminate them. They are considered unclean, and they must announce their presence from a distance so that people can move out of their path to avoid becoming unclean like them. They are erroneously considered to be cursed by God since leprosy was understood to be a curse from God upon those who have sinned (Ex. 20: 5; Is. 53: 4).

Although, the lepers kept the ritual distance from Jesus, they, nonetheless, summoned the courage to break the taboo of speaking to a rabbi. But then, what exactly did they say: "Jesus, Master, have mercy on us." We cannot say exactly that they were asking to be healed or they were asking for alms, but whichever it is they meant, they indicated: (i) that they knew who Jesus was because they even called him by name, (ii) they believed that he could be of help to them, and (iii) they were ready to take their chances.

Of utmost significance for us is that they were not specific in what they asked for. It is a lesson for us that when we seek God's favour, we should allow God give us what He deems fit, against the usual attitude of presenting a list of petitions before God. It is a total reliance and dependence on the providence of God, who knows how to give the best to His children (Mt. 7: 11). This should be the attitude of a good disciple. Whatever they were asking for, Jesus was ready to reinstate them into the society that their skin condition ostracized them from and even much more, as we see with the one who returned to give thanks. What more could they possibly have asked for that would be greater than what Jesus was ready to offer them.

The disposition of Jesus Christ towards the lepers shows us how, as Christians, we should treat others with respect and uphold their human dignity. Jesus did not hurry away from them to avoid becoming unclean. He did not ignore their plea for mercy, he did not consider the social restrictions that prevent communication between the leprous and the unleprous. He had time to spare for them, he wanted to free them from their predicament and restore them to their full dignity and place in the community. Jesus' disposition towards the lepers is an instruction to us about breaking the barriers that divide us in the society.

The faith of the lepers calls for a closer reflection. Even though they were not cleansed yet, Jesus asked them to go and do what a cleansed leper is expected to do in order to be rehabilitated into the society. Without questions about how they were supposed to do that when they were still leprous, they proceeded, in obedience to his directives. Away from Jesus, on their way to see the priest, they were cleansed. The other nine continued their journey towards rehabilitation into society, but one, a foreigner, preferred first to be reunited with Jesus before he goes to be reunited with society. Like the popular "Good Samaritan" in Lk. 10: 30-37, we see another "Good Samaritan" in today's gospel. Note that they are not good because they are Samaritans, they are good because they did the right thing.

While the other nine lepers really obeyed Jesus to the letter and continued their journey to regain their social status, the Samaritan leper thinks it better to re-establish his relationship with God first. It sounds easy but the truth is that, it takes a strong inner conviction to do what the Samaritan leper did. Here is someone who has been constantly reminded by society that he was suffering from a curse imposed on him by God and after all that humiliation, should he be grateful to God for all the humiliation? The Samaritan leper, instead of grudging over the past, was forward-looking. He was grateful to God for turning around his fortune and giving him a new future. He praised and worshipped God. His attitude of gratitude placed him in a position to receive something much more, something that even those who were never leprous are not sure of – he got salvation.

He got salvation because he had a deeper and somewhat different kind of faith from the other nine. Like the other nine, he had the faith to request, but more than the faith he shared with the other nine, he had the faith to be grateful, which the other nine lacked. So while they all got their request, in addition to being physically cleansed, the Samaritan leper got salvation. The ten lepers had faith to seek for help from Jesus, but only one of them, the Samaritan leper, had the deeper faith to go back and express his thanks. The nine lepers were healed; the Samaritan leper was not only healed, he was also saved. The faith to ask is self or problem-focused, but the faith to be grateful is self-transcending, it is solution-focused. The former focuses on our needs, but the latter looks beyond our needs to the giver.

In our second reading from 2 Tim. 2:8-13, St. Paul encourages Timothy and, indeed, all of us to endure hardship in faith. If we learn to do this, we would see the hand of God in all the circumstances of our life and realize that for those who love God, all things work unto good (Rom. 8:28). And thus, we shall always have cause to thank, glorify, praise and worship God for His deeds in our lives, just as the Samaritan leper did.

38

Allowing God into Our Lives (Lk. 7:11-17)[173]

1 Kings 17:17-24 give an account of Elijah as God's instrument in the raising of the son of the woman at Zarephath. This can easily be compared with the gospel account of Jesus raising the son of the widow in the city of Nain (Lk. 7:11-17). Both women had the similar experience of the power of God restoring the joy in their lives. Although, they both experienced the same power of God, we can nonetheless identify differences in the process by which God intervened in their lives.

First and foremost, the woman at Zarephath was the one who took her problem to the man of God, Elijah. This was not exactly the case with the widow of Nain. She was on her way to bury her son. Jesus, without being invited, but out of compassion intervened. Secondly, the woman at Zarephath had proven her faith by bringing her case to the man of God. This was not the case with the widow of Nain. She had neither proved her faith nor even attempted to do that when the death of her son came upon her. She accepted her situation and was, in her grief, going to bury her late son. Thirdly, the woman at Zarephath had shown some goodness towards the man of God by accommodating him. We can, therefore, conclude that she received the reward of her good deed. This is, however, not the case with the widow of Nain.

Nonetheless, there is something about the widow of Nain that warrants the sympathy of Jesus as shown in the gospel passage cited above. This is precisely the fact that she is a widow. The

---

173 Homily on the 10th Sunday of Ordinary Time, Year C, at St. Louis Grammar School, Mokola, Ibadan, in 2013.

scripture, especially the Old Testament, presents us with a tradition where women seem to be entirely dependent on their husbands. Thus, a widow is like a helpless woman. The future of a widow would rest on her sons, who supposedly will take care of her when they grow up to become men. Thus, the scripture presents the widow as especially close to the heart of God. And here is a widow whose only son has passed on, this implies that she has no hope for the future. To be a widow and in addition to be sonless is to virtually be reduced to a life of begging.

That Christ came to the aid of this widow is a demonstration of the unbounded love of God for those who suffer. It is also a kind of protest from Christ against laws that discriminate; in this case, against women and the less privileged, against cultural practices that encourage such discriminations, and against unjust economic policies that further impoverish the less privileged and disadvantaged in society. The sympathy of Jesus towards the widow of Nain who has become sonless demonstrates his faithfulness to his claim that he has come that we may have life in abundance (Jn. 10:10).

We may ask why some people still suffer if God shows such unconditional love, especially those who profess to be his followers. This question brings us to the theme of our reflection, namely, allowing the intervention of God in our lives. The truth is that, not many of us allow God to intervene in our lives. We have our ideas and notions of how things should be and how things should not be. We lack the patience to stop and listen to God in the situations and circumstances of our lives. We are too busy and entrenched in doing things our own ways and standards that even when God wants to come in, we do not notice or recognize the handwriting on the wall.

Let us again look at the widow of Nain whose situation is worsened by the death of her son. Engrossed in her pain and the hopelessness of the future that she would by now be staring into, it is definitely an unwelcome situation for a stranger to interfere in the process of peacefully burying her son. The first comment of Jesus to the widow was, "Do not weep." Many of us would respond to such a comment with a cynical stare at the person uttering such to a woman in such a situation. For such a stranger to go on and halt the funeral procession would be considered going too far. The most likely reaction would be to scold and push him away as an unwelcome intruder.

This, however, was not the reaction of the widow. She did not complain nor ward off Jesus, even though she did not know who he was. She maintained the stillness that enable her encounter the grace of God. She did not allow the human urge to always be in a hurry to do what has to be done steal away her moment of grace. She allowed God to intervene in her life. The Psalmist says, "Be still and know that I am God" (Ps. 46:10).

Let us learn to be still and give God a chance to intervene in our lives. As much as we are not required to be laybacks in life, we should not be so engrossed in handling our own affairs and thereby losing sight of the presence and need of God. We should always endeavour to create an atmosphere that enables us recognize the presence of God. Most importantly, we should allow God intervene in our lives.

39

Make a Straight Path for the Lord (Lk. 3:1-6)[174]

The prophecy of Baruch shows that God intervenes mercifully in favour of humankind (Baruch 5:1-9). The prophet Baruch revives the hope of Israel after their return from exile in Babylon in 538BC. According to Baruch, God has ordered the levelling of the high mountains and the filling of the valleys to make a level ground so that Israel may safely walk in the glory of God.

The gospel of Luke echoes the same call as Luke likens the preaching of John the Baptist, which was a call to repentance for the forgiveness of sins, to the prophetic claim of Is. 40:3-5. This is the voice in the wilderness that calls for the preparation of the way for the Lord. This voice lays out the pattern for the preparation of the way of the Lord. The way of the Lord is to be made straight by filling in the low valleys, bringing down the mountains and hills, straightening the crooked paths and smoothening the rough edges. If we are able to do just this, then we stand the chance of seeing God's salvation. If we make the path of the Lord straight, we open ourselves to the grace of salvation. In other words, if we allow the Lord a path into our affairs, then we dispose ourselves for the grace of salvation.

Two striking scenarios in the gospel periscope above are: (i) The efforts of the evangelist Luke to aptly time the activities of John the Baptist, and (ii) the very content of Isaiah's prophecy, which Luke equates to John's call to repentance.

---

174 Homily on the 2nd Sunday of Advent, Year C, at the Seminary of SS. Peter and Paul Chapel, Bodija, Ibadan, on the 9th of December, 2012.

Luke provides an insight into the political and religious times/atmosphere within which John the Baptist exercised his ministry. The political atmosphere was not a friendly one, neither was the religious atmosphere particularly friendly. "In the fifteenth year of the reign of Tiberius Caesar, Pontius Pilate being the governor of Judea, and Herod being tetrarch of Galilee, and his brother Philip, tetrarch of the region of Ituraea and Trachonitis, and Lysanias, tetrarch of Abilene, in the high priesthood of Annas and Caiaphas, the word of God came to John the son of Zechariah in the wilderness; and he went into all the region about the Jordan, preaching a baptism of repentance for the forgiveness of sins" (Lk. 3:1-3). Looking at this scenario as described by Luke, we see two pagan powers and two believers in power. And in the religious arena, we see two persons; Annas and Caiaphas in the same office, which clearly points to some kind of division.

Like John the Baptist, our call to serve the Lord is situated within a given timeframe and milieu. It may not be the most favourable or conducive situation, as we find in the case of John the Baptist, we are, nonetheless, expected to be faithful by willingly accepting our era and milieu, so as to make them the framework where we serve God and follow Christ as John the Baptist did.

The content of Isaiah's prophecy, which John the Baptist echoes, calls for bringing low the mountains and hills, filling the valleys and straightening crooked paths. These do not necessarily refer to the landscape of Palestine, but rather to the lives of the people. They refer to their excesses, their weaknesses, their omissions and their commissions. They refer to their sins of pride, selfishness, greed, hypocrisy, gossip, malice, adultery and fornication, lies, deceit, etc.

These sins, which are as much present to us and in us today as they were to the people in the time of John the Baptist, are what preparing a straight path for the Lord is all about. We are called to turn away from them. This is the call to repentance for the forgiveness of sins, which John the Baptist preached. It is the same repentance that we preach today, turning away from our sins, that we may experience the mercy and forgiveness of God.

When we turn away from sins, when we repent, what do we do? Where do we turn to? When we turn away from sinful ways, we turn to the corresponding virtues of our sinful ways. In other words, when we turn away from our sinful ways of pride, selfishness, greed, hypocrisy, gossip, malice, adultery and fornication, lies, deceit, etc. we turn to humility, selflessness, generosity, honesty, agape (Christian love), chastity, and straightforwardness. To make this turnaround would place us within the grace of salvation. God would, as always mercifully intervene in our lives.

Advent is a season of joyful expectation of the coming of the Lord. The Church therefore, calls upon us to stop and listen to the call to repentance. To pause a while and look into our lives, to level the excesses of our lives, fill-in the valleys of our weaknesses, straighten our crooked ways and smoothen the rough edges of our spirituality. In this way, we prepare a straight way for the Lord into our lives that we may see the salvation of our God. St. Paul speaking to the Philippians said, "... it is my prayer that your love may abound more and more, with knowledge and all discernment, so that you may approve what is excellent, and may be pure and blameless for the day of Christ, filled with the fruits of righteousness which come through Jesus Christ, to the glory and praise of God" (Phil. 1:8-11). Amen.

40

War against Sin and Evil (Lk. 12:49-53)[175]

The prophet Isaiah describes the coming Messiah as the Prince of Peace; "Unto us a child is born, unto us a child is given; and his name shall be called, wonderful counsellor, everlasting father, and the Prince of Peace" (Is. 9:5). Jesus confirmed that he is the Prince of Peace when he sent out his disciples to places where he himself was to go to. He categorically asked them to be peaceful and always firstly impart a blessing of peace to any house they enter (Lk. 10:5). It would be surprising in the light of these to hear Jesus talk about bringing division to the earth and casting fire upon the earth as stated in today's gospel passage.

The division that Jesus talks about is the division between those who follow the values of the world and those who follow the values of Christ. And the fire he wishes were already kindled is a purifying element; the fire that would purify his followers from sin, selfishness, hatred, indifference, and superficiality. It is not a fire of destruction, except we understand the destruction as the destruction of tendencies within us that are opposed to the values of thc kingdom of heaven.

When Jesus talks about casting fire upon the earth and bringing division, it is not so much about his purpose of coming among men as our human language would want us to interpret it; it is more about the inevitable consequences of his coming. He declared in Jn. 10:10 that he has come that we may have abundant life. Abundance of life is not quantitative but qualitative;

---

175 Homily on the 20th Sunday of the Ordinary Time, Year C, given at St. Joseph of the Holy Family Catholic Church, Harlem, Manhattan, NYC, August 2013.

destruction by fire and division would not be terms used in describing a phenomenon from its qualitative perspective!

Since the forces of evil and darkness are always against the forces of good and light, there is a natural tension between both, a division between the two camps; the camp of the godly and the camp of the ungodly. This is an inevitable consequence of the coming of the Messiah into the world. Evil and ungodliness are always opposed to good and godliness; a perpetual strife exists between these two groups.

As Christians, followers of Jesus Christ, we will have to perpetually war against evil and sin. It is not a war that calls for a compromise between both camps, it is not a war where we have to shift a little for each other; it is a war where we one will have to defeat the other. Christians should ensure that they defeat evil, sin, and ungodliness in their lives. To achieve the defeat of evil and sin, we have to learn to persevere. The Letter to the Hebrews counsels, "Let us run with perseverance the race that is set before us, looking to Jesus the pioneer and perfecter of our faith, who for the joy that was set before him, endured the cross, despising the shame, and is seated at the right hand of the throne of God" (Heb. 12:2-3).

In other words, Christ was met with hostilities as the gospels clearly show. He nonetheless endured and carried on the fight against sin and evil. He endured the earthly shame that the war brought upon him, because he had his eyes fixed on the victory that is to come. And when all the shame and humiliation had been endured, he rose in glory and today he is seated on the throne. Therefore, as Christians, we are called to follow in his path by remaining steadfast and fighting on in perseverance. We are called to endure the hostilities that are the hallmark of the strife, the division between good and evil, light and darkness, and the inevitable consequences of the coming of the Prince of Peace to this world.

41

"Unless a Wheat Grain Falls into the Earth and Dies" (Jn. 12:24)[176]

"How foolish!" St. Paul would exclaim, "What you sow must die before it is given new life..." (1 Cor. 15:36). In this seeming foolishness lies the truth of our Christian faith and life. In a religious community were two great brothers. Great because they were each renowned for their closeness to God. One spends six days of the week in his cell praying and fasting while the other spend six days of the week caring for the sick. Another brother confused about their opposed Christian attitude once asked an elderly member of the religious community, whose spiritual renown was equally widespread, about his opinion concerning both brothers. The simple response of the elder was, if the brother who spends six days praying and fasting in his cell was to hang himself by the noose in asceticism, all seven days of the week that will not equal one act of kindness of the one who takes care of the sick.

In the gospel verse above, Jesus Christ presents us with the amazing paradox of our Christian faith and life. At one and the same time, he says three things, which turn out to be variations of one central truth that lies in the heart of our Christian faith and life.

i. Only by death comes life.
ii. Only by spending life do we retain it.
iii. Only by service comes greatness.

"I tell you, most solemnly, unless a wheat grain falls on the ground and dies, it remains only a single grain; but if it dies, it

176 Originally delivered as a homily at the Seminary of All Saints, Uhiele, Ekpoma in 2003.

yields a rich harvest" (Jn. 12:24). In this singular statement of Jesus lies a truth, an instruction, and a call, to Christian service. We live in a world where the idea of service is in danger of getting lost, if it is not already lost! A world in which the pronouns "my" and "mine" have become the aggressive order of the day, both in business circles and in governance. This explains why in a country like ours (Nigeria), the masses suffer want in the midst of plenty. It explains why poverty keeps eating deeper into the fabric of our nation. It explains why discord, disharmony, distrust, and mutual suspicion, characterise our human relationships, even in the priesthood and among Christian brothers and sisters. It is so because the "my" and "mine" pronouns only serve the purposes of selfishness and satisfaction of unchristian desires and want.

Contrary to this self-centredness and selfishness, Christ Jesus warns us of the dangers they pose to our faith. He calls us to a closer examination of our Christian faith and life in the light of service to humanity. He uses the latter as a paradigm to be imitated by those who are called and chosen to be his followers, which includes you and me and Christians everywhere.

That a wheat grain must first die is a call in the sense that, it is an invitation that we spend our life for others so as to retain it for ourselves and for God. Only by death comes life. For as long as we preserve the grain of wheat, for so long, it remains ineffective and unfruitful, as it were, it remains safe and secure. Consequently, growth and development remains stunted and stagnant.

The history of humanity shows that it is because men and women were prepared to die that great things and events have taken place. Thus, the truth becomes clearer that only when Christian men and women bury their personal aims and ambitions that they begin to be of real use to God, which is our calling, to make ourselves, especially as priests and future priests, useful in the hands of God. That is to say, we truly become servants of God, servants in the positive sense, when we let go our personal desires and ambitions.

A survey of the men and women of all times and places we call great reveals too that these are those who have forgotten themselves in favour of something outside of themselves. Take for instances, names like Martin Luther King Jr., who gave up his life for the peaceful liberation of the African Americans. Mother Theresa, who spent her life in a tireless effort to take care of the dying beggars of Calcutta, Ken Saro-Wiwa, Kudirat Abiola, and a host of others who have laid their lives to be slaughtered for the political emancipation and freedom of the Nigerian people, held captives in their own land by their own government. And of course, the supreme example of Jesus Christ himself, of whom scripture says; "although he was Son, he learnt to obey through suffering; but having been made perfect, he became for all who obey him the source of eternal salvation" (Heb. 5:8).

Our world today is in need of service, let us think today about what this world would have lost without men and women who were ready to give up their personal safety, security, selfish gain, and self-advancement. We owe a million thanks to such who have spent their lives and strength for God and others. There is no doubt that we may exist longer, if we take things easily, avoid strain, and look after ourselves. We definitely stand the chance to exist longer, but to exist is not to live. According to Christmas Evans, "It is better to burn out than to rust out."

Jesus Christ came with a new view of life. He teaches us that only by death comes life. That we retain our lives only by spending it. And that true greatness, the greatness that counts in the sight of God comes through service. This is the truth of common sense, this is the truth of our Christian faith, this is the truth of our Christian life, and the truth Christians are called to live. It is indeed not possible to harm others without harming oneself, in the same way, it is equally impossible to help others without helping oneself. Anthony de Mello tells the story of Nasrudinn, who sang happily and carried around a bright face on this golden morning and when Musa, a friend of his tried to find out the source of his joy, Nasrudinn said, "Don't mind that idiot Ahmed who keeps slapping me on the back each time he sees me. Well, I've put a stick of dynamite under my clothing today so this time when he slaps me he'll blow his arm off." Will Nasrudinn walk away unharmed or would someone have committed suicide?

42

Human Justice vis-à-vis God's Mercy (Jn. 8:1-11)[177]

Our gospel passage for reflection narrates the story of the woman caught in the act of sin. The particular sin in question is adultery. Not wanting to take justice into their hands, the scribes and Pharisees brought the case to Jesus. This would sound a noble path, but as the evangelist John noted, they had an ulterior motive; they wanted something on which to catch Jesus and accuse him of breaching the laws of their religion. This is definitely not a noble motive.

Anyhow, from the presentation of the scribes and Pharisees, it appeared that they were seeking justice. Justice flows from application of the laws of the land. Thus, they skilfully crafted their presentation; "Teacher, this woman has been caught in the act of adultery. Now in the law Moses commanded us to stone such. What have you to say about her?" (Jn. 8:3-4). Apparently, they expected Jesus, in his characteristic way to protect the woman from their wrath, which in their understanding Moses approved of. For Jesus to do this, it would amount to disregard for Moses and the laws of the people.

Jesus aware of their unwholesome motive and the craft of their question maintained a dignified silence for a while. It was as if since you know what the law says, why bring her to me? Of course, they were already in and without an answer from Jesus it would feel awkward for them to proceed to apply the law, so they pressurised him to saying something. I'm sure somewhere in the

177 Homily for the 5th Sunday of Lent, Year C, at Our Lady Seat of Wisdom Chapel, University of Ibadan, in 2013.

corner of their mind, they would be feeling good that they had Jesus in a tight corner. Jesus is never in a tight corner. His silence did not, in any way, signify that he did not know what was the right thing to do, perhaps, it may even just be an indication of the pity he feels for them.

His eventual response indicates that the scribes and Pharisees were the ones who had driven themselves into a tight corner. Jesus' response was not to dispute their claim for justice, but to challenge them to prove that they are better off than the woman they seek to condemn. "Let him who is without sin among you be the first to throw a stone at her" (Jn. 8:6). It is not a case of she is not guilty nor was it a case of your law is wrong; it was a simple case of search yourself and beat your breast that you have never sinned! One after the other, they left. No one had the courage to stand out and proclaim himself sinless, precisely because no one is sinless.

In the eyes of the law and within the human description of justice, when you do the wrong thing, you have committed a crime and justice demands that you are punished. The punishment is to reprimand you and deter others from committing the same wrong. This was all the scribes and Pharisees demanded. Within the new teachings of Christ, the bedrock on which our Christian faith is built, there is, however, a different way of viewing things. When you do the wrong thing, you have sinned and Christian love requires that you are forgiven. This Christian approach represents the mercy of God in partnership with human justice. I use the phrase, 'in partnership' because God's mercy does not negate justice, in our common parlance, we say, "tampering justice with mercy." This was the lesson Jesus taught his followers in the passage for reflection.

When the crowds who wanted justice done as prescribed by the law had gone away, aware they too had at different points in time violated the law, Jesus turned to the woman who had done wrong. He did not praise her for winning the case against the crowds, neither did he dismiss her without a caution. "Woman, where are they? Has no one condemned you?" "Neither do I condemn you; go, and do not sin again" (Jn. 8:11).

In law, we talk about "discharged" and "acquitted." This means that one is not found guilty of the crime accused of, and therefore, he/she is allowed to go. In this case, Jesus discharged the woman but did not acquit her, he found her guilty as charged but discharged her on the grounds of mercy, giving her another chance. If he had acquitted her, he would not say, "... do not sin again." The "again" implies that she had indeed sinned. Yes, he discharged her and gave her another chance, as God always does to us.

Jesus did not approve of what the woman had done. He, however, had not condemned her. He gave her another opportunity to do the right thing. The reaction of Jesus brings to our consideration some salient points.

i. The opportunity for a second chance: God always gives us the opportunity to turn away from sin and be saved.
ii. The merciful nature of God reflected in the compassion of Jesus for the woman; a presentation of God's merciful love for his children.
iii. The challenge of the woman by Jesus to confront her bad life and replace it with the good life.
iv. The belief of Jesus in human nature that we can change if we make the required efforts to change. According to St. Augustine, "the sinner can become the saint."
v. The unspoken but firmly and emphatically implied warning; either you go back to your old life and be condemned forever, or you change your ways and be saved.

Let us also note the calmness and fraternal manner in which Jesus approached the woman in question. After the crowds had gone, he could have turned to the woman and give her a scolding of her life. This would easily be the approach of many of us. Jesus' approach was different, a lesson for us on fraternal correction. He told the woman the truth that she actually did wrong, but not in a manner of judgment. He admonished the woman not to do such again in a loving manner that respected the dignity and the personhood of the woman. This is a contradiction to our usual human ways of correcting one another.

Today's passage of reflection is a gospel of second chance, or re-sit, if you like. This is precisely what the season of lent offers us; a second chance to do the right things we had hitherto being doing wrong. Lent offers us this second chance annually as God suspends our judgment, believing in our human nature to make a change for the better. Cases abound of those who took advantage of this second chance and changed. For instance, the prodigal son did, so we too can. Zachheaus did, we too can. St. Augustine did, you too can. I can, and we all can.

43

Gaining Admittance into Heaven (Lk. 13:22-30)[178]

Today's gospel passage opens our eyes to a number of issues. First and foremost is the response of Jesus to the question on whether those to be saved are few. Jesus did not say there would be few or there would be many who are saved. His response was more on what one should do to be saved. In other words, the issue that should occupy the Christian's mind should not be about statistics and numbers but about what I should do and be as a Christian. Often, we Christians get carried away with externals and forget the most important aspect of striving for personal sanctification and union with the Lord. For instance, we get carried away with constructing beautiful church edifices, the way the institution and system of administration is run, the number of worshippers, the financial gains and losses of the church, etc. In the process, we neglect our spiritual life, which is much more important than all these.

Secondly, the response of Jesus to the knock on the door by the latecomers; "I do not know where you come from." Meanwhile, these latecomers claim; "We ate and drank in your presence, and you taught in our streets." And again, the response is; "I tell you, I do not know where you come from; depart from me, all you workers of iniquity." Apparently it's not all who come into the presence of Jesus that are recognized by him. Meaning, therefore, that going to Church on Sundays is not what makes one a child of God.

---

178 Homily on the 21st Sunday of the Ordinary Time, Year C, at St. Joseph of the Holy Family Church, Harlem, Manhattan, NYC, August 2013.

Thirdly is the fact that "... men will come from east and west, and from north and south, and sit at table in the kingdom of God." The reference to the four geographical points of the earth drives home the point that salvation is universal and not the exclusive privilege of any group of persons. Particularly, for the Jews, it is a warning to them that salvation is not their monopoly.

That salvation is universal, however, does not mean it is automatic. There are given criteria for which those to be saved will be admitted into the kingdom of God. Close association with Christ in terms of having a knowledge of him and his words is not a guarantee for admittance into the kingdom. We may know a number of facts about Jesus, like; where and when he was born, how he grew up and what his teachings are about, such knowledge does not make us his disciples. Jesus' response to those latecomers who claimed to have eaten and drank in his presence was, "... get away from me, I do not know you."

From this response, it becomes obvious that what matters is not that we know and recognize Jesus, but what matters is that Jesus recognizes us and knows us. The latecomers obviously knew and recognized him, but he does not know and recognize them. Their knowledge of Jesus was not enough to gain them admittance into heaven, what was required is that Jesus recognised and knew them.

At this point, it is imperative to ask, how is Jesus supposed to know and recognise us? The answer is very simple and straightforward; "By their fruits you shall know them ..." (Mt. 7:16). This is what Jesus said in the scriptures. It is by what we do and how we live our lives that Jesus will recognise us. The fruits we bear are the identification marks by which we are known to be children of God. Actions and deeds that proceed from love and respect directed towards our fellow human beings are the hallmarks of our personal union with Jesus, who has requested us to follow his example (Jn. 13:15). Again he says; "Love one another, for by this, they will know that you are my disciples" (Jn. 13:34-35).

The narrow gate that Jesus asked his disciples to strive to enter the kingdom through is the life of love and Christian charity. This is a life that demands humility, self-sacrifice, endurance, perseverance, and the spirit of mercy and forgiveness. These are virtues that are contrary to the generally accepted values of our world; pride, self-centeredness, and personal aggrandizement, easy and short way out, vengeance and malice, these constitute the wide and smooth path that Jesus condemns. It is the easy path taken by the majority of persons but leads to damnation.

44

Service and Friendship (Lk. 10:38-42)[179]

In Gen. 18: 1-10, Abraham showed courtesy and kindness towards three travellers. He invited them into his house, prepared them a meal and chatted with them. This encounter was entirely at the instance of Abraham. He offered them refreshment without them asking. In return Abraham was blessed with a child.

It is very instructive within the context of recent events in Florida, concerning the case of Zimmerman and Trayvon, to note that Abraham was not suspicious of the travellers. He did not attempt to guard and protect his territory from strangers. He saw human beings like himself in need of refreshment on their journey. And he saw himself as being in a position to be able to provide that refreshment.

This is a sharp contrast from Zimmerman whose first impression of Trayvon was that of a black boy whose only intention would be to bugle any store. For Zimmerman, the neighbourhood must be protected from such blacks that are of no good. Against this impression could be a nobler impression of a disadvantage black boy who has to walk unprotected in the rain back home after getting an item from the store for his mum. As it turned out to be, the latter was the case of Trayvon.

Abraham invited the visitors into his home. Shared with them and provided for them. In this process a relationship of friendship was established through the service of Abraham. How I wish this was the case between Zimmerman and Trayvon! Trayvon would still be alive, his family would have been spared of their present pain and the state of Florida would not be plunged in bad light with the "Stand your ground" ruling that set Zimmerman free.

---

179 A homily delivered in St. Catherine of Genoa Catholic Church, Harlem, Manhattan, NYC on the 16th Sunday of Ordinary Time, Year C, July 2013.

Today's gospel reconciles the issue of service and companionship. The gospel account is the story of Jesus' visit to the home of Mary and Martha. While Mary sat at the foot of Jesus to listen to him, Martha was preoccupied with preparing a fitting welcome meal for Jesus. This scenario presents Martha and Mary depicting service and companionship respectively. Both (service and companionship) are not to be separated. But there should be an order of priority, where one flows from the other.

Service is better rendered when we know the needs of the one who is served. We get to know the needs of the other person by listening to him/her. This was what Martha did not do. Abraham in the first reading had a rapport with the travellers. "... If I have found favour in your sight, do not pass by your servant. Let a little water be brought, and wash your feet, and rest yourselves under the tree, while I fetch a morsel of bread that you may refresh yourselves, and after that you may pass on..." In response, they said to Abraham, "Do as you have said."

Such rapport was not established between Martha and Jesus. Martha presumed what Jesus would be needing. As it turned out, Jesus would had preferred she sat and listened to him as Mary did. Jesus, however, did not condemn Martha's good intention and action. He nonetheless, reminded Martha not to be overly anxious but be patient to find out the need of others before setting out to meet them. Otherwise, it would be the case of doing the right thing in the wrong manner.

As Christians, we need to first listen to the Lord and know what he requires of us. The evangelist Mark tells us about the call of the apostles, "So he appointed twelve to be with him; and he called them apostles. He wanted to send them out to preach" (Mk 3:14-15). The reason he called them was to send them out, but first they had to be with him, to listen so they would know what he requires of them and how he wants it done. Christ requires that we spend time with him before we set out to be another Christ to one another. In the same vein, we need to learn to hear each other out before we can begin to assist each other. We need to be each other's companions that we may be able to be at each other's service.

45

Neighbourhood without Borders (Lk. 10:25-37)[180]

In response to the direct question, "Who is my neighbour?" Jesus told the story of the Good Samaritan. This story has become so popular within and outside the Christian world. It is a story that carries within it a lot of insight into the Christian idea of human interpersonal relationship. Strangely, but very significantly, Jesus did not, at the end of the story, say who one's neighbour is. Instead, he redirected the question to the lawyer that asked the first question. "Which of these three, do you think, proved neighbour to the man who fell among the robbers?" Without hesitation, the lawyer provided the answer, "The one who showed mercy to him." In the response of the lawyer, he defined neighbourhood without reference to boundaries, but within the framework of how people relate to one another. "Go and do likewise" was Jesus' final comment. A comment that approves of the answer of the lawyer, a comment that agrees with the definition of neighbourhood without borders.

In the story of the Good Samaritan, Jesus gives us the paradigm of neighbourhood without borders as the paradigm of Christian charity. Among other issues, the story of the Good Samaritan makes four issues categorically clear.

i. From the story of the Good Samaritan, the important question should not be, who is my neighbour? But who am I a neighbour to? There should be a shift from the

180 Homily on the 15th Sunday of Ordinary Time, Year C, given at St. Joseph of the Holy Family Catholic Church, Harlem, Manhattan, NYC. July 2013.

other person to me. This fact is made clear in the contrast between the question of the lawyer, "Who is my neighbour?" and the question of Jesus Christ, "Which of these three, do you think, proved neighbour to the man who fell among the robbers?"

ii. The story of the Good Samaritan disagrees with our human divisions between the "us" and the "them." This is shown in the contrast between the Samaritan and the Jew. The Jews usually separated themselves from the Samaritans as the chosen children of God. In like manner, we have divisions among ourselves, we have those that belong to our group or tribe or religion (the us) and those that do not belong (the them). From Jesus' story, the "us" were not there for each other. It was the "them" that was there for the "us." It was a Jewish traveller that was attacked, the first two persons that saw him were Jewish, but did nothing for their person or brother. It was the Samaritan, who did not share the same religious views with the Jews, who is seen as outside the circle of the redeemed, by the Jews, that offered the needed hand of fellowship and help.

iii. The story of the Good Samaritan highlights the fact that our humanity precedes all other things that we are and have become. We are not human because we are Americans, we are not human because we are Spanish, we are not human because we are Asians, and we are not human because we are Africans. We are not human because we are rich, we are not human because we are poor. Our humanity is not determined by our position on the social, economic, political, or cultural ladder. Our humanity, which is our common factor is predicated on the fact that we are all made in the image and likeness of God, irrespective of colour, race, tribe, language, etc.

Neighbourhood is not built on geography, politics, social, or economic status. The "us" and the "them" distinction is built on our acquired characteristics. The basic common factor about our being is our humanity, which is not determined by our acquired characteristics or designations. I am American, Spanish, Asian, African, because I am a man or a woman. I am not a man or woman because I am American, Spanish, Asian, or African.

The Good Samaritan is not "good" because he is from Samaria, he is "good" because he was able to transcend the human barriers and distinctions we have placed between ourselves. He did not see the attacked victim as a Jew. He did not see himself as a Samaritan. He saw two human beings; (i) the victim of armed robbery attack who needed help, and (ii) himself, who was in a position to help.

The Good Samaritan is "good" because he was selfless. He was ready to spend all he had on him. In fact, he was not just ready, he actually spent all he had, and was ready to spend even more, without asking how much more it will cost. How different that is from us! How often do we consider what it amounts to before we extend a helping hand to each other! What we stand to gain or lose before we come to each other's aid!

Having aided the lawyer to see the different possible ways we can relate to each other, Jesus asked him to answer his own question by deciding for himself who was a neighbour to the other. This redirection of the focus is very instructive because it teaches us that neighbourhood is not to be determined by any static parameters, but by the dynamics of our relations with one another. Neighbourhood is not to be considered from the perspective of who is my neighbour, but from the perspective of who do I prove a neighbour to.

Finally, Christ set the Good Samaritan before his listeners as the model of Christian living. "Go then and do the same." It is like saying, "Go and be a neighbour to those you meet on the path of life." As we, therefore, strive to live a good Christian life, let us "go then and do the same." Amen.

46

Salt of the Earth and Light of the World (Mt. 5:13-16)[181]

Centuries ago, Mahatma Gandhi claimed that the greatest hindrance to Christianity is the Christians themselves. The gospel narrative of Mt.5:13-16 provides the context within which Gandhi's assessment confronts us as the truth of our time. The principles of Christianity, when appropriately applied, would definitely ensure that Christians are role models and examples of what a child of God should be. Unfortunately, Christians have woefully failed in applying most of the teachings of Christ in the way they live. The lack of application of Christian principles by Christians in their everyday life is precisely what Gandhi claims as the greatest hindrance to Christianity.

Jesus refers to his followers in the passage above as the "salt of the earth" and the "light of the world." He had declared himself as the light of the world (Jn. 8:12, 9:5). So, calling his followers the light of the world is asking them to be what he himself is to the world. In other words, he is asking that his followers should live in such a way that others may see in them what he was when he physically walked the path of this earth; a shining guide and an example of what a child of God should be.

Why has Jesus chosen to use "salt" to describe his followers rather than something sweeter or tastier than salt? He could have used "sugar" or "honey" for instance. These are definitely tastier and even healthier than salt! That Jesus did not use any of these

181 This was original preached as a sermon on the 5th Sunday of the Ordinary Time of Year A in Our Lady Seat of Wisdom Chapel, University of Ibadan, Ibadan on 9th February, 2014.

points only to one thing, namely, that the issue involved here goes beyond taste. If it is not a question of adding taste to life, what is it about then?

Beyond adding taste to food, salt is also a natural preservative. This is one advantage of salt over sugar and honey. If we consider this aspect of salt in application to Jesus' use of it to describe his followers, it gives us a great insight to the message he was passing across. As salt of the earth, the Christian has the role of preserving the original dignity of God's creation as well as adding some taste of sweetness to it. This is quite in line with the responsibility God bestowed on man at creation when he gave him responsibility over his creation (Gen. 1:28).

Jesus called his followers, "Light of the world." The primary benefit of light is that it enables us get a clear vision of the things around us and thus, makes our navigation easy. Therefore, as light of the world, Christians have the divine responsibility to be guides for others to follow. By their way of life, they are to enlighten and guide others along the right path, which is the path that leads to God.

The combination of "salt" and "light" in application to the Christian passes across a very powerful message to all Christians as to the enormity of the responsibility they have as children of God. Salt and light have positive effects, which Christians are asked to imitate; to positively impact on others around them, like the Good Samaritan (Lk. 10:25-37, Mt. 22:34 and Mk. 12:28).

Christians have the mission to positively impact on the world. To do this, Christians need to be different from the world, like salt is different and separate from that which it impacts on. But it does not impact on it without first coming in contact with it. So also, although the Christian has to be different from the world, for Jesus did say, "You are in the world, but you are not of the world" (Jn. 15:19), the Christian must, nonetheless, come in contact with the world to impact on the world.

It is not right as Christians to separate yourself from others because you do not want to be corrupted. This is not an appropriate Christian attitude! Yes, it is important that we be on our guard not to follow and belong to the world, we have to constantly be aware that we live our Christian faith in the world and in relation to others in the world. Light is different from darkness, but light does not dispel darkness without coming in contact with darkness. The Christian cannot impact positively on the world without coming in contact with the world.

As Christians, we must associate with the world to impact positively on it. While we reject and avoid living by the values of the world, which separate us from the world, we must strive to impact on the world the values of the kingdom of heaven by living them out in the world. We must share ourselves with the world that the world may gain from our Christian lives. The salt preserves and sweetens by sharing itself with that which it preserves and sweetens. Same goes for light, it is in shedding its light where there is darkness that light enlightens and dispels darkness.

Many of us live under the illusion that we do not have anything or enough to share. Everyone has something good to share, all it takes is the willingness to share and you find that you have so many things to share. There is a story of a crippled student who moves around the campus on a wheelchair. On this faithful day, he observed a fellow student who was on crutches struggling with his backpack. He wheeled up to him and offered to help with his backpack while he hops along on his crutches. They strolled to the lecture hall of the boy on crutches where the boy on wheel chair handed him his backpack, wished him a quick recovery and wheeled himself away.

Here is a boy who has no hope of ever walking, helping another who can temporarily not walk! So who says we have nothing to share? Who says we need more than we already have to impact on others? Who says we cannot be salt in the lives of others and light to brighten each other's lives? Jesus obviously has not said so, in fact, he says; "You are the salt of the earth.... You are the light of the world." And goes on to say, "Let your light so shine before men, that they may see your good works and give glory to your Father, who is in heaven."

Note the last part of the sentence, "...and give glory to your Father who is in heaven." We are not to shine for self-praise and glorification; we are not to be good to others, guide and enlighten others so as to earn their praise. We are to do all these for the glory of God. As the Psalmist puts it, "Not to us Lord, not to us, but to your name be the glory" (Ps. 115:1).

47

The Christian Mission of Peace (Lk. 19:1-12, 17-20)[182]

We come to believe in Christ because we have first heard about him. We hear about Christ because someone has spoken about him. To talk about Christ to others is to preach his name, which means we have faith, or we believe because we have heard the preaching about Christ (Rom. 10:14-17). The passage of today declares the need to announce the word of God, the need for people to preach the word of God. It sets out the guidelines for the mission of preaching and encourages preachers not to be discouraged even if the results of their efforts are not apparent. The Christian life is essentially missionary and involves all Christians. It is not an exclusive preserve of a few, even though some are specifically called into the ministry of the word, all Christians are part and parcel of the evangelizing team.

This point is buttressed in Christ's appointment of seventy *others*. There is an emphasis on *others* because it brings out the fact that some had been appointed earlier. Those appointed earlier were the twelve apostles. To show that others are equally called to participate in the same mission, Christ appointed seventy others. The number seventy expresses fullness or wholeness, which implies that everyone or all are involved. Not only did Jesus appoint seventy others, he set out the outline for the mission. Within this outline, he declares the nature of the mission, the manner of mission and the method by which this mission is to be executed.

182 Homily on the 14th Sunday of the Ordinary Time, Year C, given at Our Lady Seat of Wisdom Catholic Chapel, University of Ibadan, Ibadan, 2013.

The mission is essentially the mission of Jesus Christ himself. He sent the appointed to places that he himself was about to visit. Thus, those sent were merely to announce his coming and prepare the people for his arrival. The preparation consists in helping the people dispose themselves for the grace of God that is to come into their lives. It is God who converts and bestows faith, ours is to call on the people to make themselves available for the graces of God. The mission is, therefore, not that of the missionary, but that of Christ.

The mission is a massive one, for Jesus declares that, "the harvest is plentiful but the labourers are few; pray therefore the Lord of the harvest to send out labourers into his harvest." Again, here, there is a reference to the fact that the harvest is the Lord's, "pray therefore the Lord of the Harvest to send out labourers into his harvest." The nature of this massive mission requires that everyone be involved, either as active full-time missionaries as is the case of the ordained ministers or as missionaries who announce the kingdom by their way of life in their various fields of calling.

The mission is an urgent mission, for Jesus instructs those he sends out, "... salute no one on the way." This is an admonition that they should not be distracted by frivolities. Attention should be focused on the mission at hand and attended to immediately. It is, however, not to be misunderstood as a lack of courtesy, but an emphasis on the need for the urgency of the mission at hand.

It is a difficult mission. "I send you as lambs in the midst of wolves." The mission would be met with opposition as it is always the case in the struggle between the forces of darkness and the forces of light. Missionaries would be ridiculed, maltreated, or even killed. They shall suffer rejection and taunting, even from the least expected quarters. Wolves and lambs are never friends. The difficulty of the mission, notwithstanding, is no reason to abandon the mission. Difficulty does not mean impossibility.

The mission is a mission of peace. The symbolism of the "lamb" already indicates this. Jesus emphasizes this aspect when he instructed that, "Whatever house you enter, first say, 'Peace be to this house! This announces immediately that your mission is a peaceful one. Even if, when this announcement of peace is rejected, you are not to be aggressive, as the peace shall return to you; for as Jesus says, "And if a son of peace is there, your peace shall rest upon him; but if not, it shall return to you." Either case scenario, the peace is never lost. Aggression is never a way of evangelization! Aggression is counterproductive to the message of the gospel. The missionary is sent as a "lamb" not a "wolf." So we should always bear in mind that in our Christian life, we are a people of peace, even when in the midst of wolves.

The mission is necessarily a collaborative mission as indicated in the fact that Jesus did not send out the seventy "one by one," but "two by two." He sent them out in pairs that they may provide support and encouragement for each other. That when one is weak, the other may become his strength, when one is discouraged, the other may become his inspiration. It is unfortunate that in our days, we are losing the concept of collaboration. Many of our priests are finding it difficult to live together in the rectories and work together in a parish, while our lay faithful are battling each other for unwholesome reasons. Individualism and self-interest are beclouding our genuine sense of the mission.

Since the mission is a peaceful mission, it must be executed with humility, simplicity and focus. Materialism must be shunned as it is an obstacle and distraction to the mission. "Carry no purse, or bag, no sandals..." I wonder if priests still remember this aspect of the mission. Excess luggage has become one of the prominent banes in contemporary Catholic priesthood, especially in our country. The craze for luxury cars, hi-tech communication equipment (mobile phones) and electronics, modern and expensive clothing, unnecessary oversea trips in the name of vacations, and all sorts of distractive activities that we engage in these days. Many parishioners encourage and praise their priests who entangle themselves in these distractions, by so doing, you become a clog in the wheel of the mission.

The simplicity required in carrying out the mission is further emphasized by Jesus when he instructed that, "And remain in the same house, eating and drinking what they provide, for a labourer deserves his wages." While the latter part of this instruction has been twisted by many, the first part is completely ignored. No genuine minister of the word of God is ever in want, want comes in when we begin to seek what is beyond that which is available. When we learn to accept that which is available and make do with it, we not only find joy, but most importantly, we save the providers the burden of trying to meet our desires. What we see all around us today are cases of ministers making neck-breaking demands on the flock in their care. Modern day ministers have adopted a flamboyant and lavish life style as a proof of the prosperity of their mission. A mission that is in the first place not even their own but that of the Lord.

Focus is shifted from the mission of proclaiming healing (from the disease of sinfulness) and salvation to material prosperity. Today, we count success rather than paying attention to being faithful to Christ and the mission. The success of the seventy was predicated on their faithfulness to the instructions they had received from the Lord of the harvest who had sent them out. Modern day Christianity seems to have lost focus. It is swallowed up in the raging tide of materialism and esotericism. Material prosperity and flamboyancy have become the measuring tape for the success of the mission instead of faithfulness to the Lord of the mission. Focus is now on the missionary and not on the mission as it should have been.

Christ told the seventy, "Nevertheless do not rejoice in this, that the spirits are subject to you; but rejoice that your names are written in heaven." In other words, it is not by the exploits of the missionary that his mission is adjudged successful but by his faithfulness to the Lord of the mission. Mt. 25:35 specifically outlines the criteria for having our names written in heaven. None of the criteria include the kind of exploits advertised on bill-boards, flexes, and flyers today by ministers of God. The criteria had to do with faithfully imitating the self-giving, sacrificial lifestyle of Jesus who is the Lord and owner of the mission.

48

Christianity and Suffering (Mt. 16:21-27)[183]

Contemporary Pentecostal Christianity preaches a theology of prosperity, a Christianity devoid of pain and suffering. Bill boards abound on our highways and byways advertizing Christianity. The messages we find on these boards are all about breakthrough without efforts, successes in examinations without studies, cure without treatment, etc. Although these adverts attribute all these as coming from God, it is ironical that most of the bill boards do not carry the image or picture of God, Jesus Christ, or the Holy Spirit. They are graced with the beautiful images and pictures of the miracle working pastors and their wives and the preachers of the Christianity of prosperity.

This type of Christianity seems to fit perfectly into Peter's idea of Christ's messianic profile. A superstar messiah who is above any form of humiliation, suffering and pain. A messiah for whom all things would be rosy and one who without efforts achieve whatever he wants. After all, the miracles of Jesus have shown that he had powers to do virtually all things; the cure of the leper (Mt. 8:2-3), the calming of the storm (Mt. 8:23-27), the cure of the two demoniacs in Gadara (Mt. 8:28-32), the cure of the paralytic (Mt. 9:2-8), the raising to life of the synagogue official's daughter (Mt. 9:18-26), the restoration of sight to two blind men and the power of speech to a dumb man (Mt. 9:27-34), the miracle of the loaves (Mt. 14:16-21), and Jesus walking on water (Mt. 14:25-32). One significant thing about these miracles is that

183 Homily on the 22nd Sunday of the Ordinary Time of Year A at Our Lady Seat of Wisdom Chapel, University of Ibadan, 31st August, 2014.

they were all recorded in the gospel of Matthew before the sixteenth chapter in which the narration for our reflection is recorded. Therefore, it is safe to assume that Peter was a witness to all these miracles and as such, we cannot blame him for having the superstar notion of Jesus Christ, as his action in the passage above suggests.

Naturally, therefore, in consonance with his idea that the Messiah cannot be subjected to suffering and pain, Peter took Jesus aside and remonstrated with him. "God forbid, Lord! This shall never happen to you." The response of Jesus to Peter would have come as a surprise to Peter. Jesus clearly and emphatically corrected Peter's notion that suffering and pain are not alien to his mission and his Messianic profile. He rebuked Peter in strong words. Thereafter, he turned to his followers to declare in clear terms that pain and suffering are part and parcel of his Messianic profile and anyone who would follow him should be ready to accept same as part and parcel of being his disciple. "If any man would come after me, let him deny himself and take up his cross and follow me."

The declaration of Jesus Christ that the cross is an integral part of following him obviously contradicts present day Christianity of prosperity that preaches the "crown" without the "cross." A Christianity whose theology eliminates pain and suffering or considers pain and suffering as alien and Satanically induced apparently has not taken into consideration this declaration of Jesus that his would-be followers must take up their crosses daily and follow him. We must, however, admit that not all sufferings may be considered as legitimate, in the sense that they fit into what Jesus means by the term "cross" in his declaration.

There are two types of sufferings; (i) the necessary suffering, and (ii) the unnecessary suffering. The unnecessary suffering is the type of suffering we impose on others because of our selfishness. This includes, when we break the marriages of others because of our adulterous habits, when we neglect things we ought to do and bring pain on others because of our neglect, when we carry around an unhealthy sense of guilt and cause ourselves pain because of our stupidity. The pains and sufferings that arise from these situations are avoidable and unjustifiable, and therefore, cannot be considered necessary suffering.

On the contrary, necessary suffering would include such sufferings that come with our growing up, facing our limitations, admitting our mistakes, accepting responsibilities, and giving up our bad habits, etc. These are sufferings and pains that we cannot but endure in our efforts to be responsible persons and true children of God. We need to know the difference between both types of sufferings and avoid the unnecessary suffering, while embracing the necessary sufferings. The impending passion that Jesus talks about in the passage above is a necessary suffering and he would not allow Peter dissuade him from it.

Today that we live in a "push-button" civilization, when everything is done the easy way, we need to remind ourselves of the Greek proverb that says; "The beautiful things are difficult." Easy as our world has become because of growth in science and technology, no success in any field of endeavour is achieved without enormous effort. No sportsman wins a laurel without the pain of serious training and preparations. The same applies in the fields of science, technology, and art. In relation to following Christ, same and even much more is applicable. To the man who declared that he wanted to follow Christ, Christ said; "Foxes have holes, and the birds of the air have nests, but the Son of man has nowhere to lay his head" (Mt. 8:20). This was not meant to discourage would-be followers, but to impress on them that followership of Jesus comes with its own necessary pains and sufferings.

We cannot be true disciples without enduring the necessary pains and sufferings that go with it. Habits, as we know, are easy to form but quite difficult to give up. Following Christ requires we give up our habits that are not agreeable to God's injunctions; the habits of lying, gossip and tale-bearing, fornication and adultery, stealing, quarrelling and fighting. We need to renounce worldly pleasures that offend God. We need to patiently endure and tolerate others who hurt us. We need to give up ourselves in selfless service of others.

Pain and suffering were part and parcel of Jesus' life from the outset. He was not born in a world class hospital with high grade medical facilities; he was born in a stable in Bethlehem. At a tender age, he had to endure the pain of the long journey through the desert to Egypt to avoid the assassination attempt of Herod. He did not grow up with a silver spoon in his mouth, he was a carpenter who toiled in harsh conditions. As an itinerary preacher, he was not welcomed everywhere he went, neither was his message popular among, even the religious leaders of his day. He suffered rejection, misunderstanding, misrepresentation, and misinterpretation, mostly because of envy and jealousy. To crown it all, he suffered a humiliating death on the cross. He went through all these in uncomplaining endurance. They all cumulated in the victory of his resurrection. Thus, after the cross came the crown. No Christianity without pain, no true followership of Christ without some form of suffering, no crown of salvation without the pain of the cross.

49

The Danger of Greed (Lk. 12:13-21)[184]

"Teacher, bid my brother divide the inheritance with me." This was the cry that came from someone in the crowd who supposedly was listening to the teachings of Jesus. Apparently, the owner of that voice, although in the multitude gathered around to hear Jesus, was not listening to him. His mind was somewhere else and on something else – how to get his own share of inheritance. That was more important to him than whatever Jesus had to say at that point in time. When he got the opportunity, he spilled it.

Characteristic of Jesus, following his gentle manner, and always seizing every opportunity to teach and correct those who listen to him, he responded with the parable of the rich farmer. Prior to the parable, he declared to his listeners what his message was; "Take heed, and beware of all covetousness; for a man's life does not consist in the abundance of his possessions." He warned them against being greedy as human possession is not a guarantee of human life.

According to this parable of the rich farmer, he had a great and bumper harvest and decided to build a bigger barn to store his harvest for his future enjoyment. But unknown to him, he was not going to live to build the bigger barn or even enjoy the bumper harvest. Very likely, if he knew that death awaited him that night, he would have taken a different course of action. For instance, he may have decided to call everyone around and share the harvest to them, knowing that he would not live to enjoy it himself. That

184 Homily on the 18th Sunday of Ordinary Time, Year C, given at St. Joseph of the Holy Family Catholic Church, Harlem, Manhattan, NYC. July 2013.

would have been noble and he would be fondly remembered and prayed for always.

We may begin to wonder what the rich farmer did wrong! Ordinarily, he made a wise decision to get himself a bigger store house. He had worked hard in the farming season and his hard work is rewarded by a huge harvest. He has laid out a good plan to guarantee his future by providing adequate and appropriate storage for his harvest. At least, he can take some time out and relax knowing that he has enough, or even more than enough, laid out for his future.

Is Christ accusing him of greed? Why should he accuse him of greed? Where is the greed in the rich farmer? What exactly did the rich farmer do wrong? He worked hard during the farming season and the reward for his hard work is the rich harvest that God granted him. He sat down and planned well for his future, which one would expect of every reasonable person. So, what exactly had he done wrong that Jesus would cite him as an example of greed?

Perhaps a further assessment of the plan for the future by the rich farmer may give us an insight! The first thing that might catch the attention of the person who takes a more careful and closer look at this passage is the choice of Jesus' term; against the popular and general notion that Jesus is warning against greed, which in itself is sinful, Jesus actually said; "Take heed, and beware of all *covetousness*; for a man's life does not consist in the abundance of his possessions." Although an aspect of greed, the term covetousness does not exactly mean greed. It refers to a situation where you take and keep what belongs to another, while greed refers to desiring and wanting everything within sight.

Jesus warns against covetousness because the quantity of our possessions cannot guarantee us life. The rich and wealthy also die. From the plan of the rich farmer for his future and what he intends to do with his rich harvest, it is obvious that there was no plan for sharing with others. Six times he used the "I" and never once referred to others. There was no reference whatsoever in thanksgiving to God who has given him the life, the good health, and the strength to work hard and reap a rich harvest. Without the gift of life, good health, and strength, he would never had had a rich harvest. Now the harvest is plentiful and he cannot thank God from whom came the life, the good health, and the strength.

In his plan for the future, there was also no reference to "him" or "her" but always "I." He had not thought of sharing with the less privileged. When God blesses us, it is to enable us bless others with the blessings he has given to us. To keep it to ourselves alone without sharing with others is what Jesus condemns and warns us against. This was what the rich farmer did. The word of God says; "To whom much is given, much is expected" (Lk. 12:48). The wrong of the rich farmer is not in what he did or planned to do, but in what he did not do or did not plan to do. He did not share with others and did not plan to share with others. He appropriated his rich harvest to himself alone.

There is a saying that, "Events mock at human foresight, nothing is certain, except the unforeseen." In his plan for the future, the rich farmer never envisaged that by daybreak he would no more be alive. Maybe, just maybe, if he was privy to that knowledge, he would most likely had gone around sharing out his harvest, knowing that he would not live to enjoy them. In his human wisdom, he did not reckon with the fact that he is not the owner of his life. That his life is a gift from God, who reserves the right to take it back when He deems fit. And that night, after the plentiful harvest, God was going to take back what He gave to him. In his human wisdom, he was foolish in the sight of God.

If his plan was to be rich in the sight of God, he would be generous with the blessings of God to him, he would in turn bless others with God's generosity towards him. In that way, alive or dead, he will be God's own and one with God is always life in abundance. The paradigm for judgment in Mt. 25:35-47 clearly expresses the fact that at the end of time, God is not going to ask anyone who he is and what work he did. The question on judgment day is not how much you had in your bank account or the kind of house you lived in. It is not about the kind of cars you owned or how many cars you owned. The question is simple and straightforward; it is about what you did with what you had, especially in relation to those who were less privileged than you.

Thus, riches and wealth in the sight of God is determined by your relationship with others with regard to what God has blessed you with. Did you hoard your blessings by keeping it to yourself, or you were selfless enough to share them with others?

Sir Fred Catherwood describes greed as "The belief that there is no life after death. We grab what we can, while we can, however we can and then hold on to it hard." Our rich farmer in today's gospel reading is guilty of the latter part of Catherwood's definition of greed; "... then hold on to it hard." Very many of us, with today's capitalist materialistic attitude, prefer to add and multiply what we have, instead of subtracting and dividing from what we have, for the benefit of others. Others are never part of our equation. Thus, Jesus' warning: "Take heed, and beware of all *covetousness*; for a man's life does not consist in the abundance of his possessions," is as relevant and important to us in our Christian life today as it was at the time he addressed it to his listeners.

50

Who Is Jesus in My Life? (Lk. 9:18-24)[185]

Throughout human history, people have expressed different opinions about the person of Jesus Christ. Today's liturgy of the word invites us to revisit the question of who Jesus is in our lives. This can be properly done from the following perspectives:

i. The twofold questions of Jesus Christ to his disciples.
   a. Who do people say that I am?
   b. Who do you say that I am?

ii. The response of Peter to the second question.
   a. You are the Christ of God.

iii. The twofold response of Jesus to Peter.
   a. The real meaning of being the Christ of God.
      - The Son of man must suffer many things.
      - And be rejected by the elders, and chief priests and scribes, and be killed.

   b. The invitation of Jesus to follow in the path of the Christ of God.
      - If any man would come after me.
      - Let him deny himself and take up his cross daily and follow me.

These perspectives open us to the depth of the question of who Jesus is to us and enable us to understand the true nature of the

185 Homily on the 12th Sunday of Ordinary Time, Year C, in the Seminary Chapel of SS. Peter and Paul, Bodija, Ibadan. 2013.

messianic mission of Jesus Christ. They further prompt us to apply ourselves to and affiliate with the mission of Jesus as his followers.

To begin with, Jesus asked his disciples: "Who do people say that I am?" We all have opinions about the persons we think others are. Some of these opinions may be true and appropriate descriptions of the personality of the person in question, some of the opinions may be prejudiced, and some of the opinions may be out-rightly malicious. The one true fact about these opinions is that they are personal to whoever has them. They express how the one who entertains the opinion perceives and understands the one the opinions are about. Invariably, however, these opinions shape how we relate with one another.

We may, therefore, ask the same question of Jesus Christ in the general form in which he himself first put it to his disciples. Who do people say Jesus is today? As the apostles were able to outline the different opinions of the people of the time of Jesus Christ concerning his person, for instance, that he is John the Baptist, Elijah, or one of the old prophets who has risen, so we too, in our time can easily identify some popular opinions of the generality of people concerning the person of Jesus Christ.

For very many people today, Jesus Christ is the great provider. For such persons, Jesus is instrumentalized as a means to meet their needs. These are the group of people who will seek Jesus Christ for breakthroughs without efforts. People who seek miracles in achieving success in life without making the human efforts towards that which they seek.

For some others, Jesus is the mighty healer. For people who share this opinion about Jesus, they would rather pray or visit a man of God for prayers when they are sick instead of seeking medical help from specialized and trained medical personnel. Entrenched in this opinion is the sister opinion that sicknesses are usually a result of demonic attacks. Natural ailments are viewed from spiritual perspective by those with this opinion of Jesus.

Yet another popular opinion of Jesus in our time is the idea that Jesus is the undefeated warrior in battle. The slogan that captures this opinion is, "No weapon fashioned against me shall prosper." Those with this opinion see all life's situation from the battlefront perspective. They hardly see life as a celebration of the gift of God. It is all about one battle or another and Jesus is the mighty conqueror who will lead them to victory over their enemies.

It is true that Jesus can and does fit into these opinions, however, he is, by far, not limited to any of these opinions and he is much more than any of these opinions can express about him. This is the same case with the opinions of the people in the time of Jesus as expressed by his apostles. Thus, Jesus probed further. This time, he needed to know the personal opinion of his disciples. It is important that he knows what they, as his personal and very close friends and associates, think about him because he was going to entrust his mission to them eventually, when he physically departs from the earth.

The second question, "But who do you say I am?" came as a subtle, but firm admonition from Jesus to his apostles not to allow themselves be swallowed up in the tide of public opinion. Yes, it is good to be aware of public opinion, nonetheless, we should have our personal opinion that is grounded upon our conviction. This applies to us today as it was to them then. Maybe, even more seriously in our time that is so immersed in materialism and consumerism. A time where emotions seem to be more in control of our decisions than reason.

The response to the second question was not as fast in coming as the response to the first. In fact, it was Peter who took the bull by the horn. "The Christ of God," Peter answered. Our Catechism teaches us that the word 'Christ' means anointed. So to call Jesus 'the Christ of God' is to say he is 'the anointed one of God.' Jesus had said of himself, quoting from the prophecy of Isaiah, "The spirit of the Lord is upon me. He has anointed me ..." (Lk. 4:18). It means then that Peter got it right. What, perhaps, Peter would not know then is what it means to be the anointed one of God. It is always one thing to identify a concept, and yet another to understand the meaning of the concept. So, while Peter identified Jesus as 'the Christ of God, Jesus was to explain to him and his colleagues what it means to be 'the Christ of God.' This is where the twofold response of Jesus to Peter come in.

Acknowledging that he is the anointed one of God, Jesus went on to explain what his anointing is about. He has been anointed to suffer and be killed. Thereafter, to rise again. This is the summary of his mission, the same mission for which he is anointed. "The Son of man must suffer many things." These many things can be summarized in the "three misses;" misunderstanding, misrepresentation, and misinterpretation. These were precisely the things that led the scribes and Pharisees to want to kill Jesus.

The religious leaders rejected Jesus. They were supposed to confirm him and provide appropriate logistics for his mission as the religious leaders of his time. Instead of doing this, they had their own agenda, into which, apparently, Jesus' *modus operandi* did not fit. So they thwarted and attempted to frustrate his mission as 'the Christ of God.' This same attitude is very prevalent amongst us today. It is a clear fact that within and outside the Church, we have people with their own personal agenda. These people include both the clergy and lay faithful, people in high and low places within and outside the Church, who will stop at nothing to frustrate and thwart the ministry of others because it does not favour their personal agenda, which more often than not, is never a noble agenda.

Lastly, Jesus invites his apostles to follow him, not on their own terms, but according to his terms. One fact about the invitation is that it is optional; "If any man would come after me ..." It is not mandatory to follow him. It is a free and personal choice. No one is compelled to follow him. If you choose to follow him, then there are guidelines, namely; you must deny yourself, take up your cross daily and follow him. The words that we should not miss out here are; "deny yourself" and "daily."

Self-denial is not a negation of one's being, but a willingness to submit one's desires to that of God. Taking up your cross demands that you first of all accept the cross. The cross can be viewed from either the negative perspective as problems or difficulties, which is not Christ-like or positively as challenges that are to be surmounted, or opportunities to prove our commitment to Jesus. Jesus insists that acceptance and subsequent carrying of the cross is a daily affair. It is not a once and for all thing. It is an ongoing process, because we meet with challenges in life on a daily basis. It is a lifelong process. To follow Jesus means we cannot be doing things our own way, we have to do what we do the way Jesus requires that we do it. Follow Christ on his terms and not on our own terms, as many Christians want to do today.

Today's liturgy of the word tells us what it means to know Jesus. To know Jesus is to follow Jesus in the midst of the challenges of our everyday life. To seek shortcuts that often compromise our Christian values is to be guilty of following Jesus on our own terms. The implication of this is appreciated in the analogy of the man who chooses to reduce the length of his cross to fit the size that is convenient for him to carry. On arrival at a gully where you have to lay your cross over to walk on to the other side, he discovered that his cross was too short to reach out to the other end of the gully. Thus, he could not cross over. Is my knowledge of Jesus fitted into my personal opinion or am I open to accepting him as 'the Christ of God?'

51

Zacchaeus: God's Availability and Our Response (Lk. 19:1-10)[186]

With man, God crowned His work of creation on the sixth day. He made man in His own image and likeness, and looking at what He had done, "God saw all that he had made, and it was very good" (Gen. 1:31). Zacchaeus, the central character of our gospel passage for this reflection, is part of this very good creation of God. As such, even though he is despised and seen as evil by his fellow humans, God was available to him by sending his Son, Jesus Christ to seek him out for salvation. Today's gospel, therefore, shows us God's availability, patience, and love. The question is, what is our response to these gifts of God.

Zacchaeus was a wealthy tax collector of the city of Jericho. As a tax collector, he was not on fixed salary. He was required by the Roman authority to turn in certain amount as tax from the Jews within his city of operation, but he was at liberty to collect whatever amount he wishes as tax, remit what was required, and keep the balance for himself. This explains the source of his wealth, his sole authority to determine how much tax he wishes to collect from the Jews, as long as whatever he collects accommodates what he was expected to remit to the Roman authority.

Being a tax collector, the Jews saw Zacchaeus as a traitor, who exploited his own people for the benefit of the Roman authority and acquisition of his own illegal wealth. He associated with the pagan authority as he worked for them and therefore, he was

186 Homily on the 31st Sunday of Ordinary Time, Year C, at Our Lady Seat of Wisdom Catholic Chapel, University of Ibadan, Ibadan. 2013.

unclean. He was, in their eyes, a public sinner. He is hated in the city and alienated from his people, and they considered him alienated from God as well. Therefore, we could say that although Zacchaeus was wealthy, he was a lonely man.

The gospel brings out an aspect of Zacchaeus that we need to note; he was a man full of determination. He wanted to see who Jesus was but could not. He was a man of small stature and the crowd would not allow him see Jesus. Yet he was not discouraged, rather, "He ran on ahead and climbed up into a sycamore tree to see him, for he was to pass that way." Zacchaeus was ready to do whatever it was going to take him to see Jesus. He did not mind the crowd neither was he bothered about his rich man status; if climbing the sycamore tree would make him catch a glimpse of Jesus, so shall it be. He put aside his pride and dignity and did what only boys and slaves should do; climb a tree.

When Jesus got to the tree, he looked up and asked Zacchaeus to come down. He invited himself to his house. Jesus' attitude towards Zacchaeus was in contrast to that of the crowd. While the crowd despised Zacchaeus, Jesus esteemed him by voluntarily offering to go to his house. "Zacchaeus, make haste and come down; for I must stay at your house today." Against a judgmental crowd, Jesus refused to condemn Zacchaeus, rather he extended a hand of friendship towards him to the disappointment of the crowd. "And when they saw it they all murmured, 'He has gone in to be the guest of a man who is a sinner."

Zacchaeus was overwhelmed by Jesus' display of love for him. Without scolding him, without even as much as a word of reproach, Jesus' availability to Zacchaeus spoke volumes and Zacchaeus felt compelled to respond. Once a pastor paid a visit to a laid-back parishioner, who for subsequent Sundays had been absent from Church. Opening the door to behold the pastor, he immediately started preparing a defence in his mind in view of his expectation that the pastor would soon question him on his absence from Church. The pastor greeted him warmly and sat with him by the fire. They engaged themselves in various interesting discussions and the pastor would add another firewood to the fire as it goes down. He never questioned the parishioner on his absence from Church. At the end of his visit, on his way out, still without raising the issue of his absence from Church, the parishioner could no longer hold back on the subject of his absence from Church, not in the face of so much love and friendliness from his pastor, he quietly told the pastor; "Father, I will see you in Church next Sunday." This is the power of love and availability at play.

The basic message of this narrative is the availability of God. In the action of Jesus Christ, we see the availability of God to his children. God makes Himself available to us always, He is patient with us and awaits our positive response towards His presence. Jesus did not make demands on Zacchaeus as he did not make demands on the woman caught in the act of sin and the prodigal father did not make demands on the prodigal son (Lk. 15:11-13). God does not make unnecessary demands on us; He makes Himself available to us and waits for us to acknowledge His presence and respond in generous self-giving.

Zacchaeus responded accordingly; overwhelmed by the love and availability of Jesus, even when he had not committed himself to turning away from his misdeeds, he could not but respond likewise. "And Zacchaeus stood and said to the Lord, 'Behold, Lord, the half of my goods I give to the poor; and if I have defrauded any one of anything, I restore it fourfold." I wonder what might be left of his wealth after the generous giving to the poor and the fourfold restitution. This was obviously not a concern for Zacchaeus; he has found something worth more than material wealth, he has found spiritual wealth, he has found peace in the presence of the saviour.

Note that Jesus did not go to drag Zacchaeus to himself. Zacchaeus simply desired to catch a glimpse of Jesus, he roughed the tide of the aggressive crowd and weathered the storm of humiliation by climbing the sycamore tree. Jesus rewarded his efforts by inviting himself to his house; something Zacchaeus never dreamt of nor even had the courage to do. The grace of God always fills up the spaces left when we have done our bit.

Zacchaeus' response to Jesus' availability and love is best described as a genuine desire that refused to be procrastinated. A determination that is backed up with action. A smart and wise move by Zacchaeus to take the opportunity of God's loving presence and patience. The positive response of Zacchaeus won him salvation. "And Jesus said to him, 'Today salvation has come to this house, since he also is a son of Abraham. For the Son of man came to seek and to save the lost." It is so reassuring to hear Jesus refer to a public sinner like Zacchaeus as, "also a son of Abraham." It means no one is ever a "cast away" in the sight of God. For as long as we repent and turn away from our misdeeds and respond to the availability of God like Zacchaeus did, salvation is close to us.

Like Jesus, we must take steps to seek out and show love to the many Zacchaeuses; men and women, hiding in the trees we pass under every day. We do this by not intimidating them, not being judgmental about one another, and not condemning one another. And like Zacchaeus, we should not allow the opinions of others about us block our ways and dampen our spirits to take advantage of the availability of God. We should not be intimidated by the many self-righteous people around us. We should be focused and brave, and promptly respond positively to the loving presence of God, for today is our day of salvation.

52

Rising to Life in Christ (Jn. 11:1-45)[187]

The prophet Ezekiel says, "Thus says the Lord God: Behold, I will open your graves, and raise you from your graves, O my people; ... And I will put my Spirit within you, and you shall live..." (Ezk. 37:12-14). This prophecy is fulfilled in the gospel passage of our reflection, the raising of Lazarus from the dead by Jesus. The resurrection to new life is not only a phenomenon that comes after physical death, it is also a phenomenon that comes after spiritual death. We may still be physically alive, but spiritually dead. Christ, like he did to Lazarus in the gospel passage, is ready to raise us back to a healthy spiritual life, if and only if, we cooperate with him.

The traditional belief of the Jews is that the soul of the dead remains with the body until three days after death before it departs. This explains why Martha in today's gospel passage was reluctant to open the tomb of Lazarus at the request of Jesus because it was four days already after he died. It is curious that despite the love Christ had for Lazarus, he delayed in responding to the news that he was ill. He stayed two more days before going. And by the time he arrived, Lazarus was four days dead. Yet, when he was told that Lazarus was ill, Jesus had said that "This illness is not unto death; it is for the glory of God, so that the Son of God may be glorified by means of it." Apparently, Jesus had a plan in mind.

The first good news of this passage is the response of Jesus; his response to Martha is a pointer to the fact that with God there is

187 Homily delivered at Our Lady Seat of Wisdom Catholic Chapel, University of Ibadan, Ibadan, on the 5th Sunday of Lent, Year A, 6th April, 2014.

no situation that is hopeless. It can never be too late with and for God to revive and revitalize a situation or a person. Yes, Lazarus was ill. Yes, Lazarus was physically dead by the time Jesus arrived at the scene. That was the perfect situation in which the glory of God is to shine as the Lord of life. Three days have gone by so no one would say that the soul of dead Lazarus was still within his body. Yet Jesus was going to reunite soul and body by a mere command, "Lazarus, come out."

In this command of the Lord is the key to revival. Obedience to the Lord's command is the key to our new life, our resurrection from the grave of spiritual death. For us to rise to life in Christ, for us to be revitalized and brought back to spiritual vibrancy, God needs our cooperation, a cooperation that simply requires that we obey his command. This is lucidly expressed in the gospel narration of today; practical obedience to the will of God.

In this narration of Jesus raising Lazarus back to life, three commands were issued by Jesus;

i. Take away the stone.
ii. Lazarus, come out.
iii. Unbind him, and let him go.

The first command to "Take away the stone" met with an initial resistance from Martha. She protested on the basis of the fact that by now the corpse will be decomposing, and therefore, will produce a foul odour. At this, Jesus questioned her faith; "Did I not tell you that if you would believe you would see the glory of God?" Remember that he had earlier told his disciples that this illness is not unto death but it is for the glory of God, so that the Son of God may be glorified by means of it. Martha submitted in faith and perhaps, gave instructions that the stone covering the tomb be taken away. If Martha had not submitted to this command of Jesus, the resurrection of Lazarus would not have commenced. It would have been a human clog in the wheel of divine interference in the life of Lazarus.

Taking away the stone at this point did not make sense to Martha, but it made sense to her that the Lord had asked that it be done. It is the submission of reason to faith, a very important and necessary aspect of authentic followership of Christ. She had put aside all other considerations, like, the foul odour, the embarrassment of the crowd at the stench of such odour, and of course, the hard labour of taking away the stone. Very often, we consider things like these and declare that it does not make sense to follow some moral injunctions. Very often, we place reason over faith and rationalize the demands of our Christian followership. Very often, we become the clog in the wheel of God's intervention in the life of his children by our attitudes of unbelief.

With the stone out of the way, Jesus proceeded with step two. I'm curious to learn from scripture scholars why Jesus did the next thing as the second step and not the first. He lifted up his eyes, and called upon the Father. He prayed. Was it the case that he needed to be sure that the human cooperation would be there before calling on the Father? If they had not taken away the stone, would he still had proceeded to call on the Father? These are questions I cannot answer. But one thing is sure, our human cooperation is required for God to work his wonders in our lives. In this case, that was taken care of by Martha's cooperation to take away the stone.

The next command was to the dead man; "Lazarus, come out." Nothing is dead before God. For us humans, the dead cannot hear but Lazarus, who was dead, heard the voice of God. This is simply a testimony to the fact that no situation is out of control for God. Lazarus, not only heard, he obeyed and came out. "The dead man came out, his hands and feet bound with bandages, and his face wrapped with a cloth." It is strange that he was not assisted to come out in such a position as described in the narrative. He was still bound when he came out. Again, it is another defilement of natural law. But is God within the limits of natural law? Of course, not; God is not and cannot be restricted by time and space or the forces and laws of nature.

The third command is again directed to the living humans around; "Unbind him, and let him go." God has done it; we have to activate his deeds in our lives. If again Lazarus was left bounded, it would mean that, although, the grace of God has been given, we have refused to make it active – while Lazarus has been brought back to life, we have refused to allow him live by keeping him bound. I liken this to purchasing a TV, setting it up and refusing to switch it on. It will remain there and it would be said we have a TV, but it would never function as one, until we switch it on. Again, human compliance is required here. The work of bringing to life is done, the work of living out the life is ours.

One fact that run through the commands is the obedience of those concerned to the commands. Let us make no mistakes, the commands are not easy commands to carry out, nonetheless, they were obeyed. Out of place as they sound, they were obeyed. Obedience to the commands brought to realization the miracle of Lazarus' coming back to life. The commands also show that we all have a role to play individually and collectively in realizing the will of God for us in our lives. The first two commands were directed to individuals; Martha and Lazarus, the third command was directed to the crowd; "Jesus said to them..."

As individuals and communities, we have fallen victims to the death of sin. Many of us are already in the tomb of hopelessness and decay because of our sinful habits and attitudes. The Lenten season is a season of grace, if we cooperate with the grace of God by listening to his voice and obeying it, he will revive us. All that is required of us is to "take way" the obstacles that separate us from God's reviving grace. Such obstacles include the following:

i. Our habits of gossip.
ii. Our moral depravity.
iii. Our rascality and laziness.
iv. Our excessive materialism that expresses itself in senseless fashion and trending things.

Are we willing to unbind one another by forgiving those we begrudge and those who hurt us? God is waiting for us to take the first step of taking away the obstacles so that He can fill us with his grace of new life. After which we are required to activate that grace of new life in our daily dealings with one another.

53

Sing unto the Lord all the Earth (1 Chr. 16:23)[188]

> Sing to the Lord, all the earth; day after day proclaim his salvation! Declare his glory among the nations, his marvels to every people! (1 Chr. 16:23).

The practice of singing to the Lord is age long. When the Lord delivered Israel from the land of their slavery in Egypt, they gathered together on a piece of land beside the sea of reeds to joyfully sing to Yahweh. They extolled His mighty name and deeds in their lives (Ex. 15:1ff). Thus, it has always been the practice in ancient Israel whenever they are victorious in battle to sing songs of praise to the Lord. The Psalms are replete with such songs of praises to God. Such singing is usually accompanied with drumming, rejoicing, and dancing. They went as far as calling on all God's creation to praise His name (Dan. 3:57-90).

The kings of Israel institutionalized professional singers who had the job of singing the praises of God during liturgical celebrations and to compose beautiful songs for such occasions (2 Chr. 20:21). This is, perhaps, the beginning of the choirs in liturgical celebrations, which today have become an indispensable part of our liturgical worship. Following from this, we can rightly say that singing joyfully to the Lord is a medium of prayer, wherein the faithful praise His name, His deeds, acknowledge His sovereignty, as well as ask for His blessings.

188 Homily given at the Provincial Choir Competition at the Ambrose Alli University, Ekpoma, on 26th October, 2002.

The Evangelist, Matthew, at a very important point in his gospel, namely, the institution of the Eucharist, remembered to note that psalms were song before Jesus and his disciples left for the Mount of Olives (Mt. 26:30). Thus, he who has come not to abolish the law but to fulfil the law (Mt. 5:17) preserved the aged practice of singing unto the Lord.

Little wonder then that the practice of singing unto the Lord found its rightful place in the Early Church. Among the early Christians, even when Christianity was a *religio illicita,* the practice did not die. From here it has evolved through the ages in our liturgical celebration. So, it is proper to offer befitting songs; inviting us to praise and worship the Lord, to exalt His holy name and deeds, to ask Him to receive our sacrifice of His Son, and mercifully heed our supplications.

Singing for us Christians, should therefore, be seen as a gift from God. A gift that enables us to raise our hearts and minds to God in a fitting gesture of recognition of His sovereign reign over all. Hence, St. Augustine exclaimed that he who sings well prays twice. Much earlier before him, the Apostle to the Gentiles, St. Paul, encouraged and urged the Churches he founded to be joyful always and sing praises to the Lord (1 Cor. 14:15, 1 Thess. 5:18).

Whenever we sing joyfully to the Lord, we join the angels and saints to praise the Lord. That is, the church militant becomes one with the church triumphant, in the praise and worship of God (Rev. 14:3, 15:3). In this, therefore, we have a foretaste of what eternity shall be like, an eternal joyful worship of the Lord.

On a day and occasion like this, it is only right and proper that some relevant issues that afflict our Church today be addressed. This, especially affects the youths where you as members of the National Fellowship of Catholic Students (NFCS) belong. We have heard time and time again that the Catholic Church is boring, antiquated, and lacks the spirit to move forward. One of such areas that have prompted such opinion is the area of singing. What we see in Christian gatherings today is a 'disconized' version of liturgical songs, which the Church makes efforts to avoid, so that the spirit of liturgical music may not be eroded. It is definitely not true that the Church is antiquated, boring, and uninteresting.

Without being apologetic, the Church encourages her faithful to improve and constantly update her hymns without losing sight of the all important aspect that singing in the Church is to enable better worship rather than gratifying unnecessary emotions that negate the spirit of a loving response to a salvific call.

Finally, dear friends, as youths, you are virile and full of enthusiasm, let your voices be used, therefore, to praise God now. It is indeed noble to sing praises to the Lord, to proclaim His wonders day by day, to tell of His love in the morning and His faithfulness in the watches of the night. And may God bless you as you sing. Amen.

54

Watching and Preparing for the Lord's Coming (Mk. 13:33-37)[189]

Three times in today's gospel, Jesus urges his disciples to 'watch' so that they will not be caught unawares, when the Lord comes. In the very short gospel passage, Jesus presents a scenario in which servants were entrusted with responsibilities for which they will account when the master returns. The twist in the story is the time of the master's return. This time is unknown. Perhaps the master knows, but certainly, the servants do not know. The doorkeeper had an exceptionally challenging responsibility. Imagine that the master returns and he is not at his doorpost. The master would be kept waiting outside.

The gospel scenario is very realistic rather than far-fetched. We are God's servants, entrusted with various responsibilities for which we shall account when we return to God. At our individual deaths, the time comes for us to account for how we have carried out our responsibilities. As it were, we do not know when this will be.

Just imagine that when the time comes, you are not at your duty post like the doorkeeper. For instance, while you are supposed to be at adoration with your parishioners, you left the deacon or seminarian to conduct the prayers and you were taking a little longer nap in your room. Or when you were supposed to be instructing catechumens you were receiving a visitor at home. It is worse, when you are at one immoral or sinful activity.

---

189 Homily on the 1st Sunday of Advent, Year B, given at SS. Peter and Paul Major Seminary, Bodija, Ibadan on the 3rd of December, 2017.

All these could be a result of getting too familiar with the repetitiveness of what we do and allow it to become mere habit, or worse still, become careless about it or even negligent. Thus, advent is a season that reminds us to be constantly on the watch that we may not be found asleep when the master comes.

Like the frog, Christians need to be jolted out of the habit of routine. When you throw a frog into a pot of hot water, it jumps out of it immediately, but when you place the same frog in a pot of cold water and slowly boils the water, the frog will just sit right there. This is because of its primitive nervous system that needs sudden jolts to realize that it is in danger.

Advent is a wakeup call for Christians at the beginning of every new liturgical season. We can, and we do fall into the habit of following our Christian worship as a matter of routine. We listen regularly to the readings from scripture but no longer hear them. We listen to homilies so regularly that we no longer hear or remember them. We pray the office four times daily that they become mere recitations to us.

Advent jolts us from becoming Christians by habit only. It is a call to wake up. A call to shake off the dust of routine and let Christ come alive in us. Advent is a season of preparation for the coming of the Son of God into our world. It is a reminder that our entire Christian life is a preparation towards our return to the Father. As we prepare to welcome the infant Jesus, the season points to the second coming of Christ, to which today's gospel directs our attention. That we should keep watch and not be taken by the surprise of the Lord's coming, any time, no matter what the time. 'Any time' is the wrong time for the unfaithful servant, but for the faithful servant, 'any time' is the right time.

The important question we need to ask ourselves this season is how to prepare for the Lord's coming. Living in a world today where the Church and Christians seem to be taking directions from the society, instead of *vice versa*, it is imperative that we clearly identify the appropriate way to prepare for the Lord's coming. Christmas, the day we celebrate the birth of the Son of God is about the most popular celebration in the world. Christians

and non-Christians alike celebrate it with equal pomp and pageantry.

Non-Christians, who do not share the theology of Christmas consider it a social activity and prepare for it as such; without any spiritual connotation. For them, it is a time for traders to make more money by hiking the prices of goods, while criminals intensify their activities to make more money, to have enough, to party and lavish at Christmas. Weddings and celebrations are fixed and prepared for. It is a timeline to finish projects, acquire a new car, and pick up a new girlfriend. In all these, the most significant reason for Christmas – the birth of the Son of God is ignored. And so, we have a celebration of Christmas without Christ.

Unfortunately, many Christians are toeing this path of preparation and neglecting the most significant aspect of preparing the manger of their hearts for the baby Jesus. This is what the advent call jolts us to. To be watchful that we do not become comfortable with the usual ways of the world at the detriment of our souls.

Preparing for the infant Jesus is not a time to get rich quick, it is not a time to disenfranchise others so that we can celebrate Christmas in a lavish and worldly way. It is a time to deeply reflect on God's loving kindness, His generosity to us in taking on our mortal nature. A time to reawaken in us the consciousness to reciprocate God's love and kindness by being good to others, love others, respect others, reach out to the poor, the needy, the weak, and the sick.

Isaiah, in today's first reading begins by acknowledging the greatness of God: "You, O Lord, are our Father, our Redeemer from old is your name." He progresses to a lamentation: "O Lord, why do you make us err from your ways." And then expresses hope in God: "Return for the sake of your servants, the tribes of your heritage. O that you would tear the heavens and come down" (Is. 63:16-17, 64:1). Isaiah captures the reality of our situation; we constantly stray away from God and need to return to Him for our salvation. It is this salvation that we hope the coming of Christ will accomplish for us. Thus, advent awakens us to that hope, and

requires that we expectantly prepare to embrace the offer of salvation that comes with the birth of Christ.

Although Paul was specifically referring to the seconding coming of Christ (Parousia) in the second reading (1 Cor. 1:3-9), his encouragement that we remain faithful as we wait for this coming of Christ is *ad rem* to this season of advent. As Paul rightly noted, we have been enriched and given the grace of God in Christ. This is to strengthen us in our wait for Christ's coming. God's grace opens us to the Holy Spirit who will teach us to prepare well. Operating within the grace of God and the guidance of the Holy Spirit, we will know the items we need to prepare well for the welcoming of the infant Jesus.

Today's gospel warns: "Take head, watch and pray" (Mk. 13:33). This is a call to be careful lest we stray, to be alert that we may not be deceived, and to solicit the assistance of the Holy Spirit through prayer. We can easily follow the spirit of the world, providing rational justification for our actions, without knowing that we are straying away from God. If we prepare everything and every place well without preparing a manger for the infant Jesus in our lives, our preparation would be in vain. It will be like the story about the woman who cleaned up her house and made all the physical preparations in view of the visit of Jesus Christ. Thrice Jesus came, she failed to recognize him and sent him away. She was physically prepared, she was spiritual not ready; Jesus indeed came, and the house was prepared for his visit, she did not recognize him because she was not ready. The physical preparation on which she expended her time, energy and resources, blinded her perception of the spiritual.

Dear friends, the four weeks of advent afford us the opportunity to constantly ask ourselves, how we can best prepare to welcome the infant Jesus. How do I prepare a manger for him in my life, so that he can be born anew in me? May the Lord bless us, strengthen and guide us with his Spirit that we may adequately prepare to receive him into our lives, through the same Christ our Lord. Amen.

55

See Lord, I Have Come to do Your Will: Discipleship (Ps. 40:8-9)[190]

Ps. 40:8-9 summarizes the theme of our reflection; discipleship. In simple terms, discipleship is all about following a master, in this case, Jesus Christ our Lord. The authenticity of discipleship lies in the faithfulness of a disciple to abide by the instructions and teachings of the master. A disciple who deviates from the master's teachings and recommended ways is not a faithful disciple. Discipleship is not measured in terms of achievements, as we often and erroneously assume, in the exercise of our various Christian and priestly ministry. It is measured in terms of faithfulness to the teachings of Christ.

Christian discipleship is a call-response phenomenon. God calls His children to follow Christ on the path of salvation and the child of God responds wholeheartedly by following wherever Christ leads. It is not as simple as hearing a voice calling and issuing instructions on what to do and which path to take. It involves careful discernment, more so, in a world like ours that is characterised by the loudness of so many misleading voices. Our response is retarded by various internal and external factors that weaken the determination of the spirit to follow on the path of righteousness. In the same vein, the quality of our response is enhanced by our availability and disposition to Christ.

Today's readings seem to have departmentalized some of these basic requirements of discipleship. The first reading (1 Sam. 3:3-10. 19), talks about discernment, while the second reading (1 Cor.

190 Homily for the 2nd Sunday of Ordinary Time, Year B, at SS. Peter and Paul Major Seminary, Bodija, Ibadan, on the 14th of January, 2018.

6:13-15. 17-20) directs our thought to obstacles to discipleship, and the gospel (Jn. 1:35-42) impresses on us the need to be available and positively disposed to Christ. Departmentalized as this may seem, there is a cross-fertilization among the readings in terms of presenting us specific examples to follow.

Three times the Lord called Samuel and three times, Samuel was mistaken in his response. More than the initial mistaken response of Samuel is the striking fact that, he always willingly responded. Like many of us would prefer to do nowadays, Samuel was not laidback in responding at any time. As soon as he heard the voice, he did not wait for a second call or pretend not to have heard, he responded as soon as possible. One would also expect that after the first and second calls to which he responded, and Eli denied calling him, he would just ignore the next call. No, he still answered the third call.

Eli's role in guiding Samuel is an example for all of us priests and seminarians. We occupy positions that most people look up to for guidance. Some have the courage to approach us, most people do not, yet they watch us and listen to us, hoping to be guided by our examples and teachings. Thus, we must be careful in our speeches and behaviours. As it is said, sometimes, our life is the only Bible some persons have the opportunity to read. And the voice of our action can be, and it is always, louder than our voice.

Eli patiently observed the situation and wisely guided Samuel's response to the Lord's call. He was not rash, hasty, or even offended by Samuel interrupting his own rest. He paid attention to the little lad and gently attended to his concern. This is what we should do anytime those who are confused and need our guidance come to us. Proper discernment is key to a faithful response. Where our discernment is mistaken, we would be responding but responding in error. It is like running fast but outside the track, which invariably means our effort comes to nothing.

St. Paul, in the second reading, using fornication as a classic example of immorality points out the relationship between immorality and spirituality. Immorality of any type is always an obstacle to our faithful response to the Lord, and therefore, counterproductive to spiritual growth. I would not know if it is foresight on the part of St. Paul or just divine wisdom that he zeroed down on fornication. The sin of the flesh is clearly one of the most widespread acts of immorality today. It has become socially acceptable to keep a friend for sexual purposes. And it is assumed that something is wrong with you, if after attaining the age of 18, you do not have a girlfriend or boyfriend. Cheating in a relationship, within or outside marriage is gradually becoming a norm. Fornication and adultery prevails everywhere; the old and elderly, priests, religious, seminarians, pastors, prophets, evangelists, youths, and even the underaged, educated and literate, as well as the uneducated and illiterate, the rich and the poor are involved. Although, it looks like a physical and biological thing, it impacts, and negatively so, on the spiritual.

Immorality, whether initiated from within us (internal) or caused by external factors, is the greatest obstacle that retards our faithful response to God's call. In today's Nigeria, and the world at large, there are so many loud voices of immorality howling at us and demanding our attention. Ranging from the urge to satisfy our sexual desires, the lure for material riches, the tendency to abuse office, power, and position, the unbridled clamour for unrestrained freedom and unwillingness to be mentored, the tendency towards examination malpractices, to laundering our personal image while destroying others by gossip, backstabbing and outright lying against others. The voices calling out on us toward these acts of immorality can be subtle and veiled. We need, therefore, to be guided in our discernment and be courageous in refusing to heed them.

The evangelist John weaves together the guidance of Eli and the response of Samuel in the concrete, practical example of John the Baptist and two of his disciples. John the Baptist did what many of our pastors and preachers would not do today; he clearly, firmly and humbly guided his disciples to Christ by pointing at Jesus Christ as the one to be followed. He made no attempt whatsoever to restrain his disciples from leaving him to follow Christ; a clear testimony on his part, of a preacher who is walking his talk. He had earlier said: "I baptize you with water. But one who is more powerful than I will come, the straps of whose sandals

I am not worthy to untie" (Lk. 3:16; Mt. 3:11; Mk 1:8). Most of our preachers today seem to direct their congregation to themselves rather than to Christ. They would rather, in practice retain their members while theoretically talking about Christ. This happens among us too, as some of our priests, rather than preach, the authentic and right theology, embellish doctrinal teachings to suit their personal agenda. Although some of them ignorantly do so, but then, a priest's ignorance of basic theology is unjustified and unjustifiable. What did he spend his theology classes in the seminary doing?

The response of the two disciples of John to immediately follow Jesus and willingly accept Jesus' invitation to come and see is very instructive. Like Samuel's "Speak, Lord, for your servant hears." The two disciples of John were open to whatever Jesus wanted them to do. They stayed with the Jesus and found in him, the Messiah. Take for instance that they had not stayed, would they have found the Messiah? The follow-up of Andrew to bring his brother Peter into the picture is what disciples should do. Having found and experienced the Lord, they should bring others to him. It is the missionary dimension of discipleship.

The natural consequence of faithful discipleship is to put on a new way of life that configures him/her to the path laid out by the master. This takes us back to the second reading's advice that we jettison immorality if we want to keep ourselves free for the habitation of the Holy Spirit of God. For when immorality pollutes us, we become foul and uninhabitable for the Spirit. We are weakened in our response to follow Christ.

Today, God calls us as He does always in several ways and in various situations. He awaits our positive and faithful response. Let us be bold and courageous to say with Samuel, "Speak, Lord, your servant hears" and with the Psalmist, "See, I have come, Lord, to do your will."

55

Transcending the Boundaries of Division (Mk 1: 40-45)[191]

To be a Christian is a call to face and take up the challenges of being a child of God daily, as we meet and relate with one another. These challenges take different forms and sometimes require that we contradict the status quo. Today's readings present us with one of such challenges side by side with the status quo and the response of our Lord Jesus Christ, who is the model of Christian living.

The first reading (Lev. 13:1-2, 44-46) presents to us a status quo which encourages segregation, exclusion, and stigmatisation. While we can justify this divisiveness based on worldly and material safety; that is, the contagious and incurable nature of leprosy (the disease in question), we cannot run away from the fact that such divisiveness, no matter its justifiedness, is not acceptable in the sight of God. Therefore, should not be part of the practice of the Christian life. The gospel (Mk 1:40-45), presents the response of Jesus to such unacceptable status quo that divide and exclude some of the children of God. Jesus' willingness to relate with and touch that which the status quo forbids him to relate with and touch is a clear message to the child of God not to practice and allow divisions, segregation and exclusions in his/her life. Every Christian is bound to imitate Christ as Paul, his convert servant is doing, so much so that Paul can boast that others should imitate him, as he does Christ (1 Cor. 10:31-11:1). Paul's boast is a call on all Christians to make their lifestyle an example for

191 Homily for the 6th Sunday of Ordinary Time, Year B, at SS. Peter and Paul Major Seminary, Bodija, Ibadan, on the 11th of February, 2018.

others to follow. That their faith should be lived, rather than just professed.

Let us take a closer look at the nuances of today's readings. For a better comprehension let us consider them under the following headings: (i) The inhumanity of the Levitical law of exclusion, (ii) The Leper's response to societal stigmatisation and enslavement, and (iii) Jesus' response to the leper.

Leprosy, which is a bacterial infection (1873 discovery) is a disfiguring, contagious skin disease. It has been surrounded by many religious and social taboos in history, and one of such taboos is what we read in today's first reading (Lev. 13:1-2, 44-46). Because of the ancient erroneous notion that leprosy is the consequence of one's sins, a leper was to be pronounced unclean by the priest. With such pronouncement, the leper would have to dehumanise him/herself by wearing torn clothes, leave his/her hair unkempt, cover his/her mouth when s/he speaks, and announce him/herself unclean and unfit to be related with by others. Such a leprous person is subjected to living alone away from others. This is clearly enslavement.

Fully aware of his exclusion from the society, living under the burden of stigmatization, the leper would be an unhappy person. Daily he would have to wake up to rejection by others and worse still, forced to reject himself. And he was to remain so for as long as the disease last, which means till he dies, for at that time (until the 1940s) there was no medical treatments for leprosy and therefore, it was considered incurable. The leper in today's gospel had to take his destiny in his own hands. He braced up to the challenges and made a move to free himself from the shackles of rejection. In any case, he stood to lose nothing even if Jesus would not heal him, but if Jesus did, he stood to gain everything.

One striking but hidden fact is that, even though society tries to force him to reject himself, deep within him, this leper refused to reject himself. That provides the plausible explanation why he had the courage to approach Jesus. He refused to wallow in the self-rejection and pitiable state society confines him. He takes the initiative to approach Jesus, summoned the courage to transcend the religious custom of his day to challenge Jesus, by humbly asking him, how far he is willing to go to heal someone.

In facing his challenge of rejection, the leper was humble, respectful and courteous. He did not demand healing from Jesus as a right, but pleadingly said: "If you will, you can make me clean," which means, "if you don't want to heal me, no *wahala*." His courage to challenge his challenges did not translate into full-headedness or stubborn arrogance. He recognized that Jesus was at will to do as he pleased with him. This is a sharp contrast to popular ways of praying in modern Christianity, where God is instructed, blackmailed, and commanded, giving God time limit and schedule to answer our prayers.

Jesus' response was sharp and swift. Simultaneously, he acted and spoke: "I will; be clean." Jesus was moved with pity and acted. His pity did not make him wish but made him act. Situations that require our active compassion abound around us at different levels and in different forms. And they challenge us to respond to them as Jesus did in today's gospel reading.

Jesus' healing of the leprous man by touching him broke the Levitical rule of exclusion, which demonstrated how far Jesus was willing to go to uplift the pain of the suffering. The question for us is, how far are we ready to go in helping others? Do we hide behind traditions and customs to abdicate on our Christian responsibilities? Are we ready to challenge traditions and customs that separate us by going beyond them to positively touch the lives of each other?

My brothers and sisters, our country Nigeria is, today, a fractured society. Nigeria is fractured by tribe, ethnicity, economic and social status, political affiliation, and worse still, religious beliefs. The sufferings and pains, occasioned by corruption that has penetrated our national fibre and the maladministration prevalent at all levels in our country have deepen these lines of division. This has become very visible even in our church and Christian communities. Within our immediate community, these divisions are expressed in the formator/formandi, theologian/philosopher, my diocesan brother and those not from my diocese, the talented/gifted and the untalented brother. Consciously or unconsciously, we have allowed these divisions inform our relationships with one another. We have created the mentality of "the Us" as different from "the Them". This mental othering separates us and restricts our ability to be there for one another. We gratify that which divides us instead of promoting our common humanity.

This is where St. Paul cautions us in today's second reading. "Brethren: ... whatever you do, do all to the glory of God." Doing all to the glory of God necessarily excludes actions that inherently cannot glorify God. For instance, there is no adultery, stealing, lies and dishonesty, murder, kidnapping, cheating in an examination, deceit, injustice, betrayal, etc. that can glorify God. Which means these manners and attitudes of behaviour are not to be found among the children of God. On the contrary, all human actions inspired by love and compassion would always glorify God. Thus, St. Augustine said, "Love and do whatever you like" because in true Christian love you would do no wrong.

Dear friends, let us eschew favouritism, let us scale over the lines of division that separate us, let us be courageous like the leper to challenge the status quo that deny our common humanity. Like Jesus, let us not allow anything restrict our compassion and willingness to be there for each other. Let our actions and lives bring healing and upliftment to those around us. In doing all these, let humility, respect for one another, and courtesy of speech be our watch word.

Index

Printed in Great Britain
by Amazon

40906364R00169